Affirming the Imamate

The Institute of Ismaili Studies

Ismaili Texts and Translations Series, 26

Editorial Board*:* Farhad Daftary (general editor), Wilferd Madelung (consulting editor), Orkhan Mir-Kasimov (series editor), Carmela Baffioni, Nader El-Bizri, Heinz Halm, Hermann Landolt, Mehdi Mohaghegh, Roy Mottahedeh, Azim Nanji, Ismail K. Poonawala, Ayman F. Sayyid, Paul E. Walker

Previously published titles:

1. Ibn al-Haytham. *The Advent of the Fatimids: A Contemporary Shiʿi Witness*. An edition and English translation of Ibn al-Haytham's *Kitāb al-Munāẓarāt*, by Wilferd Madelung and Paul E. Walker (2000).
2. Muḥammad b. ʿAbd al-Karīm al-Shahrastānī. *Struggling with the Philosopher: A Refutation of Avicenna's Metaphysics.* A new Arabic edition and English translation of al-Shahrastānī's *Kitāb al-Muṣāraʿa*, by Wilferd Madelung and Toby Mayer (2001).
3. Jaʿfar b. Manṣūr al-Yaman. *The Master and the Disciple: An Early Islamic Spiritual Dialogue*. Arabic edition and English translation of Jaʿfar b. Manṣūr al-Yaman's *Kitāb al-ʿĀlim wa'l-ghulām*, by James W. Morris (2001).
4. Idrīs ʿImād al-Dīn. *The Fatimids and their Successors in Yaman: The History of an Islamic Community*. Arabic edition and English summary of Idrīs ʿImād al-Dīn's *ʿUyūn al-akhbār*, vol. 7, by Ayman Fuʾad Sayyid, in collaboration with Paul E. Walker and Maurice A. Pomerantz (2002).
5. Naṣīr al-Dīn Ṭūsī. *Paradise of Submission: A Medieval Treatise on Ismaili Thought*. A new Persian edition and English translation of Naṣīr al-Dīn Ṭūsī's *Rawḍa-yi taslīm*, by S. J. Badakhchani with an

introduction by Hermann Landolt and a philosophical commentary by Christian Jambet (2005).

6. al-Qāḍī al-Nuʿmān. *Founding the Fatimid State: The Rise of an Early Islamic Empire.* An annotated English translation of al-Qāḍī al-Nuʿmān's *Iftitāḥ al-daʿwa*, by Hamid Haji (2006).
7. Idrīs ʿImād al-Dīn. *ʿUyūn al-akhbār wa-funūn al-āthār.* Arabic critical edition in 7 volumes by Ahmad Chleilat, Mahmoud Fakhoury, Yousef S. Fattoum, Muhammad Kamal, Maʾmoun al-Sagherji and Ayman Fuʾad Sayyid (2007–2014).
8. Aḥmad b. Ibrāhīm al-Naysābūrī, *Degrees of Excellence: A Fatimid Treatise on Leadership in Islam.* A New Arabic Edition and English Translation of al-Naysābūrī's *Ithbāt al-imāma*, by Arzina Lalani (2009).
9. Ḥamīd al-Dīn Aḥmad b. ʿAbd Allāh al-Kirmānī. *Master of the Age: An Islamic Treatise on the Necessity of the Imamate.* A critical edition of the Arabic text and English translation of Ḥamīd al-Dīn Aḥmad b. ʿAbd Allāh al-Kirmānī's *al-Maṣābīḥ fī ithbāt al-imāma*, by Paul E. Walker (2007).
10. *Orations of the Fatimid Caliphs: Festival Sermons of the Ismaili Imams.* An edition of the Arabic texts and English translation of Fatimid *khuṭbas*, by Paul E. Walker (2009).
11. Taqī al-Dīn Aḥmad b. ʿAlī al-Maqrīzī. *Towards a Shiʿi Mediterranean Empire: Fatimid Egypt and the Founding of Cairo.* The reign of the Imam-caliph al-Muʿizz, from al-Maqrīzī's *Ittiʿāẓ al-ḥunafāʾ bi-akhbār al-aʾimma al-Fāṭimiyyīn al-khulafāʾ*, translated by Shainool Jiwa (2009).
12. Taqī al-Dīn Aḥmad b. ʿAlī al-Maqrīzī. *Ittiʿāẓ al-ḥunafāʾ bi-akhbār al-aʾimma al-Fāṭimiyyīn al-khulafāʾ*. Arabic critical edition in 4 volumes, with an introduction and notes by Ayman F. Sayyid (2010).
13. Naṣīr al-Dīn Ṭūsī. *Shiʿi Interpretations of Islam: Three Treatises on Theology and Eschatology.* A Persian edition and English

translation of Naṣīr al-Dīn Ṭūsī's *Tawallā wa tabarrā*, *Maṭlūb al-mu'minīn* and *Āghāz wa anjām*, by S. J. Badakhchani (2010).

14. al-Mu'ayyad al-Shīrāzī. *Mount of Knowledge, Sword of Eloquence: Collected Poems of an Ismaili Muslim Scholar in Fatimid Egypt*. A translation from the original Arabic of al-Mu'ayyad al-Shīrāzī's *Dīwān*, translated by Mohamed Adra (2011).
15. Aḥmad b. Ibrāhīm al-Naysābūrī. *A Code of Conduct: A Treatise on the Etiquette of the Fatimid Ismaili Mission*. A critical Arabic edition and English translation of Aḥmad b. Ibrāhīm al-Naysābūrī's *Risāla al-mūjaza al-kāfiya fī ādāb al-du'āt*, by Verena Klemm and Paul E. Walker with Susanne Karam (2011).
16. Manṣūr al-'Azīzī al-Jawdharī. *Inside the Immaculate Portal: A History from Early Fatimid Archives*. A new edition and English translation of Manṣūr al-'Azīzī al-Jawdharī's biography of al-Ustādh Jawdhar, the *Sīrat al-Ustādh Jawdhar*, edited and translated by Hamid Haji (2012).
17. Nāṣir-i Khusraw. *Between Reason and Revelation: Twin Wisdoms Reconciled*. An annotated English translation of Nāṣir-i Khusraw's *Kitāb-i Jāmi' al-ḥikmatayn*, translated by Eric Ormsby (2012).
18. al-Qāḍī al-Nu'mān. *The Early History of Ismaili Jurisprudence: Law and Society under the Fatimids*. An Arabic edition and English translation of al-Qāḍī al-Nu'mān's *Kitāb minhāj al-farā'id*, edited and translated by Agostino Cilardo (2012).
19. Ḥātim b. Ibrāhīm al-Ḥāmidī. *The Precious Gift of the Hearts and Good Cheer for Those in Distress. On the Organisation and History of the Yamanī Fatimid Da'wa*. A critical edition of the Arabic text and summary English translation of Ḥātim b. Ibrāhīm al-Ḥāmidī's *Tuḥfat al-qulūb wa furjat al-makrūb*, by Abbas Hamdani (2012).
20. Abū Ṭāhir Ismā'īl al-Manṣūr bi'llāh. *The Shi'i Imamate: A Fatimid Interpretation*. An Arabic edition and English translation

of al-Manṣūr's *Tathbīt al-imāma* attributed to Abū Ṭāhir Ismāʿīl al-Manṣūr bi'llāh, edited and translated by Sami Makarem (2013).

21. Idrīs ʿImād al-Dīn. *The Founder of Cairo: The Fatimid Imam-Caliph al-Muʿizz and his Era*. An English translation of the section on al-Muʿizz from Idrīs ʿImād al-Dīn's *ʿUyūn al-akhbār*, edited and translated by Shainool Jiwa (2013).
22. Ibn al-Walīd. *Avicenna's Allegory on the Soul: An Ismaili Interpretation*. An Arabic edition and English translation of Ibn al-Walīd's *al-Risāla al-mufīda*, edited by Wilferd Madelung and translated and introduced by Toby Mayer (2015).
23. Ḥasan-i Maḥmūd-i Kātib. *Spiritual Resurrection in Shiʿi Islam: An Early Ismaili Treatise on the Doctrine of* Qiyāmat. A new Persian edition and English translation of the *Haft bāb* by Ḥasan-i Maḥmūd-i Kātib, edited and translated by S. J. Badakhchani (2017).
24. Muḥammad Ḥasan al-Ḥusaynī, Aga Khan I. *The First Aga Khan: Memoirs of the 46th Ismaili Imam*. A Persian edition and English translation of the *ʿIbrat-afzā* of Muḥammad Ḥasan al-Ḥusaynī, also known as Ḥasan ʿAlī Shāh, edited and translated by Daniel Beben and Daryoush Mohammad Poor (2018).
25. Muḥammad b. ʿAbd al-Karīm al-Shahrastānī. *Command and Creation: A Shiʿi Cosmological Treatise*. A Persian edition and English translation of the *Majlis-i maktūb* by Muḥammad al-Shahrastānī, edited and translated by Daryoush Mohammad Poor (2021).

Affirming the Imamate

Early Fatimid Teachings in the Islamic West

An Arabic critical edition and English translation
of works attributed to
Abū ʿAbd Allāh al-Shīʿī and his brother Abu'l-ʿAbbās

by

W. Madelung and Paul E. Walker

I.B.TAURIS
LONDON • NEW YORK • OXFORD • NEW DELHI • SYDNEY
in association with
THE INSTITUTE OF ISMAILI STUDIES
LONDON, 2021

I.B. TAURIS
Bloomsbury Publishing Plc
50 Bedford Square, London, WC1B 3DP, UK
1385 Broadway, New York, NY 10018, USA
29 Earlsfort Terrace, Dublin 2, Ireland

In association with The Institute of Ismaili Studies
Aga Khan Centre, 10 Handyside Street, London N1C 4DN
www.iis.ac.uk

First published in Great Britain 2021

Cover design: Adriana Brioso

A catalogue record for this book is available from the British Library.

A catalog record for this book is available from the Library of Congress.

ISBN: HB: 978-0-7556-3732-4
PB: 978-0-7556-3713-7
ePDF: 978-0-7556-3733-1
eBook: 978-0-7556-3734-8

Series: Ismaili Texts and Translations Series

Typeset by RefineCatch Limited, Bungay, Suffolk
Printed and bound in Great Britain

The Institute of Ismaili Studies

The Institute of Ismaili Studies was established in 1977 with the object of promoting scholarship and learning on Islam, in the historical as well as contemporary contexts, and a better understanding of its relationship with other societies and faiths.

The Institute's programmes encourage a perspective which is not confined to the theological and religious heritage of Islam, but seeks to explore the relationship of religious ideas to broader dimensions of society and culture. The programmes thus encourage an interdisciplinary approach to the materials of Islamic history and thought. Particular attention is also given to issues of modernity that arise as Muslims seek to relate their heritage to the contemporary situation.

Within the Islamic tradition, the Institute's programmes promote research on those areas which have, to date, received relatively little attention from scholars. These include the intellectual and literary expressions of Shiʿism in general, and Ismailism in particular.

In the context of Islamic societies, the Institute's programmes are informed by the full range and diversity of cultures in which Islam is practised today, from the Middle East, South and Central Asia, and Africa to the industrialized societies of the West, thus taking into consideration the variety of contexts which shape the ideals, beliefs and practices of the faith.

These objectives are realized through concrete programmes and activities organized and implemented by various departments of the

Institute. The Institute also collaborates periodically, on a programme-specific basis, with other institutions of learning in the United Kingdom and abroad.

The Institute's academic publications fall into a number of inter-related categories:

1. Occasional papers or essays addressing broad themes of the relationship between religion and society, with special reference to Islam.
2. Monographs exploring specific aspects of Islamic faith and culture, or the contributions of individual Muslim thinkers or writers.
3. Editions or translations of significant primary or secondary texts.
4. Translations of poetic or literary texts which illustrate the rich heritage of spiritual, devotional and symbolic expressions in Muslim history.
5. Works on Ismaili history and thought, and the relationship of the Ismailis to other traditions, communities and schools of thought in Islam.
6. Proceedings of conferences and seminars sponsored by the Institute.
7. Bibliographical works and catalogues which document manuscripts, printed texts and other source materials.

This book falls into category three listed above.

In facilitating these and other publications, the Institute's sole aim is to encourage original research and analysis of relevant issues. While every effort is made to ensure that the publications are of a high academic standard, there is naturally bound to be a diversity of views, ideas and interpretations. As such, the opinions expressed in these publications must be understood as belonging to their authors alone.

Contents

Introduction 1

Translation of BL OR 8419 15

Translation of *Kitāb mafātīḥ al-niʿma*, The Book of the Keys to Grace 79

Select Bibliography 107

Index 109

Qurʾanic index

Arabic index

Arabic Text of BL OR 8419

Arabic Text of *Kitāb mafātīḥ al-niʿma*

Introduction

For the earliest phase of the Fatimid caliphate, and of its Ismaili precursor, we now possess a fairly rich array of source material, the most recent addition to which is the memoir of Ibn al-Haytham, a young recruit to the cause at the time of the establishment of the new state, who was to recall those events more than three decades later. We brought this source into modern scholarship in an earlier volume, *The Advent of the Fatimids: A Contemporary Shiʿi Witness.*[1] But there are a number of other accounts to consider as well, all of which together allow us a more complete picture of that period than of many later stages in the development of the empire. Here, in the present volume, we bring to this body of sources two more of major importance and high significance. Both have heretofore not been included simply because they were previously either not known at all or had never been studied sufficiently. Moreover, the attribution of authorship that we now propose for them is not without some uncertainties. In our opinion they are two works from the earliest Fatimid *daʿwa* in North Africa, consisting of a record of sermons by Abū ʿAbd Allāh al-Shīʿī and a letter by his brother Abu'l-ʿAbbās on fiscal obligations to the Imam.

In the latter case, where the material in question has never been carefully scrutinized previously, we have what appears to be a treatise (actually, a letter) composed by Abu'l-ʿAbbās, the brother of the great founding *dāʿī* of the Fatimid state, Abū ʿAbd Allāh al-Shīʿī. Its Arabic title, as it has come down to us, is *Mafātīḥ al-niʿma* (The Keys to

[1] London: I. B. Tauris, 2000.

Grace) and it has been preserved for the intervening centuries by the Ismaili manuscript tradition where it has always been considered by those who maintained and catalogued the items held by them to be the work of the famous al-Qāḍī al-Nuʿmān (d. 363/974). Reading the treatise itself carefully, however, quickly dispels that idea. It is certainly not by al-Nuʿmān and the internal evidence in it clearly points to Abu'l-ʿAbbās, even though he is not mentioned by name in it as such.

The other work is somewhat more of a mystery in part because it is not one of those found in the known Ismaili collections. Moreover, it exists at present solely in a single defective manuscript now housed in the British Library, where it has been catalogued as a work in the genre of *qiṣaṣ al-anbiyāʾ* (stories of the prophets). The manuscript (BL OR4819) also lacks a title and carries no citation, or even direct suggestion, of authorship. Pages are missing from the beginning and the end with at least five breaks of undetermined length in between. Thus it has remained anonymous. Internal evidence, however, seems to suggest an origin in the North African Ismaili mission, its *daʿwa*, in the period prior to the advent of the first Imam-caliph al-Mahdī, whose appearance it anticipates. Its author, therefore, or at least its source, we suggest, is Abū ʿAbd Allāh al-Shīʿī himself. In his role as head of the *daʿwa* in the Maghrib, this man spent nearly two decades of the late 3rd/late 9th–early 10th century patiently propagating the Ismaili cause and teaching and preaching among his North African, mainly Berber, congregations with the purpose of instilling among his audience, and all those who would listen to him, a devotion to the Family of the Prophet and specifically the line of Imams descended from ʿAlī b. Abī Ṭālib who were, he said, then about to rise and restore true religion and proper faith in place of the decadence and corruption in the Islamic community all around.

But it is certainly noteworthy that we have in this case two treatises that have both lost their proper identity, either by being ascribed to someone else or now missing whatever credit of authorship they might have had. A ready answer to why such material may have been either neglected, as with the *Mafātīḥ*, or simply not preserved by the *da ʿwa*, as with BL OR4819, is to be most likely associated with the tragic fate of the two brothers and the subsequent ignominy attached to their names. Barely over a year after the proclamation of the Fatimid caliphate, charges of plotting to overthrow al-Mahdī by the two and a few of their Berber colleagues led him to order their execution. Although the disgrace that followed fell most heavily on Abu'l-ʿAbbās, and not Abū ʿAbd Allāh, both suffered severely. Thus, for example, although its contents were valued, his name as its author was not preserved.

Still, by the period of the writing of Ibn al-Haytham's memoir – towards the middle of the 4th/10th century – it had become possible apparently to recall the brothers with affection and respect.[2] Ibn al-Haythan's account of his meetings and discussions with both offers valuable first-hand testimony to the talents of the two men who played such a substantial role in the founding of the state. It is amply clear, from what Ibn al-Haytham reports, that they were extremely learned, with a deep knowledge of a wide range of the sciences and of Islamic history and doctrine.

In what follows we offer both texts in a critical edition of the Arabic text of each accompanied by an annotated translation and explain how and why they came to our attention.

BL OR 8419 attributed to Abū ʿAbd Allāh al-Shīʿī

The first text, which we can only cite by its British Library catalogue number OR 8419, was brought to light by Michael Pregill of Elon

2 In fact Ibn al-Haytham's work is the best source for information about the two brothers, but most especially for Abu'l-ʿAbbās, Other accounts deal with Abū ʿAbd Allāh, particularly al-Qāḍī al-Nuʿmān's *Iftitāḥ al-daʿwa*, which is now available in English translation in Hamid Haji's *Founding of the Fatimid State: The Rise of an Early Islamic Empire* (London, I. B. Tauris, 2006).

University in an article in the *Journal of Qur'anic Studies*[3] entitled 'Measure for Measure: Prophetic History, Qur'anic Exegesis, and Anti-Sunnī Polemic in a Fāṭimid Propaganda Work (BL Or. 8419)'. Pregill had apparently been drawn to this manuscript because of his interest in the genre of *qiṣaṣ al-anbiyā'* only to discover that this particular work did not really belong to it. In fact, as he himself realized, it uses material of that type, not for its accounts of earlier prophets as such, but for a polemical purpose to show how the errors and mistakes of previous religious communities, mainly the Israelites have been, and are continuing to be, repeated by the Muslims, here meaning the Islamic authorities who have failed to recognize the divinely sanctioned line of Imams that stems from ʿAlī b. Abī Ṭālib and the *ahl al-bayt*.

However, once carefully studied, it is possible to be more precise in characterizing it and its purpose. Pregill himself did not try to identify the author and he suggested it was written 'some time after the establishment of the Fatimid caliphate in Ifrīqiya in 297/909'. Yet the text clearly states that the Mahdī has not yet appeared but was about to in the near future. The author then would be Abū ʿAbd Allāh al-Shīʿī, whose revolutionary preaching among the Kutāma Berbers is described by al-Qāḍī al-Nuʿmān in his *Kitāb Iftitāḥ al-daʿwa* as well as by the Sunni author Ibn ʿIdhārī al-Marrākushī in his *Kitāb al-Bayān al-mughrib*. These sermons were presumably recorded and assembled as a book by one of his followers.[4] They evidently date from the time of Abū ʿAbd Allāh's armed struggle to overthrow the Aghlabid regime in Ifrīqiya after the Fatimid Imam al-Mahdī had decided in 292/905 to seek refuge in the Maghrib rather than the Yemen. They describe in stark terms the disobedience of the Sunni majority to the

[3] Vol. 16 (2014), pp. 20–57.

[4] Curiously, the last folio of the manuscript, not included here, contains an unconnected fragment of a probably Muʿtazilī text of some sort which suggests that the whole of the original manuscript included several items not necessarily related to each other.

Prophet Muhammad and his legitimate successors. As the text proceeds, it moves cautiously from stories of how Muhammad's role as prophet – his miracles – were prefigured in the Biblical Israelite tradition to the special relationship of ʿAlī and his family and then ultimately to a clearly Shiʿi message, with many examples of the evil acts committed by the Muslims against ʿAlī's family and descendants. Evidently such atrocities still continue. They will not be brought to an end until the Mahdī appears, a fact stated in slightly different ways three times in our text. It is an event soon to happen.

Although the context and message are fairly obvious, pointing to the North African mission of Abū ʿAbd Allāh, the work itself does not display the typical characteristics of Ismaili doctrinal writings, including terms, as for example for the ranks of the religious hierarchy, that appear in that literature and nowhere else. It has none of these. But, as it stands, it was not designed for internal *daʿwa* use but rather for public preaching to an audience unlikely to have included the Shiʿis, let alone loyal Ismailis. Its principal aim is to convert, to bring non-Shiʿis into the fold. It is, moreover, not really a treatise, a work in which an author sets out to compose an argument or discourse. Instead it has the feel of someone in the process of teaching or preaching orally, following and developing a theme. Accordingly, what we have is most likely not his sermons themselves, but a record of Abū ʿAbd Allāh's proselytizing and of the techniques he employed to that end. Thus it also remains less polished than if it had been a final draft of a written text.

The text presents an appeal to a broad audience more inclusive of Muslims not previously affiliated to the Ismaili cause. It thus commences with citations of several *ḥadīth* and a series of historical incidents that prove the prophecy of Muhammad, all of commonly accepted reports. It then slowly introduces material to establish that Muhammad regarded ʿAlī as his brother, eventually explaining that he had said that ʿAlī was to him as was Aaron to Moses with all that is implied in that claim. Next is the importance of the *ahl al-bayt*, here specifically including only ʿAlī, Fāṭima, al-Ḥasan and al-Ḥusayn. One striking image is the comparison of ʿAlī to the staff of Moses. Eventually our author brings up the denial of ʿAlī's succession by those he calls the pharaohs of the Islamic community and the subsequent violence directed by them against al-Ḥusayn and his family. These oppressors of the *ahl al-bayt* continue to dominate the Muslim community unjustly and perfidiously. They wage jihad against the small select few who have upheld the truth. As the author says:

> Likewise the pharaohs of our community caused fear over the manifestation of the family of Muhammad by the tongue of their friends: 'Truly we fear that the family of Muhammad will gain ascendency over you and so will change your religion which you manifest, since God made them forefathers and models for those who will come later.' So the community believed in jihad against the family of Muhammad as an obligation out of fear that the changes and deviations from what is sound would alter their religion, as with the customs of the family of Pharaoh, in accord with their *sunna* and in imitation of them.

And he finally concludes that they will only be overcome when the Mahdī rises.

The references to the rising of the Mahdī are thus a key to the time and place and that in turn indicates who the author was. Those critically important passages are the following:

> Our prophet was taken by death and did not absent himself as had done Moses. So the worshippers of the calf in our community persisted in their error repeatedly, without their repenting, without remembering the unbelief that had infused in their hearts up to the day of God's vice-regent the Mahdī. The day of the calf of our community, on account of the nobility of the prophet, is extended prior to the advent of the Mahdī, on whom be peace, without killing. When the deputy of the Mahdī comes out, the gates to repentance shall be shut against the

> worshippers of the calf of our community, just as they will be shut against all who did not believe prior to the sun rising in the west. God has said: 'the day when some signs of your Lord shall come, their faith will benefit none who did not believe before or acquired in their faith good deeds' [Q 6: 158], and that is the rising of the sun from the west. For the worshippers of the calf, there is no Day except for him who puts trust in the calf and obeys the Sāmirī. He who obeys the brother of their prophet and his successor, they deem him weak, as had done the Israelites with Aaron and his partisans. 'They said: kill the sons of those with him who believe and spare their women' [Q 40: 25] in conformity to the custom of the Israelites and in imitation of them.
>
> The Mahdī is the one of Muhammad's family who will rise.
>
> And when our community disobeyed the legatee of the Apostle of God, God became angry with them, so that they wandered in the land for eighty years confused about the religion as their punishment for having contravened the order of their guardian. The time of the Umayyads was for this community like the wandering in the wilderness of the Israelites, exactly the same.
>
> . . . among the community of Muhammad, there is 'a community that guides to the truth and acts justly' [Q 7: 159]. They are towards the west, as were the people of Moses towards the east, in the territory of the descendant of Idrīs b. Idrīs; the rule of the Book is manifest among them and apportioning is equitable, and justice for the subjects prevails; they are the opposite of what is there of the Murjiʾa in the justice of their imams and their conduct.
>
> God will manifest His religion at the hands of His vicegerent, the Mahdī, may the blessings of God be upon him.

Note further the references to the 'rising of the sun from the west' and the community of Muslims 'towards the west', surely here signifying the nascent Ismaili appeal recently established and spread in the West (Maghrib) by Abū ʿAbd Allāh himself.

***The Book of the Keys to Grace (K. Mafātīḥ al-niʿma)* attributed to Abu'l-ʿAbbās**

The *Mafātīḥ al-niʿma*, in contrast to BL OR 8419, represents a letter carefully crafted and argued by its author, specifically intended for a loyal Ismaili audience, one for whom the technical language and terms of the *daʿwa* were certainly appropriate. In fact their appearance here provides important evidence of how early they were commonly applied and used.

The misattribution of Abu'l-ʿAbbās's work to al-Qāḍī al-Nuʿmān probably began long ago, perhaps because it was once preserved among the latter's personal papers. Moreover, somehow several paragraphs of additional extraneous material became attached to it at the end. They commence with an item recording a comment of the caliph al-Muʿizz to al-Nuʿmān in which he is named. Thus, his name appears in this fashion, although in a section at the end, which comes after the original treatise itself has concluded. It is amply clear that the portion by Abu'l-ʿAbbās himself both opens and closes as one would expect with a work of this kind. The extra items are a later addition.

Nevertheless, the Ismaili *daʿwa* continued to regard the text as al-Qāḍī al-Nuʿmān's. Al-Majdūʿ's eighteenth-century catalogue of Ismaili works, *Fihrist al-kutub wa'l-rasāʾil*, ascribes it to him.[5] In addition, al-Majdūʿ also explained clearly what it dealt with and therefore we can be sure it is the same text. Ismail Poonawala in his *Biobibliography* repeats this information as well[6] and, when the Syrian Ismaili scholar Muhtadī Muṣṭafā Ghālib came to publish an edition of it in Salamiyya, he, too, claimed it as a work by al-Nuʿmān.[7]

5 Ed. ʿAlī Naqī Munzavī (Tehran, 1966), p. 187.
6 Ismail K. Poonawala, *Biobibliography of Ismāʿīlī Literature* (Malibu, CA, 1977), p. 66.
7 This edition, issued apparently in 1982, is exceedingly rare and would be otherwise unknown to us except for Samer Traboulsi who managed to obtain a copy and supply us with a pdf of it. We were able to consult it thanks to him.

The identity of the real author, however, is obviously based on internal evidence provided by passages in which he mentions 'my brother (*akhī*) Abū ʿAbd Allāh'. The context, moreover, excludes the possibility of this being a friendly or honorific usage. The larger part of the *K. Mafātīḥ al-niʿma* reproduces a letter of stern reproach by an unknown author to an unnamed recipient. The author can safely be identified as Abu'l-ʿAbbās Muḥammad, the elder brother of Abū ʿAbd Allāh al-Shīʿī, by the references to the latter as his brother. The recipient cannot be identified by name, but must have been a chieftan in a Berber clan other than the Kutāma. From the letter it is apparent that he was converted to the Ismaili faith, not by Abū ʿAbd Allāh al-Shīʿī, but by a certain Abu'l-Ḥasan al-Baghdādī, evidently a companion *dāʿī* of Abū ʿAbd Allāh. Abu'l-Ḥasan al-Baghdādī found the Berber neophyte to be exceptionally intelligent and eager to acquire knowledge of the *bāṭinī* esoteric truths. He sent a warm recommendation for his higher initiation to Abu'l-ʿAbbās, who at that time was residing in Silyāna, a region in Ifrīqiya north-west of Qayrawān. Favourably impressed by the recommendation, Abu'l-ʿAbbās answered and invited Abu'l-Ḥasan al-Baghdādī's pupil to visit him. When the latter, however, arrived at his residence in Silyāna, Abu'l-ʿAbbās happened to be absent. Abu'l-ʿAbbās apologized in a letter to the Berber chieftan and directed him to join his brother Abū ʿAbd Allāh for further initiation, expressing a hope of later meeting him personally. Abu'l-ʿAbbās also sent a letter recommending him to his brother Abū ʿAbd Allāh. Soon, however, this man began to complain and criticize Abū ʿAbd Allāh for withholding some of the four-fifths of the war booty to which his volunteer supporters were entitled under Islamic law. Abū ʿAbd Allāh himself may not have been pleased with having to deprive his volunteer warriors, who, like the early Muslims in the age of the prophet, armed themselves and fought at their own expense, from receiving their legal share of the booty. He sent the letters of complaint from the Berber chieftan on to his brother. The latter now wrote the letter of severe reproach to the discontented Berber chief that is preserved in the *K. Mafātīḥ al-niʿma*. He explained to him that faithful supporters of the Imam ought voluntarily to turn over part of their material gains to the Imam for their own ultimate spiritual benefit, even though he, the Imam had no need of their financial support. The higher the level of spiritual initiation reached by any of the faithful, the greater was his obligation to surrender voluntarily part of his material gains to the Imam.

Knowing who composed it also provides a clue as to its date. The work itself indicates that the Mahdī had already appeared, implying the advent of the Fatimid Imam-caliph al-Mahdī who was liberated from house arrest in Sijilmāsa in 297/909 and proclaimed ruler in Raqqāda in early January 910. Over the ensuing twelve months the two brothers retained their high status and authority and that lasted until they fell victim to events that produced their execution in Jumāda 298/February 911. Abu'l-ʿAbbās's *Mafātīḥ* therefore dates from this exact period of barely over a year after the foundation of the Fatimid caliphate.

The compiler of the book, who gave it the title *Mafātīḥ al-niʿma*, must have had access to the documents and notes in al-Qāḍī al-Nuʿmān's library after his death. He may well have been a son of al-Qāḍī al-Nuʿmān. The original letter of Abu'l-ʿAbbās was, however, a personal one, not intended for dissemination by the *daʿwa* and as such did not have the book title *Mafātīḥ al-niʿma*. Al-Qāḍī al-Nuʿmān presumably obtained a copy of it from Abu'l-ʿAbbās in his youth. Later the compiler of the *K. Mafātīḥ al-niʿma* evidently recognized that the letter, though conceived as a personal one, could be useful for the *daʿwa* in general as a work detailing the obligations of the faithful initiates towards the Imam.

The main themes of the treatise as we have it commences with the author responding to a complaint about this matter, from a member of the *daʿwa* voicing a concern about dues and fees that have been imposed on him by his *dāʿī*. He is seeking an explanation and some assurance that paying the amount asked for is proper and accords with his religious obligations. Has the *dāʿī* demanded too much and is he the one to collect such payments? Abu'l-ʿAbbās answers by saying that his brother requested his views on this issue and that he writes this letter to explain both explicitly and generally the subject of obligatory and voluntary fees and dues (*zakāt* and *ṣadaqa*), to whom they should be paid, and for what purpose. A key issue in what follows is the connection between willingly paying and access to instruction by the *dāʿī* about the esoteric interpretation (*taʾwīl*) of the law and scripture, and of the hierarchy of authorities who determine it. Alms given to God's guardians, says Abu'l-ʿAbbās, serve three aims.

> . . . the religion of God, both the outward and inward, exist so that His unique oneness, both outwardly and inwardly, leads to three conditions and three benefits. One of them is the worship of God. The second of them is that by means of which the world flourishes, that is, by His commandments and judgments. The third is that it points to the inner meaning of the law, the interpretation of the revelation, and to the spiritual and the physical hierarchy. The surface of the law is that by which it is determined, fixed and set, leading thereby to those who are the causes of salvation and through whom there is the ascent to the abode of the Return.

He readily admits that payments can create a hardship but he insists that it is nevertheless an obligation imposed by God in order to test the sincerity of the individual believer. It constitutes a method of ascertaining whether the novice is worthy of access to the esoteric meaning of religious matters.

> God orders him [the *dāʿī*] to examine the believers who seek the benefits of the religion to test out their secrets. If they bear the trial with patience, it is licit for the teacher to initiate them and raise them in the interpretive sciences. A person who breaks and perishes

and does not bear up during the trial and ordeal is forbidden to be initiated.

On the subject of who is authorized to receive the alms, Abu'l-ʿAbbās shows that the eight classes of people mentioned in the Qurʾan as those to whom it is payable are actually eight ranks of the Ismaili religious hierarchy (the *daʿwa*).

> These are eight kinds [religious ranks] whom God made the pillars of His religion and the treasurers of its science. He made it a duty for the people to know them and obligated them to obey them and ordered that offerings and alms be paid to them and put in their proper place with them, so that those of them who are not an Imam can convey it to the Imam who will expend it for the benefit of religion.

The individual believer, the entry-level novice at the bottom of this hierarchy, is to respond to the directive of his *dāʿī*:

> As for the believer, he pays what he pays on the measure of his sincerity and in accord with what his *dāʿī* determines for him in order to test him. If he pays that once, he has fulfilled the basic requirement of the religion and thus fulfilled the necessary obligation, by his fulfilment of which he distinguishes himself from the people of outward meaning and he departs from their ranks. If he pays a second time, his *dāʿī* knows the goodness of his intention and the firmness of his certainty and then he reveals to him the secrets of the interpretation. If he pays out a third time, his status with God's guardian rises and his rank similarly rises among the believers.

This, in brief, is the principal message of the *Mafātīḥ*. Its author repeats the same points several times and provides a number of explanatory interpretations based on the esoteric understand of key scriptural passages. This treatise is especially important both for them and for the technical terms and language he uses, all strictly for the internal consumption of the *daʿwa*. No one not a member is likely to have had access to it.

The Editions

Long before learning about the printed edition of the *Mafātīḥ*, we prepared an edition of the Arabic based on two manuscripts held by the Institute of Ismaili Studies in London. They are Mss 105 and 955, the former described in Adam Gacek's work *A Descriptive Catalogue of Arabic Manuscripts in the Library of the Institute of Ismaili Studies*, vol. 1 (London, 1984), pp. 21 and 58, the latter in Delia Cortese's *Ismaili and Other Arabic Manuscripts* (London, 2000), p. 104. Although we have subsequently used the printed version, the variants listed here are those in these two manuscripts, the first signified by the Arabic *alif* and the second by *bāʾ*.

For BL OR 8419 the edition is based solely on this unique manuscript which is, on the whole, fairly legible. Corrections to its text are so noted in the apparatus. As stated above, one folio or more is missing at the beginning and at the end. In addition, there are breaks in the text in several places: between folios 46a and 46b; 64b and 65a; 72b and 73a; 74b and 75a; 79b and 77a (folio 79a-b has been bound out of place); and 80b and 81a.

BL OR 8419

An Untitled Work attributed to Abū ʿAbd Allāh al-Shīʿī

…'(O People of the Book there has now come to you Our Apostle making matters clear to you after the interval among the messengers, lest you claim that there has neither come to us) a bearer of glad tidings nor a warner. In fact there has come to you a bearer of glad tidings and a warner; and God has power over all things' [Q 5: 19]. Thus they became blind after [having been given] the explanation and denied after [having been given] certainty. They differed after clear evidence and guidance, in revolt on their part and out of envy in their very souls. It is as God, glory to Him, has said about past nations and bygone centuries: 'they did not differ except after the explanation had come to them, in revolt between them' [Q 45: 17]. And He has said: 'God wishes to explain to you and to guide you with the right practice of those who came before you' [Q 4: 26]. He also said: 'Do not be like those who divided and differed after the explanations had come to them' [Q 3: 105]. And He said: 'God does not lead a group astray after having guided them unless He has made clear to them what they should guard against' [Q 9: 115]. Thus the Apostle of God, may the blessings of God be upon him, and give him and his family peace, warned his community against disunity and mutual difference and he informed them that they will perpetrate what the nations that came before them perpetrated. And so he, on him and on his family be the most excellent of peace, said, 'Surely you will follow the practice of the Israelites in a completely identical manner, exactly alike.' ʿAmr b. ʿAuf b. Ṭalḥa al-Muzanī[1] reported, 'We were sitting in his mosque with the

Apostle of God. Gabriel brought him the revelation. He covered himself with his cloak and remained so a long time. Then Gabriel went away and he took off his cloak. He was sweating profusely and obviously he was holding on to something. At that he said, "Do any of you know what comes forth from the date palm?" The Anṣār said to him, "O Apostle of God, may our father and mother be your ransom, nothing of the date palm is unknown to us and we are masters of date cultivation." Then he opened his hand in which there was a date stone and said, "What is this?" So they replied, "O Apostle of God that is a date stone." He said, "A stone of what thing?" They replied, "*Sanh*."[2] He said, "You are right. Gabriel came to you to contract with you concerning your faith that you shall keep to the path of those who came before you in a completely identical manner and to take after them exactly, whether inch by inch, cubit by cubit or yard by yard, to the point that, were they to enter the burrow of a lizard, you would enter it as well."'

ʿUbāda b. al-Ṣāmit[3] narrated saying, '"How is it that your Qurʾan readers and your scholars fled to the tops of the mountains out of fear of being killed with you?" They answered, "Yes." He said, "Was not the Torah with the Jews and they lost it, the Gospels with the Christians and they lost them? One evil only follows another evil."' Al-Mustawrid b. Shaddād[4] said, 'The Apostle of God said, "This community will not abandon the practice of previous generations just as this thumb leads the one that follows it."' Ḥudhayfa b.

1 ʿAmr b. ʿAuf b. Ṭalḥa al-Muzanī was a Companion of the prophet and one of the earliest Muslims. On him see Ibn ʿAbd al-Barr, *al-Istīʿāb fī maʿrifat al-Aṣḥāb* (Cairo, n.d.), vol. 3, p. 1196.

2 'A *nakhla sanhā*' is a palm-tree that bears one year and not another', Edward Lane, *Arabic-English Lexicon*; 'a *sanh* is a date palm that produces no fruit for many years', Steingass, *Persian-English Dictionary*.

3 ʿUbāda b. al-Ṣāmit was a Companion of the prophet.

4 Al-Mustawrid b. Shaddād was another of the Companions. See ʿAbd al-Barr, *al-Istīʿāb*, vol. 4, pp. 1471–1472.

al-Yamān[5] said, 'There was nothing with the Israelites but that its like will be with you.' A man said, 'Will we be monkeys and pigs?' He answered, 'What causes you to doubt about that, may your mother perish?'[6] And, in another *ḥadīth* reported of him, he said, 'What excellent brothers of yours are the Israelites, all sweetness is yours and all bitterness is theirs.' ʿAbd Allāh b. ʿUmar[7] said, 'The Apostle of God said, "You will surely follow the path of those who came before you inch by inch, cubit by cubit, exactly alike, to the point that, should they enter the burrow of a lizard, you would follow them into it." They said, "O Apostle of God, of the Jews and the Christians?" He replied, "The Jews and the Christians."'[8] God, may He be exalted and thanks be to Him, has said: '*Alif lam min*; do the people reckon they can escape by saying "We believe" and thus not be tried; truly We tried those before them and thus did God come to know those who speak the truth and those who are liars' [Q 29: 1–3] in regard to their true faith. Then God said: 'The custom of God is that which was in effect from before and you will find no alteration in the custom of God' [Q 48: 23] and 'you will not find that the law of God changes' [Q 35: 43]. He has said: 'So you find enjoyment in your lot just as those who came before you found enjoyment in theirs and you are so engrossed as were they' [Q 9: 69]. He has said: 'They will be humbled just like those who came before were humbled' [Q 58: 5] and He said: 'Likewise those who came

5 Ḥudhayfa b. al-Yamān was another of the Companions, ʿAbd al-Barr, *al-Istīʿāb*, vol. 1, pp. 334–335.

6 Literally: 'May you have no Mother.' Compare with the following *ḥadīth* that ʿAbd Allāh b. ʿAmr narrated: 'The Prophet said: "My *umma* will face what the Banū Isrāʾīl faced step by step, even if one of them approached his mother publicly (sexually) there will be one of my *umma* who will approach his mother."' (Tirmidhī, #2651). In another *ḥadīth*, Abū Salama and Abū Hurayra narrated the same. Ibn Majāh, *Sunan*, '*Kitāb al-fitan*', #3981.

7 ʿAbd Allāh b. ʿUmar b. al-Khaṭṭāb was the son of the second caliph, a prominent Companion and an authority on *ḥadīth* (d. 73/693).

8 As reported in the *Ṣaḥīḥ*s of both Bukhārī and Muslim, 'The Prophet Muhammad said: "You will follow in the path of those who came before you, inch by inch, yard by yard, so that even if they were to go into a lizard's burrow, you would follow them into it." His Companions asked him: "You mean the Jews and Christians?" He replied: "Who else?"' *Ṣaḥīḥ al-Bukhārī* (#7320) and *Ṣaḥīḥ Muslim* (#2669).

before them said the same thing, being like them in their hearts' [Q 2: 118].

Jacob and Esau were twins and then Esau disobeyed God in regard to Israel and wronged him. So God blessed the progeny of Israel and made among them prophets and pure souls (*al-aṣfiyā'*). Similarly Hāshim[9] and 'Abd Shams were twins; but Umayya opposed Hāshim Muḍar. So God blessed the descendants of Hāshim and placed among them the lord of prophets and the seal of the executors (*al-awṣiyā'*).[10] The [original] name of Israel was Jacob and so when he travelled in the night he was called Israel.[11] Subsequently, his name became dominant to the point that when 'the family of Jacob' was said no one understood it unless it was called 'the family of Israel'. Similarly, the name of Hāshim was 'Amr. When he broke up the bread for the soup of his people, he was called Hāshim ('the crusher').[12] That name became so prevalent that when someone said 'the family of 'Amr' it was not understood unless 'family of Hāshim' was said, in exactly the same fashion.

Truly did the Apostle of God encounter the same suffering at the hands of the unbelievers of his people as the messengers experienced at the hands of their people, in being called liars, accused of sorcery and being slandered. Indeed Pharaoh and his notables said to Moses: 'Whatever sign you bring before us with which to bewitch us we will not believe in you' [Q 7: 132] and he said: 'If you

9 Hāshim b. 'Abd al-Manāf was the great grandfather of Muhammad and the founder of the Banū Hāshim sub-clan of the Quraysh. He was also, as stated here, the brother of 'Abd Shams, who was the father of Umayya, the founder of the Umayyad sub-clan of the Quraysh and thus the ancestor of the Umayyad dynasty. On the former see M. Watt, 'Hāshim b. 'Abd al-Manāf', *EI2*. The use of 'Muḍār' should be taken as a reference to his noble tribal lineage.

10 'The lord of prophets' and 'the seal of the executors' are respectively Muhammad and 'Alī.

11 *Isrā'* (as in *isrā'il*) means 'nocturnal journey'.

12 Hāshim 'was the first to provide *tharīd* (broth in which bread is broken up) in Mecca. Actually his name was 'Amr, but he was called Hāshim because he broke up bread in this way for his people in Mecca', Ibn Isḥāq, *Sīrat rasūl Allāh*, ed. F. Wüstenfeld as *Das Lebens Muhammed* (1st ed. Stuttgart, 1864), tr. A. Guillaume (London, 1955; rpr. Karachi, 1997), ed. Wüstenfeld, p. 87, tr. Guillaume, p. 58.

have come with a sign, then bring it forth if you are one of those who speak the truth; so he threw out his staff and it became a live serpent and he drew out his hand which then became white to those who observed' [Q 7: 106–108]. At that the notables said: 'Truly he is a skilled sorcerer' [Q 7: 109] and they said: 'This is clearly sorcery' [Q 27: 13]. In a similar way the unbelievers among the Quraysh said to the prophet, 'Split this moon for us.' So he called upon his Lord and the moon was split into two halves. When they saw it, they said, 'Muhammad has bewitched the moon.'[13] God then said: 'The hour drew near and the moon has become split, and when they see a sign they turn away and say, "This is the same sorcery as before"' [Q 54: 1–2]. And He said by way of explanation to His prophet: 'Messengers before you were accused of lying; so they bore patiently the falsehood said of them and the malice until Our help reached them' [Q 6: 34]. 'But they said: "What is this prophet who eats food and walks about in the marketplace?"' [Q 25: 7]. And God said: 'We did not send before you messengers who did not eat food and walk about in the marketplace' [Q 25: 20]. Then next He said: 'Nothing is said to you that was not said to the messengers before you' [Q 41: 43]. And He said: 'What is there to prevent people believing when guidance comes to them or from seeking forgiveness of their Lord except should the custom of the ancients come upon them or the punishment appear immediately before them?' [Q 18: 55]. And the Exalted One said: 'Even if We had sent to you a document written on parchment so they could touch it with their hands, those who disbelieve would say, "This is nothing but plain sorcery"' [Q 6: 7].

[13] This incident is reported in the traditions and repeated there by many authorities. Early traditions and stories explain this verse as a miracle performed by Muhammad, following requests of some members of the Quraysh. The verse Q 54: 2, 'But if they see a Sign, they turn away, and say, "This is (but) transient magic"', is understood to support this view. A tradition transmitted on the authority of Anas b. Mālik states that Muhammad split the moon after the pagan Meccans asked for a miracle.

God said: 'When Jesus, son of Mary, said: "O Israelites, I am the messenger of God to you confirming what I have of the Torah and bringing glad tidings of a messenger who will come after me whose name is Aḥmad"; but, when he came to them with the evidence, they said: "This is clearly sorcery"' [Q 61: 6]. The Apostle of God said to the family of ʿAbd al-Muṭṭalib[14] on the day on which was revealed 'And warn your close family relations' [Q 26: 214], 'O family of ʿAbd al-Muṭṭalib, verily I bring to you explanatory signs; I come to you with the glory of the religion and the nobility of the afterlife. So be in this affair the leaders; do not be the followers.' So when he brought signs consisting of feeding of forty men with the leg of a lamb, a *ṣa*ʾ measure of barley[15] and a bowl of milk, and [any one] man of them could have eaten a [whole] lamb (*jidh*ʿ) and drunk a *farq*[16] [of milk], they [the Quraysh] said, 'Your master has bewitched you' and then they laughed together and said to Abū Ṭālib, 'He ordered you to listen to and obey this youth',[17] just like Pharaoh and his notables. God said: 'And when he brought to them Our clear signs, they laughed' [Q 43: 47] and He, glory be to Him, He has no partners, said: 'Ridiculing of prophets occurred before you but those among them who mock are entrapped by what they have ridiculed' [Q 21: 41]. The Israelites said to Jesus, the son of Mary: 'Ask Your Lord to bring down for us a table from heaven' [Q 5: 112].[18] Similarly, the unbelievers among the Quraysh said to the Apostle of God, 'Ask your Lord, O Muhammad, to make for us out of

[14] ʿAbd al-Muṭṭalib was the son of Hāshim and grandfather of Muhammad. See M. Watt, 'ʿAbd al-Muṭṭalib b. Hāshim', *EI2*.

[15] Regarding the measurement of a *ṣā*ʾ, which was a measure of grain in parts of Pre-Islamic Arabia, which was fixed by the prophet after the *hijra*, see A. Bel, 'Ṣāʾ', *EI2*.

[16] A *farq* or *faraq* is a measure of liquid (Steingass). Lane provides more detail, especially of Hijāzī usage, which regards a *farq* as a measure of liquid capacity of large size, several pints or more.

[17] This story is recounted in detail by Ibn Isḥāq/Ibn Hishām, tr. Guillaume, pp. 117–118 (Wüstenfeld, p. 166; Ṭabarī, p. 1171). Ṭabarī, pp. 1171–1173, tr. M. Watt, pp. 89–90.

[18] The Qurʾanic passage cited here is slightly different; it reads: 'When the disciples (al-Ḥawāriyyūn) said, "O Jesus, son of Mary, can your Lord send down to us a table [set with food] from heaven?"' Jesus then does as they request. Q 5: 112–115.

this rock gold.' Truly the unbelieving Quraysh ridiculed the Apostle of God as the unbelievers who came before him had done. God said: 'When they see you, they accept you only in mockery saying, "Is this the one God sent as a messenger?; he might have turned us away from our gods were we not steadfastly with them"' [Q 25: 41–42]. God said to the unbelieving Quraysh: 'We have destroyed followers of yours before; does anyone remember?' [Q 54: 51]. Then he recounted about those of earlier centuries who asserted that the messengers were lying and so he brought down on them His punishment, vengeance and violence until He reached mention of the people of Pharaoh and said: 'Truly the warning came to the people of Pharaoh; they rejected all of Our signs; so We seized them with the grip of power and might' [Q 54: 41–42] Then He said: 'Are your unbelievers any better than they were, or are you absolved of that in the Psalms?' [Q 54: 43]. The Apostle of God appealed to God against the inhabitants of Mecca. He said: 'O God, bring years like the years of Joseph';[19] so they came to eat bones and corpses.

Verily God, when He afflicted the Israelites in the wilderness because of their having disobeyed, the Israelites prayed for rain and Moses used to carry with him a stone. God said: 'We said: "Strike the stone with your staff", and then there sprang from it twelve springs' [Q 2: 60], for the twelve tribes, a gift from God, a great blessing, an honour and an enhancement of the proof of his prophecy. In a similar way the companions of God's Apostle during one of their raids became thirsty, their water supply having been exhausted, so they asked the Apostle of God to pray for rain, whereupon he found a small amount of water in the hide belonging to a man. So he filled his mouth with water and chewed on it. Thereafter he watered from it a great army, as a gift from God, a blessing, an honour and an enhancement

[19] This reference is to a well-known *ḥadīth* related from Abū Hurayra in which the prophet asks God to make or bring upon [them] years like those of Joseph (*Allāhumma ij'al sinīn ka-sinī Yūsuf*).

of the proof of his prophecy.[20] Thus he made them realize the blessedness of his saliva and spittle in exactly this manner.

God gave His spirit and His word to Jesus so that he could raise the dead and provide them with what they ate and what they stored up in their houses. In a similar way, God gave His prophet Muhammad knowledge. So a lamb roasting on spit(?) cried out in front of him.[21] It said, 'Do not eat me, O Muhammad, for I have been poisoned.'[22] And the prisoners ransomed themselves with what they had stored up in their houses. So he said to his uncle al-ʿAbbās, 'Where are the dinars that you hid with Umm al-Faḍl?'[23] So the proof of his prophecy was enhanced beyond the proof of the prophecy of Jesus in that God appraised him of what was in people's hearts, while God did not appraise Jesus about people's hearts [but] just about what they could

[20] Several narratives relate a version of a prophetic miracle of Muhammad in which water becomes plentiful where little existed previously. One story has him place his hand in a vessel containing a small amount of water and then much of it flows from between his fingers. The other concerns the Muslim army trying to obtain water from a well that went dry. He sits at its edge, calls for the little water they have, drinks a drop and spits it out into the well, whereupon they find in it more than enough to water the whole army and its mounts. Perhaps our author has conflated the two accounts.

[21] The Arabic here is uncertain.

[22] 'When the Apostle had rested, Zaynab bt al-Ḥārith, the wife of Sallām b. Mishkam, prepared for him a roast lamb, having first enquired as to what joint he preferred. When she learned that it was the shoulder, she put a lot of poison in it poisoning the whole lamb. Then she brought it in and placed it before him. He took hold of the shoulder and chewed a morsel of it, but he did not swallow it. Bishr b. al-Barāʾ b. Maʿrūr, who was with the Apostle, took some of it as the Apostle had done, but he swallowed it, while the Apostle spat it out, saying, "This bone tells me that it is poisoned." Then he called for the woman and she confessed, and when he asked her what had induced her to do this she answered, "You know what you have done to my people. I said to myself, if he is a king, I shall rid myself of him and, if he is a prophet, he will be informed (of what I have done)." So the Apostle let her off. Bishr died from what he had eaten.' Ibn Isḥāq, ed. Wüstenfeld, tr. Guillaume, p. 516.

On this, Bishr, who according to the prophet was chief of the Medinan clan of Salima, see Watt, *Muhammad at Medina*, p. 234. Sallām was a prominent member of the Jewish al-Nādir clan of Medina, see W. M. Watt, *Muhammad at Medina* (Oxford, 1956), p. 212.

[23] Ibn Isḥāq, ed. Wüstenfeld, p. 463, tr. Guillaume, pp. 312–313, with the full story confirmed from Ṭabarī a portion of which is as follows: when the Prophet demands a ransom from al-ʿAbbās, the latter says at one point, 'I have no money.' The Prophet replies, 'Then where is the money which you left with Umm al-Faḍl bt al-Ḥārith when you left Mecca? You were alone when you said to her, "If I am killed so much is for al-Faḍl, ʿAbd Allāh and Qutham and ʿUbayd Allāh."' Al-ʿAbbās then exclaims, 'By him who sent you with the truth, none but she and I knew of this and now I know that you are God's Apostle.'

eat and what they stored up in their houses. God appraised the lord of His messengers of what was in men's hearts on the day Abū Sufyān b. Ḥarb[24] came to greet him. When the Apostle of God saw him, he said to himself, 'Surely I shall be this man's enemy.' So the prophet said to him, 'Do you greet me with war?' He replied, 'I testify that you are the Apostle of God in truth.' Just as it was with the Israelites in the wilderness having no shelter to shade them from the heat of the sun, which was unbearable for any soul except with shelter sheltering them, when God bestowed on them shelters as a sign, a proof, an enhancement of the proof, an honouring, a favour for them to remember, so God provided shade for His prophet on the day his caravan returned to Khadīja from Syria. Baḥīrā[25] observed them, and he saw a cloud shading them. So he invited them to eat with him. They left the Apostle of God with the pack animals, but the cloud stood still, sheltering him. So he [Baḥīrā] invited him and the cloud moved with him wherever he went.[26] God made it a shelter shading, an honouring and a blessing, a first proof for His prophet.

The Israelites drew an omen about Moses and those with him and they said, 'We have been harmed before you came to us and after you reached us.' He said, 'Perhaps your Lord will destroy your enemy and make you vice-regent over the land.' In a similar way the Quraysh said to the Apostle of God, 'Our war through you has become violent.' He replied, 'God surely shall complete this matter and grant me victory over all religion, even though the idolaters hate it. Let the treasures of

[24] Abū Sufyān, as the chief of the Banū Umayya and leader of the Quraysh, was a staunch opponent of Muhammad until his fairly late conversion and acceptance of Islam.

[25] 'Baḥīrā is the name of a Christian monk. Ibn Saʿd and Ibn Hishām offer two parallel traditions, confirmed by al-Ṭabarī (1, 1123 ff.), according to which Muḥammad, when either nine or twelve years old, whilst accompanying the Meccan caravan to Syria, in the company of Abū Bakr or Abū Ṭālib, found himself in the presence of a Christian monk or hermit, who is said to have revealed the young man's prophetic destiny, either by finding on him the stigmata of prophecy, or by noting the miraculous movement of a cloud, or the behaviour of a branch, which persisted in affording him shade, irrespective of the course of the sun.' A. Abel, 'Baḥīrā', *EI2*.

[26] A version of this event is recounted in Ibn Isḥāq, *Sīra*, ed. Wüstenfeld, pp. 115–116, tr. Guillaume, pp. 79–81, specifically p. 80.

Khusraw and Caesar be spent for the cause of God. If only one day remained for the earth, God will prolong that day until He shall give a man from my descendants possession of it and shall fill the earth with equity and justice as it was full of tyranny and injustice. Truly God will open for him the east of the earth and its west.' The hypocrites, in whose heart was malice, said, 'God and His Messenger promise us nothing but illusions. Muhammad claims that he will take control of the east of the earth and its west, while he has entrenched himself behind a trench.' So God revealed: 'Your people claim it is a lie but it is the truth' [Q 6: 66].

Pharaoh said to his people who wanted the finery of worldly life: 'Am I not better than he who is contemptible and cannot express himself clearly; why were there no bracelets of gold thrown to him, nor angels come with him as his companions; thus he made light of this to his people, and they obeyed him; they were truly a wicked people' [Q 43: 52–54]. Like that, one of the pharaohs of the Quraysh said to his followers, who had become rich with the luxuries of this world, on the day the Apostle of God said, 'I have asked my Lord for the brotherhood of ʿAlī, on whom be peace, and his ministry, and He has granted it to me.' So the fellow said, 'A leather skin in which there are some dates is dearer to me than what Muhammad has asked of his Lord. Why not ask for an angel to assist him or riches to spend?' Thereupon God revealed: 'Perhaps you may omit some of what was revealed to you and may be dishearten hearing them say: "Why has no treasure come down to him or angels accompany him; truly you are only a warner"' [Q 11: 12], exactly the same as the earlier case.

They said to Noah: '"Are we to believe you when only the vilest follow you?" He replied: "I have no knowledge of what they have been doing." Taking their account falls solely to my Lord were you to be aware. I am not the one to drive away believers"' [Q 26: 111–114]. In a similar way al-Aqraʿ b. Ḥābis al-Tamīmī and ʿUyayna b. Ḥiṣn al-Fazārī came and found the Apostle of God sitting with ʿAmmār,

Khabbāb and Ṣuhayb among people who were believers of low status.[27] So when they saw them, they were disdainful of them, saying, 'The only thing that prevents us from sitting with you is these slaves and the smell of their *jubbas*.[28] Send these people off and convene for us a meeting session with you so that the Arabs may know that we are close to you. Delegations of Arabs shall come to you and we would be ashamed that the Arabs see us together with these slaves. So should we come to you, have them stand away from us. If we stand up, sit with them if you will.' So God revealed in answer on behalf of His prophet: 'Do not turn away those who call upon their Lord morning and evening desiring His face' [Q 6: 52] and the Exalted said: 'When those who believe in its signs come to you, say to them, "Peace be upon you", your Lord has written for Himself mercy' [Q 6: 54] and He said: 'And keep your soul content with those who call on their Lord morning and evening' [Q 18: 28], and He said: 'Do not turn your eyes away from them desiring the adornment of the present life' [Q 18: 28] and He said: 'Do not obey the one whose heart We have made neglectful of remembering Us and who followed his whims and his affair is in excess' [Q 18: 28]. The meaning is: Do not keep company with the nobles, just as it was said to Noah, in exactly the same way.

The unbelievers among the Israelites have said about the Torah and the Gospels, 'They are a pair of sorcerers alike and we renounce both' [Q 28: 48]. And God said: 'Say [Muhammad], bring a book from God that guides better than these that I may follow it, if you speak the truth' [Q 28: 49]. In a similar manner the unbelievers among the Quraysh said: 'We will not believe in this Qur'an, nor in what was before it'

27 Al-Aqraʿ b. Ḥābis al-Tamīmī and ʿUyayna b. Ḥiṣn al-Fazārī were two members of tribal nobility, the former of Tamīm and the later of Ghaṭafān. The three of low status were ʿAmmār b. Yāsir, Khabbāb b. al-Aratt and Ṣuhayb b. Sinān, all freed former slaves with weak affiliation and protection in Mecca. On them see W. M. Watt, *Muhammad at Mecca* (Oxford, 1953), pp. 90, 95. A version of this incident appears in Ibn Isḥāq, ed. Wüstenfeld, p. 260, tr. Guillaume, pp. 179–180.

28 In the time of the prophet, a *jubba* was a woollen tunic with sleeves, see Y. K. Stillman, 'Libās, i. In the central, eastern Islamic lands', *EI2*.

[Q 34: 31] and: 'those who disbelieved in the truth said when it came to them: "This is nothing but obvious sorcery"' [Q 46: 7]. And that is like when the Israelites reached being freed during God's testing of them by the punishment of Pharaoh and he menaced them and he said: '"You have come to believe it before having permission; surely it is your chief who has taught you magic; I will cut off your hands and legs alternately and I will crucify you on the trunks of a palm tree; you will come to know which of us is more powerful in inflicting punishment and longer in doing so." They said, "We will not prefer you over against the signs that have come to us and the one who created us; so decree for us as you will judge on us. Your decree affects us solely in the present life"' [Q 20: 71–72]. And the pain of the punishment did not touch them. So it happened during the trial of their brothers in our community; they were crucified on a tree, and their bones were broken on the rack, as were ʿAmmār and his companions, and Ḥabīb b. ʿAbd Allāh. It was said to Ḥabīb while crucified, 'Would you wish that what is happening to you happened instead to Muhammad so that we release you?' He replied, 'No thorn must pierce him', measure for measure.[29]

God said: 'When he [Moses] came to the water of Midian, he found at it a group of people using the water and he found a short distance from them two girls holding back. He said: "What concerns you?" They said: "We cannot use the water until the shepherds depart and our father is an old man." So he drew water for them and turned away moving into the shade' [Q 28: 23–24]. They were used to taking water

[29] The Ḥabīb b. ʿAbd Allāh mentioned here would appear to be the same as Ḥabīb b. Zayd whose story is related by Ibn Hishām as follows: 'Musaylima, the liar, the Ḥanīfī chief of the Yamāma got hold of Ḥabīb and began to say to him, "Do you testify that Muḥammad is the Apostle of God?" And when he said that he did, he went on, "And do you testify that I am the Apostle of God?" he answered, "I do not hear." So he began to cut him to pieces member by member until he died. He tried putting the same questions to him again and again, but he could get no different answers.' Ibn Isḥāq, ed. Wüstenfeld, pp. 312–313, tr. Guillaume, p. 212. This Ḥabīb's brother was ʿAbd Allāh (b. Zayd) but he himself was not an ibn ʿAbd Allāh.

with a group of relatives. So it was one of his proofs, as he was fleeing towards his Lord. One of the two girls[30] described to their father what she saw of power and trustworthiness in him: 'O Father, employ him; surely the best man to hire is the strong and trustworthy one' [Q 28: 26]. When the Apostle of God appeared before Medina, he stopped with Umm Maʿbad al-Khuzāʿiyya. He milked her lean sheep that had suffered from hardship and exhaustion. It provided plenty of milk for him. He filled a cup and drank and gave drink to a whole group. And he left behind with them much milk. It was one of the many signs of his prophethood while he was fleeing to his Lord. Then she reported to her husband and described his light and beauty.[31] She made him see evidence of his blessing like that the daughter of Shuʿayb had described to her father. He said, 'By God, this is the master of the Quraysh.' Thus, she detected in the prophet of God what the daughter of Shuʿayb detected in Moses in exactly the same manner.

And the day the canine tooth of God's Apostle was broken,[32] he thought to inveigh against them. Then he said, 'May the mercy of God

[30] The girl in question here is, in the Islamic tradition, Ṣafrāʾ bt Shuʿayb, not as in the Bible, Zipporah (Arabic Ṣafūra) daughter of Jethro a priest of Midian. In the Qurʾanic context she is the daughter of the Arabian prophet Shuʿayb. Even so. the story related here is that of Exodus 2: 18–20.

[31] There are various reports of this event. Here is one: 'Umm Maʿbad al-Khuzāʿiyya, she was ʿAtiqa bt Khālid al-Khuzāʿī. She was a gracious lady who sat at her tent door with a mat spread out for any chance traveller that might pass by the way. Fatigued and thirsty, the Prophet . . . and his Companions wanted to refresh themselves with food and some milk. Umm Maʿbad told them that the herd was out in the pasture and the goat standing nearby was almost dry since it was a rainless year. The Prophet . . . touched the goat's udders, reciting over them the Name of God, supplicated and, to their great joy, plenty of milk flowed out of them. After seeing that every Companion of his was satisfied and full, that was the only time the Prophet . . . drank and said, "The cup-bearer drinks last." Before he left, he milked the goat another time and filled the container and gave it to Umm Maʿbad. After their departure, Umm Maʿbad's husband, Aktham b. Abi'l-Jawn al-Khuzāʿī, came herding an emaciated flock of sheep. When he saw the milk in the container, he said, "Umm Maʿbad, what is this? Where have you got the milk when there is no goat with milk here?" His wife answered, "A blessed man passed by us." Abū Maʿbad, who was delighted to have had his senses stimulated by the news told him by his wife, said, "Describe him." Umm Maʿbad gave her husband a description of the Prophet.'

[32] At the Battle of Uhud Muhammad was wounded in the face and at least one of his incisors was broken. There are several reports of this incident in Ibn Isḥāq, ed. Wüstenfeld, pp. 571, 576, tr. Guillaume, pp. 380, 382. See also al-Qāḍī al-Nuʿmān, *Sharḥ al-akhbār fī faḍāʾil al-aʾimma al-aṭhār* (Beirut, 1994), vol. 1, p. 277.

be upon my brother Moses. He was hurt in the cause of God more than this. Yet he bore that with patience.' The unbelievers of the Quraysh did not miss an opportunity to follow the practice of the early unbelievers in everything they did to the Apostle of God, to the degree that Abū Lahab[33] revolted against him from among his own people, just as Korah had revolted against Moses among the people of Moses. He was the son of Moses's paternal uncle just like Abū Lahab was the paternal uncle of the Apostle of God. The Apostle of God left Mecca in fear, lying, guarding himself in the cave, just as Moses had left Egypt for Midian in fear guarding himself. God, to Whom be glory and thanks, said: 'Remember when those who disbelieve devised a trick to capture you or kill you or expel you, they plotted but God plotted and God is best at planning' [Q 8: 30]. Then the Almighty said, informing His prophet that this trial always occurred to all of the prophets: 'Every nation intrigued against their messenger in order to seize him' [Q 40: 5]. And the Apostle of God returned from Medina [to act] against the infidels of his people just as Moses returned from Midian [to act] against Pharaoh and his people. And God sent down upon the enemies of Moses the drowning flood. Similarly He sent down the sword [for use] against the enemies of His prophet. In the same way, God gave the friends of God's Apostle the inheritance of his enemies' land on the day Mecca was conquered just as He gave the Israelites an inheritance of gardens, springs, treasures and noble position. This is the custom of God with regard to the unbelievers of the Israelites, exactly in the same manner.

Then truly God chose, for all the worlds, from the family of Muhammad, just as he had chosen from the family of 'Imrān. Khadīja was the equal of Āsiya, the wife of Pharaoh. She was the first female believer in Muhammad. 'Alī, peace be upon him, was [the first male

[33] Abū Lahab was the prophet's paternal uncle. His opposition to Islam was so strident and unrelenting he was condemned by name in the Qur'an. *Sūra* 111 reads in part: 'Perish the hands of Abū Lahab; perish he; no profit to him from all his wealth and all his gains.'

believer]. Aaron had been the first to follow Moses and ʿAlī, peace be upon him, was the first to follow Muhammad. So God said: 'None believed in Moses except some youths in his people in fear that Pharaoh and his nobles would persecute them' [Q 10: 83]. And none believed in Muhammad, except some youths of his people such as Jaʿfar[34] and ʿAlī, out of fear that the pharaohs of the Quraysh would persecute them. His (ʿAlī's) position with respect to our prophet was the position of Aaron with respect to Moses, except that there will be no prophet after our prophet. Muhammad, the prophet, and ʿAlī, the legatee, prayed together seven years in Mecca in fear, just as Moses had tarried [a period of] eight pilgrimages with Shuʿayb out of fear of his people. Therefore God's Apostle said, 'The angels prayed for me and ʿAlī for seven years. No male prayed with me other than him.'

Fāṭima, peace be upon her, was the equal of Maryam; God selected her and purified her over the women of the two worlds, like Maryam the daughter of ʿImrān. May God protect her and her offspring from the accursed Satan. Then God said: 'God wants to drive impurity out of you, O people of the House, and to cleanse you by purifying' [Q 33: 33]. The Apostle of God said, 'This verse was revealed about five of us, about me, about ʿAlī, Fāṭima, al-Ḥasan and al-Ḥusayn, so that I and my family may be those purified of filth and rendered immune to the accursed Satan.' God caused a table to descend from heaven to Fāṭima, just as He had descended a table to Maryam, daughter of ʿImrān, on the day she entered her *miḥrāb* and prayed two *rakʿa*s. Then she said, 'O Lord, this is Muhammad Your prophet and this is ʿAlī the cousin of Your prophet. I am Fāṭima, daughter of Your prophet and these are al-Ḥasan and al-Ḥusayn, the two grandsons of Your prophet. O God, make descend on us a table from heaven just as You caused it to descend on the Israelites, though they refused to believe in it. Our Lord, if You cause it to come down, I will not refuse to believe in it.' At

[34] This is ʿAlī's brother Jaʿfar b. Abī Ṭālib who was, therefore, like ʿAlī, a cousin of Muhammad. He was also a very early convert to Islam.

that, behold, there was by the side of the *miḥrāb* a plate of *tharīd* (broth)[35] and on it was meat from which exuded the smell of musk. Fāṭima carried it and placed it in front of the Apostle of God, may the blessings of God be upon him and his family. The prophet turned towards it and ate, with ʿAlī watching. So he said, 'O Abu'l-Ḥasan, eat and ask not. Praise be to God who has shown us in you and her what Zakariyāʾ saw in Maryam.' 'Whenever Zakariyāʾ came in to see her in the *miḥrāb,* he found with her food; he said: "O Maryam, from where comes this to you"; she said: "It is from God, truly God provides food to whomever He wills without a reckoning"' [Q 3: 37].

Aaron, son of ʿImrān, did not stay behind his brother Moses except twice: the day 'he turned his face towards Midian' [Q 28: 22] 'so he went out from it fearing in anticipation' [Q 28: 21] and the day Moses went out to the mountain and he appointed his brother Aaron in his place. ʿAlī never stayed behind his brother the Apostle of God, except on two occasions: the day he set out for the cave and went from it in fear and anticipation, and the day the Apostle of God left for Tabūk and he deputised his brother ʿAlī, peace be upon him, in his place. So ʿAlī went to him and said, 'O Messenger of God, the Quraysh claim that you find me burdensome and loathe my company.' He replied, 'Are you not satisfied that you are to me in the position of Aaron with Moses, except that there will be no prophet after me?' He said, 'Indeed I am, O Messenger of God.' He said, 'Return, there is no one suitable there except me and you.'[36] Al-Ḥasan and al-Ḥusayn were the equals of Shubayr and Shabar, the

35 *Tharīd* was a broth made from crumbled bread of which the prophet was said to be particularly fond, see M. Rodinson, 'Ghidhāʾ', *EI2*.

36 Ibn Isḥāq, ed. Wüstenfeld, p. 897, tr. Guillaume, p. 604, reports the following: The apostle left ʿAlī behind to look after his family, and ordered him to stay with them. The hypocrites spoke evil of him, saying that he had been left behind because he was a burden to the apostle and he want to get rid of him. On hearing this ʿAlī seized his weapons and caught up with the apostle when he was halting in al-Jurf and repeated to him what the hypocrites were saying. He replied: 'They lie. I left you behind because of what I left behind, so go back and represent me in my family and yours. Are you not content, ʿAlī, to stand to me as Aaron stood to Moses, except that there will be no prophet after me?'

two sons of Aaron.[37] And on the day the prophet gave an order to block the gates that opened the path for them to his mosque but to leave [open] his gate and the gate of ʿAlī, he said, 'Truly, God revealed to Moses and Aaron: "Build houses for your people in Egypt and make your houses a direction of prayer"' [Q 10: 87]. Then he said, 'O God, surely I shall never allow anyone to enter the mosque out of fear or in a state of impurity except ʿAlī, Fāṭima, al-Ḥasan and al-Ḥusayn.'

God has said: 'And when his Lord tested Abraham with words and he fulfilled them' [Q 2: 124]. The test was for him to sacrifice the most beloved of God's creatures to him, his son Ismāʿīl. So he said: 'O my son, I saw in a dream that I was sacrificing you; consider what you see'; he said: 'O father, do what you have been ordered; you will find that I am, God willing, one of the steadfast' [Q 37: 102]. Thus he found him steadfast to what he promised his father. God the Exalted, said: 'Remember in the book Ismāʿīl, truly he was true to the promise and was a messenger prophet' [Q 19: 54]. He tested Muhammad with the creature most beloved to him, saying to him, 'O ʿAlī, the infidels of the Quraysh think to kill me tonight. Can you, O ʿAlī, sleep in my bed?' He said, 'O Apostle of God, will you save yourself?' He replied, 'Yes.' So he slept in his bed convinced of his own destruction.[38] But God saved him from being killed as He saved Ismāʿīl and he was thanked for his effort. God said: 'Among the people there is the one who sells himself seeking the pleasure of God and God is compassionate with the servants' [Q 2: 207]. The Apostle of God wished to leave ʿAlī as his

[37] In the Biblical tradition (Numbers 3: 2–4) the sons of Aaron are Nadab, Abihu, Eleazar and Ithamar. The first two died after offering 'strange fire' thus only the latter two survived. They became progenitors of a priestly line. In this context they could represent a type that indicates the role of ʿAlī's offspring as Imams. Calling them Shabar and Shubayr reflects a specifically Shiʿi understanding, one that emphasises the parallels between Aaron and ʿAlī, in this case in the naming of their sons. Refer to al-Naysābūrī, *al-Mustadrak ʿalā al-Ṣaḥīḥayn*, vol. 3, pp. 265 and 168, See also Mahmoud Ayoub, *Redemptive Suffering in Islam* (The Hague, 1978), index under Shubayr.

[38] This incident is confirmed by Ibn Isḥāq, ed. Wüstenfeld, pp. 325–326, tr. Guillaume, pp. 222–223, although with a difference that makes the threat to ʿAlī personally all but disappear.

successor in his community and to make him a minister from his family and executor among his people. It was like Moses asking his Lord, saying: My Lord, 'make for me a minister from my family, Aaron my brother; strengthen me through him and have him share my cause' [Q 20: 29–32]. He feared being called a liar by his people. So God revealed to him His guidance and the safety of his appointment of his brother from the foolish and He ordered him to make that known. Thus He said: 'O Messenger, make known what has been revealed to you from your Lord' [Q 5: 67], that is, make known the position of the *walī* of the message,[39] 'for, if you do not, you will not have made known His message and God will safeguard you from the people; truly God does not guide unbelieving people' [Q 5: 67]. The Apostle of God said, 'I was unable to bear it and I knew that the people would consider me a liar, so my Lord threatened me that I make it known or He would punish me.' So he stood up at Ghadīr Khumm and took the hand of ʿAlī, peace be upon him, and appointed him to his own position. So affirmation of his truthfulness was faith and accusing him of lying was unbelief and wanton conduct, and he entrusted him with what counsel, summons to the good and the way of guidance, that had been conveyed to him, as when Gabriel appointed him on the order of the Lord of the worlds in his conveying what Isrāfīl had conveyed to him. Thus his obedience was obedience to God and obedience to His Messenger a lesson for people and a mercy from God for His servants. So he had him stand beneath two tall trees and he said to his Companions, 'Am I not closer to the believers than they are to themselves?' They answered, 'By God, yes.' Then he said, 'Whosoever I am master of, ʿAlī is his master; and whoever I am his prophet, ʿAlī is his commander; of whoever I am closer to his soul than he himself, this one is closer to his soul than he himself; O God, be a friend to his friend and an enemy to his enemy; support whoever supports him

[39] Or, 'the succession of the friend of God to the Apostle of God'.

and forsake whoever forsakes him.' And he ordered his Companions that those present make this known to those absent. Then he said, 'O ʿAlī, the likeness of you in this community is like the saying "Say: He is God the unique" in the Qurʾan. He who recites it once it is as if he has recited a third of the Qurʾan, whoever recites it twice, it is as if he has recited two thirds of the Qurʾan, and whoever recites it three times, it is as if he has recited the whole Qurʾan. So whoever loves you, O ʿAlī, and Fāṭima, for him is the like of the wage of a third of this community, and whoever loves you in his heart and supports you with his tongue, for him is the like of the wage of two-thirds of this community, and whoever loves you in his heart, supports you with his tongue and aids you with his sword, for him is the wage of the whole of this community.'

Then God revealed: 'Today I have perfected for you your religion and completed my bounty to you' [Q 5: 3], that is, I shall not reveal a commandment after it, ever. So the Apostle of God said, 'God is the greatest regarding the perfection of the religion and the completion of [His] bounty.' The Apostle of God confirmed the authority [*wilāya*] of ʿAlī b. Abī Ṭālib, peace be upon him, and Moses did not do more than this for his people in appointing Aaron his successor, but his succession consisted of one word. He said: 'Take my place among my people and put things right; do not follow the path of those who corrupt' [Q 7: 142]. The Apostle of God confirmed for his people the deputyship [*khilāfa*] of ʿAlī by what he had affirmed at Ghadīr Khumm. Then he sent out from Medina all those whom he feared would oppose ʿAlī in his successorship and authority [*khilāfatihī wa wilāyatihī*] by putting them under the command of Usāma b. Zayd,[40] his client, and by ordering that none of them should remain in Medina. And he confirmed that it would be so until the succession of ʿAlī

[40] Usāma b. Zayd was the son of a freed slave who had been adopted by the prophet and treated as a son. He held important commands in the Muslim armies, especially the one sent to Syria. See the entry by V. Vacca, 'Usāma b. Zayd', *EI2*.

b. Abī Ṭālib was fully clear. Thus it was inevitable for this community to follow precisely the example of the Israelites when the Apostle of God promised them that they would follow the *sunna* of the Israelites and what God had promised them in the Book and that they would be seduced as those before them had been. The Apostle of God said, 'O ʿAlī, if I were to return during their sedition, I would take you by your head and your beard and you would reply to me with what Aaron replied to Moses that the people considered me weak and nearly killed me. So do not cause the enemy to rejoice over my misfortune. Know that for him there is malice in the breast of people which they will not make manifest until after his death.'

Then they asked him, saying, 'To whom shall we have recourse after you, O Apostle of God, and who is your successor among us?' But when he informed them, that vexed them. The Exalted, who has no partner, said: 'O you who believe do not ask about things that, if revealed to you, would vex you; but, if you ask about them when the Qurʾan is being revealed, it will be made clear to you; God forgives you for them and God is all-forgiving and forbearing. A people before you asked about such things, then they disbelieved in them' [Q 5: 101–102]. God said to the Companions of His prophet: 'Do you want to question your messenger as Moses was questioned earlier; but he who substitutes unbelief for faith has strayed from the straight path' [Q 2: 108]. So they asked the Apostle of God, 'What did the companions of Moses ask when he had them pass through the sea and had them witness the wonders, and he passed by some people "who were devoted to their idols; they said, O Moses, make for us a god like their god"? [Q 7: 138].' Thereupon the Companions of the Apostle of God said, 'O Apostle of God, would you make for us a standard on which to suspend pendants like the one they have?' The Apostle of God replied, 'God is the greatest, you speak as spoke the Israelites, make for us a god like the one they have.' Then he said, 'You are seeking to return to the custom of those before you.'

God said in answer to His prophet, 'O Muhammad: "Inquire of those of Our messengers We sent before you who were asked about whether We made gods to be worshipped other than the Most Merciful" [Q 43: 45].'

God, the Exalted, praise be to Him, said to the Companions of His prophet: 'Do not be like those who caused Moses pain' [Q 33: 69]. So one of his Companions said, 'Muhammad has sat between the thighs of our women. So, by God, if he dies, I will marry ʿĀʾisha.' So God revealed: 'It is not allowed to you to cause pain to the Apostle of God nor that you ever marry his wives after him' [Q 33: 53]. Moses used to inveigh against Pharaoh and his people, and Aaron would say, 'Amen, "Destroy, O Lord, their wealth and harden their hearts" [Q 10: 89].' God said: 'Your joint appeal has been granted so stand upright' [Q 10: 89]. So God made as their thanks his prevention. If something distressed the Apostle of God and troubled him, he summoned ʿAlī, and so the prophet would pray and ʿAlī would say Amen, like Moses and Aaron.

The Pharaoh's people said to Pharaoh: 'Put him and his brother off a while and send to the cities heralds to bring you every trained sorcerer; and the sorcerers came to Pharaoh and said: "Is there a reward for us if we are successful?" He said: "Yes, you shall be among those who stand close." They said: "O Moses, will you cast [your staff], or are we to cast first." He said: "You cast." When they had cast, they bewitched the eyes of the people and terrified them and brought about a great sorcery. We inspired Moses [telling him], "Cast your staff." Whereupon it swallowed up their conjuration. So truth was upheld and what they practised proved false. So they were bested and belittled there' [Q 7: 111–119]. In like manner, God sent the satans of the Quraysh on the Day of the Confederates assembled in their clans. They brought about a monstrous affair and hearts came up to their throats, supposing of God a vile supposition. He said: 'Those in whose hearts is disease, said: "God and His Messenger promised us nothing but deceit" [Q 33: 12].' And ʿAmr[41] challenged them to a duel saying, 'Either you stand or I stand against you.' So the Apostle of God sent out to them his brother ʿAlī. 'Whereupon it swallowed up their conjuration' [Q 7: 117]; 'So truth was upheld and what they practiced proved false. So they were bested and belittled there' [Q 7: 118–119] God, may He be praised, said: 'God drove those who did not believe back in their fury and they gained no advantage; God sufficed for the believers in the fighting' [Q 33: 25] through ʿAlī, just as He sufficed the Israelites through the staff of Moses.

God brought together in the shirt of Joseph three proofs: the day 'they came to their father at nightfall weeping' [Q 12: 16], and the day 'they brought out his shirt with false blood' [Q 12: 18], and the day the wife of ʿAzīz the minister slandered him with false testimony 'a witness from her family testified: if his shirt is torn from the front . . . (to the end of this verse)'[42] [Q 12: 26–27], and the day he sent his brothers to his father, saying to them: 'Go with this shirt of mine and place it on my father's face to restore his sight' [Q 12: 93]. In a similar way God brought together for Muhammad many proofs regarding his brother ʿAlī. God set him up on the day of the parties in the place of the staff of Moses so that 'it swallowed up their conjuration' [Q 7: 117] and on the Night of the Cave when God used him in his plot. God said: 'When those who disbelieve plotted to seize you or to kill you or expel you, they contrived against you, but God also plotted and God is the best of plotters' [Q 8: 30]. ʿAlī was God's plot in the bed of the Apostle of God. To the satans of the Quraysh, when they sought to kill the Messenger, He made him [ʿAlī] appear like him, just as He made

[41] During the Battle of the Confederates (6/627, also called the Battle of the Trench), the Muslim defence of Medina held against the assembled army of the Quraysh and others in the confederation. At one key point ʿAmr b. ʿAbd Wudd led a Quraysh party that managed to cross the trench whereupon he issued this challenge which was accepted by ʿAlī who defeated him. There is a report with much greater detail in Ibn Isḥāq, ed. Wüstenfeld, pp. 677–678, tr. Guillaume, pp. 454–456.

[42] 'Then she is telling the truth and he is lying. But if his shirt is torn from the back, then she is the liar and he is telling the truth.'

Stephen (Iṣṭibānūs)[43] appear like him [Jesus] to the Jews when they intended to crucify Jesus. For the Apostle of God, his sacrifice was like the ram for Ismāʿīl. He was, in his community, like the ship of Noah and like the gate of Ḥiṭṭa[44] among the Israelites. Indeed, there were in ʿAlī and the Quraysh signs for the believers, just as 'there were in Joseph and his brothers signs for those who inquire' [Q 12: 7].

When the prophet of God, Moses, proposed to his people to fight the tyrants who were in Jerusalem, part of their answer was 'they said: "O Moses, there are in it a people who are powerful"' [Q 5: 22] and 'We will never ever enter it as long as they are in it; so go, you and your Lord, to fight; we will stay here' [Q 5: 24]. He said: 'O Lord, I control only myself and my brother' [Q 5: 25]. 'Two men of those who feared but on whom God showed favour said: "Charge in on them by the gate. When you enter it, you will certainly be victorious. Place your trust in God if you are believers"' [Q 5: 23]. In a way similar the Apostle of God 'on the day of the face off of the two sides'[45] did not control any except himself and his brother, the rest rushing upwards, none heeding his fellow. The Messenger appealed to them from the rear.[46] ʿAlī and Abū Dujāna[47] stood in the position of Joshua b. Nūn and Caleb b. Jephunneh,[48] the two men who feared and whom God

43 The Qurʾan declares outright that Jesus was not crucified but it was only made to appear so. However the identity of the substitute is not clear and there are various versions of who and how it happened. Simon of Cyrene is often mentioned, as are Sergius and Judas. Stephen is an extremely unexpected choice. See further, G. S. Reynolds, 'The Muslim Jesus: Dead or Alive?', *BSOAS*, 72 (2009), pp. 237–258, see pp. 240–243, for various accounts and explanations of this event in the writings of Muslim authors.

44 One of the northern gates of the Ḥaram al-Sharīf. However, Shiʿi tradition states that God commanded the children of Israel to enter the Holy land through the gate of Ḥiṭṭa so that thereby God would forgive their sins, and the *ahl al-bayt* are likened to the gate. Thus the gate is a metaphor for the *ahl al-bayt* and ʿAlī b. Abī Ṭālib. See, for example, al-Ṭabarānī, *al-Muʿjam al-ṣaghīr*, ed. Muḥammad Shakūr Maḥmūd al-Ḥājj Amrīr (Beirut, 1405/1984), vol. 2, p. 82.

45 Q 3: 155.

46 Compare with Q 3: 153.

47 Abū Dujāna (d. 11/632) was a well-known Companion, an expert swordsman and one of Muhammad's most skilled fighters.

48 The Arabic here reads Kawkab b. Yaqnī, which is most likely a corruption or distortion of Kalib b. Yifunna (i.e. Caleb b. Jephunneh).

favoured, so they put their trust in God and fought in front of the Apostle of God until God gave the victory to His prophet. The near angels marvelled at the consolation of ʿAlī for the prophet. So Gabriel said: 'Truly the angels marvel at the consolation of ʿAlī for you.' He replied, 'What would prevent him doing that, he being of me and I am of him?' Gabriel said: 'And I am of you both',[49] as long as some of the customs of the ancients last in the life of the Apostle of God, in exactly the same way.

When the Apostle of God departed this world, the majority of his community turned on their heels, just as the past communities had done after [the death of] their prophets. As Ibn ʿAbbās said, 'God has not sent a prophet and then taken him away but that after him occurred a conflict from which hell was filled.' God said: 'Muhammad is nothing but a messenger before whom there were other messengers; so if he dies or is killed, will you turn on your heels? He who turns on his heels harms God not at all. God will reward those who show gratitude' [Q 3: 144]. So they turned on their heels and abandoned the brother of their prophet, and their minister, and the appointee of the Apostle of God and his executor among his people, and his successor over his community, just as the Israelites had done with Aaron after Moses absented himself from them and the calf was adopted [as an idol] by the Israelites for ten days. God made commitments to Moses for thirty nights and completed them 'with ten, so the term of his Lord ended up as forty nights' [Q 7: 142]. The Sāmirī[50] led them astray and bewitched them and ordered them to worship the calf after the thirty nights. He said: 'This is your god and the god of Moses' [Q 20: 88]. 'So Moses returned to his people angry and sorrowful,' and said: 'Did not your Lord make you a better promise; did the covenant take too long

[49] The prophet's saying: 'He being of me and I am of him' and Gabriel's saying: 'And I am of you both' are reported by al-Qāḍī al-Nuʿmān, *Sharḥ al-akhbār*, vol. 1, pp. 93–96, p. 94.

[50] The Sāmirī, according to the Qurʾan, was the person who created the Golden Calf and seduced the Israelites away from the true faith and into worshipping it instead, in part by making the calf give forth a lowing sound.

for you? Or did you wish to have the anger of your Lord fall on you?' [Q 20: 86]. So he put them right and their penance was to be killed. God said to them: 'Turn to your Creator in repentance; kill yourselves; that is better with your Creator' [Q 2: 54]. He sat down the worshippers of the calf wrapped in their cloaks in front of Aaron and his partisans. Whichever of them raised a glance or opened their cloaks, for them he did not accept repentance. Aaron and his followers put them to the sword until he ordered them to stop. Our prophet was taken by death and did not absent himself as did Moses. So the worshippers of the calf in our community persisted in their error repeatedly, without their repenting, without remembering the unbelief that had infused in their hearts up to the day of God's vice-regent, the Mahdī. The day of the calf of our community, on account of the nobility of the prophet, is extended up to the advent of the Mahdī, on whom be peace, without killing. When the deputy of the Mahdī comes out, the gates to repentance shall be shut against the worshippers of the calf of our community, just as they will be shut against all who did not believe before the sun rising in the west. God has said: 'The day when some signs of your Lord shall come, their faith will benefit none who did not believe before or acquired in their faith good deeds' [Q 6: 158], and that is the rising of the sun from the west. For the worshippers of the calf, there is no Day except for him who puts trust in the calf and obeys the Sāmirī. He who obeys the brother of their prophet and his successor, they deem him weak, as did the Israelites with Aaron and his partisans. 'They said: "Kill the sons of those with him who believe and spare their women"' [Q 40: 25] in conformity to the custom of the Israelites and in imitation of them.[51]

When Noah knew that his community would be drowned in the water, he got himself a ship before the deluge and called upon the

[51] Killing or slaughtering the sons of those who believe and sparing their women here and later refers to the outcome of the Battle of Karbalā' in which al-Ḥusayn and the adult males of his family were killed and the women taken captive but later spared.

people to ride aboard it. They mocked him and scoffed at him. Only a small few boarded it with him. Others supposed that something other than this ship would keep them safe from the water. So they stayed away and were drowned, thus being sent to hellfire. Our prophet, when he knew that his community would be subsumed by seditions, as had the people of Noah, he warned his community against seditions, saying, 'Truly I foresee seditions falling upon your houses like rain.' Then he pointed out to them the ship of salvation, saying, 'Indeed the people of my household are like the ship of Noah; whoever rides aboard it is saved, whoever stays behind drowns.'[52] This is to say: whoever follows their path and adopts their *sunna* will not drown in the seditions, as did the people of Noah in the water who then entered the fire with the damned. God said: 'Then we drowned the rest' [Q 26: 120] 'they were drowned and so entered the hellfire' [Q 71: 25]. They supposed that their path would be like the path of the rest of them. Of his community, only a few followed their path, just as of the people only a few rode with Noah aboard his ship. Of his people there rode with Noah only his three sons Sām, Ḥām and Yāfath. So whoever pursued the way of ʿAlī was saved. Among the companions of the Apostle of God, Salmān, Abū Dharr and al-Miqdād[53] did not oppose him (ʿAlī), in accordance with the custom of those before them and in imitation of them.

Moses selected, from among his people, seventy men for the meeting of his Lord on the day of Mount Sinai. So they heard the words of their Lord and witnessed marvels. But, when they returned to the Israelites, they distorted 'the words out of their context'

[52] A well-known *ḥadīth* states: 'The likeness of the People of my house is similar to that of Noah's ark. Whoever embarks with it will certainly be rescued, but the one who opposes boarding it will certainly be drowned.'

[53] The three persons mentioned here are Salmān al-Fārisī, Abū Dharr al-Ghifārī and Miqdād Aswād al-Kindī. All three, along with ʿAmmār b. Yāsir, were the Companions who, according to the Shiʿa, remained most loyal to ʿAlī.

[Q 5: 41] and 'forgot some of what they were warned about' [Q 5: 13]. The Apostle of God selected from among his people companions but they distorted the words afterwards out of their context and also distorted the book of their Lord, in accord with the custom of the Israelites and in imitation of them.

God has said: 'Has a report come to you concerning the disputants who climbed over the wall to the sanctuary where they entered upon David and he was frightened by them? They said, "Do not be afraid. We are two disputants. One of us has assaulted the other. So judge between us fairly; do not be unjust and guide us to the true path. Truly this one who is my brother possesses ninety-nine ewes and I have one only. So he says, 'Have me take charge of it', and he bested me in the argument." He (David) said, "Surely he has wronged you in asking for your ewe to add to his ewes. Truly having many in a mix harms some of them with the others with the exception of those who believe and do righteous things – but they are few." David supposed that We were only trying him, so he begged his Lord for forgiveness falling down bowing and repenting' [Q 38: 21–24]. In a similar way ʿAlī and al-ʿAbbās brought a case for judgment to Abū Bakr concerning the estate of the prophet. Al-ʿAbbās said, 'On what basis do you adjudge that the estate of the prophet belongs to ʿAlī, seeing as I am the uncle of the prophet and he is the son of his uncle?' Abū Bakr replied, 'On the expert you attacked, do you remember, O ʿAbbās, the day we were with the kin of Abū Ṭālib forty men, and there was no one with you but me? The Apostle of God then said that there has not been a prophet before who did not leave an executor [*walī*] and successor [*khilāfa*], "So who among you shall be my executor, my successor and heir to my affairs, will settle my debts, fulfil my promise and acquit my responsibility?"' He said, 'You remained silent and no one answered him. Then you, O ʿAbbās, said, "Who would be capable of that when you are more generous than the wind?" Then he rose for the third time and said, "O assembled tribe of Hāshim, be the leaders in Islam;

do not be the followers. It shall be among you, otherwise it will be among others than you." So the most slender in shanks of you stood up and the greatest in belly, and this is he.' And he pointed to ʿAlī. 'So ʿAlī stood up and said, "I will be your executor, your deputy, the heir of your affairs. I will settle your debts, fulfil your promises, and acquit your responsibilities." Don't you know this about him, O ʿAbbās, from the Apostle of God?' He answered, 'Yes, O Abū Bakr.' He said, 'For what reason then are you contending with him while you know this declaration for him by the Apostle of God?' Al-ʿAbbās said to him, 'And you, O Abū Bakr, why do you claim to rule him in regard to his rights while you know about this from the Apostle of God?' So Abū Bakr said, 'Get the two of them away from me. Truly this is a ruse of the Banū Hāshim.' The two of them were seeking a ruling in the same way as the one we have just mentioned sought a ruling (from David). Neither of the two owners was transgressing, but they both asked for his judgment. So he knew that he was being tempted, but he repented and turned away. God said, and to Him belongs thanks: 'So We forgave him that; he has with Us a high rank and a fine place of return' [Q 38: 25]. Similarly neither of these two was the offender, meaning ʿAlī and al-ʿAbbās, even though both of them sought his judgment. And if he had repented, he would have found God most forgiving and merciful, exactly alike.

God has said: 'Have you not seen those who were given a portion of the Book believing in the demon and the evil one and they say to those who do not believe, "These are better guided than those who have faith in the way, they are those whom God cursed"' [Q 4: 51–52]. Similarly, the party hostile to the family of Muhammad said to their followers, 'The unbelievers, the Jews and the Christians, are better guided on the way', in exactly the same manner.

Indeed, the Jews and the Christians have taken their rabbis and monks as lords apart from God when they allowed them what is forbidden and forbade them from what is permitted, and they obeyed them in that. In the same way our community has taken their jurists and scholars as lords apart from God. Whenever they were reminded of their contravention of the Book and the *sunna*, they said, 'So and so is knowledgeable of the Book of God and the *ḥadīth* of God's Apostle.' And so, they came to know things that differ with the *sunna* and the Book. Those whom they took as lords aside from God tell lies about God, as did those who came before them when they permitted and forbade what God had not allowed, as a lie against God, in accord with the *sunna* of the Israelites and in imitation of them.

Truly the Jews and the Christians, when the time lasted long for them and their hearts hardened, they cast the Book of God behind their backs, that is, they no longer performed the commandments and prohibitions contained in it, nor did they uphold the divine penalties and rules. It was as Ḥudhayfa b. al-Yamān[54] said, 'Surely the Book is before them and the work is behind their backs.' So God reprimanded them for it. God said: 'They cast the book of God behind their backs as though they did not know of it' [Q 2: 101]. So when the time grew long on our community and their hearts hardened, they neglected the divine penalties and rules and what the Qur᾽an contains of things permitted and forbidden and they cast it behind their backs as though they did not know of it, in accord with the *sunna* of the Israelites and in imitation of them.

When the Jews and the Christians neglected what is in the Torah and the Gospels as a command and prohibition and as lawful and illegal, they strengthened the letters and decorated the Torah and the Gospels with gold and silver and they wrapped it in brocade. Then they recited night and day in their synagogues and churches without acting

[54] In the *ḥadīth* it is related that this was one of the Companions, and one of the *ahl al-ṣuffa*, a group of Companions who, due to poverty, lived in the portico of the prophet's mosque in Medina; the prophet made him the blood brother of ʿAmmār b. Yāsir, a Companion loyal to ʿAlī, and he died in 36/656. See, R. Tottoli, 'Ahl al-ṣuffa', *EI*3.

on what was in it. God reprimanded them for that in His statement: 'The likeness of those who were made to bear the Torah but then did not bear it is like the donkey who carries a load of books; how wretched is the likeness of the people who deny as false the signs of God' [Q 62: 5]. And God said: 'O People of the Book you have nothing to stand on until you uphold the Torah and the Gospel' [Q 5: 68]. God also said: 'If only they had upheld the Torah and the Gospel' [Q 5: 66]. Surely you do not know the meaning of the Book and the explanation that We explained to you. Thus they attributed truth to them in that and did not heed the words of him who possesses knowledge of the Book. Then, the scholars of our community followed their example and they falsified the Book and the *sunna*. They explained its verses according to their own opinions and according to their personal whims. They claimed that whatever the community requires their exegetes have already explained that for them. And so they went astray. The explanation of the Book rests solely on its partner who does not depart from it, to the truth stemming from the offspring of the chosen one, those in whose houses the wisdom and Book were revealed, and among whom was the continuous descent of the angels and by their tongue was the Book revealed. But the community denied what the lesser weight expressed about the greater weight.[55] Thus there is no explanation of the Book with them other than what their exegetes provided for them, and they are those whom they have taken as lords apart from God, just as there is no explanation with the Jews other than the explanation provided for them by their rabbis and monks whom they took as lords apart from God, in accord with the *sunna* of the Israelites and in imitation of them.

[55] A well-known *ḥadīth* states: 'I am leaving among you two weighty things: the one being the Book of God in which there is right guidance and light, so hold fast to the Book of God and adhere to it. He exhorted (us) (to hold fast) to the Book of God and then said: The second are the members of my household I remind you (of your duties) to the members of my family.' Thus the 'greater weight' or 'that which carries greater weight' (*al-thiqal al-akbar*) is the Qur'an and the 'lesser weight' or 'that which carries lesser weight' (*al-thiqal al-aṣghar*) is 'Alī and descendants.

When the Jews neglected the times of prayer and followed their own desires, they said, 'We long to see our prophets.' So they set up pictures of their prophets in their places of prayer and synagogues. Thus they decorated the places of prayer and synagogues and neglected the times of prayer. God said: 'They neglected the prayer and followed desires; so they will meet with error' [Q 19: 59]. And error is a valley in hellfire whose bottom is far and its air putrid. They asked the Apostle of God to let them embellish the mosque. He answered, 'The hypocrites will marvel when you decorate your Qurʾan copies and embellish your mosques. So the destruction will be on you, and it will be said: your mosques are crowded and yet they are ruins of mud brick. So they will gather together in mosques but among them there will be no believer.' So when they demolished the mud brick and built it with clay and embellishment, they set up in it *miḥrāb*s like the altars of the Christians, in imitation of them and in accord with their custom.

God has said: 'And then after them others than they inherited the Book; they take up the passing things of this lower world and claim that it will be forgiven us and yet if passing things like them come to them they take it. Was not the covenant of the Book taken from them not to say about God anything but the truth?' [Q 7: 169]. In the same way those who imitated them of our community said, 'It will be forgiven us' after having taken to the passing things of this lower world. And they said, 'The Apostle of God, "If only you would not sin. God reviled peoples who sin and then forgives them."' And God says: 'I have not created the jinn and men but that they worship Me' [Q 51: 56]. But they say, 'He created them to disobey Him.' Has the covenant of the Book not been taken from them not to say about God anything but the truth? And when God raised Mount Sinai over the Israelites, He raised it in the air above their heads because of their disobeying their prophet Moses. God thus frightened them and instilled them with dread. Moses informed them that if they did not offer the oath and covenant in obedience to him, the mountain would fall on them. So they feared that if they disobeyed it would fall on them and thus crush them. Then Moses began to take from them the pact and oath of allegiance. Every time he imposed on them a condition of obedience, they nodded their heads in affirmation due to their being afraid and frightened. That indicated to him that they would hearken and be obedient. The Jews assert that, when they moved their heads that day out of fear and dread of the mountain, they made the movement a second commemoration during the recitation of the Torah as a legal obligation of the law upon them. And that, they claim, was because he was reciting the Torah to them and what God required of them in it; with each commitment God imposed on them or obligation He required of them in the Torah, there were oaths of allegiance and obedience. They were responding in haste, nodding their heads out of fear in their hearts of the mountain, scared and frightened. They say that the movement of their heads that day in anxious haste to obey Moses was an affirmation. They were required to nod their heads during recitation. So whenever they affirm it is in order that they remember and not forget that day, that frightful sign from which they were saved. Thus they worship God each day as a commitment of their souls and [then] break it on the spot by their violation of the Torah. God said: 'When they dishonoured their pledge, We cursed them and We hardened their hearts; they changed the words from out of their place' [Q 5: 13]. Thus they know the proof God has against themselves when, on every day since, they insist that they are hearing and obeying the commitment to Him in remembrance and not forgetting, but yet heedless of the truth. In the same way the Apostle of God took the covenant of his Companions and imposed on them what he imposed on the women, which was to never associate God with anything, not to steal or commit adultery, not to put forward slander which they forge before them, nor to disobey Him in what is proper. Thus each night they renew their oath to God on themselves and break it by day. And God said: 'O you who believe, why do you profess what you do not act upon; professing what you do not act upon is odious to God' [Q 61: 2–3]. So they pledge allegiance to God in their nightly voluntary (*witr*) prayers,[56] saying, 'We put off and leave behind those who sin against You, O God,' and yet they break it in the day when they sin themselves and obey offenders, as did the Jews secretly in exactly the same manner.

God has said: 'Cursed were those who disbelieved among the Israelites on the tongue of David and Jesus, son of Mary. That was because they rebelled and transgressed; they used not to rebuke one another for the reprehensible things they did. How vile was what they did; you see many among them taking as friends those who disbelieve; how evil is what they have put forth for themselves so that God is angry with them and they are eternally in punishment' [Q 5: 78–80]. Similarly, you see many in this community taking as lords those who disbelieve in the rule of the Book and the *sunna*. And they call them vicegerents of God in His land with authority over His servants after having heard God forbid them from association with those who contravene God and His Messenger, even if they were their fathers or their sons or their brothers or their kin. So God associated them with those with whom they associated and He fills hell with them. How evil is the outcome. They followed the path of the offenders of the tribe of Israel and became cursed as they were cursed, in exactly the same manner.

The Jews and Christians took their feast days as a game and amusement. God said: 'O Muhammad, "leave alone those who take their religion," that is their feasts, "as a game and amusement; this earthly life has seduced them" [Q 6: 70].' Thus, our community takes their feasts as a game and amusement, so that the day of their feast is a day of adornment. On the day of their feast, the kings and the rich

[56] The *witr* prayer can be offered at night after the regular night-time prayer (*'ishā'*) but before the dawn prayer (*fajr*).

ride in procession wearing fabrics for display. The dissolute among them drink wine and sing. They adorn their slave girls and womenfolk. Their youths play polo and their boys play by the pool (*ḥawz*) and at dice and go out merrily and heedlessly until they return. The Apostle of God used to go out, he and his Companions, on the day of the feast apprehensively, fearfully, humbly imploring God with submissive hearts and humble bodies, weeping eyes, not knowing whether what they did was accepted or not. Our community has abandoned that *sunna* on the feast days. They thus resemble the Jews and Christians in accord with their *sunna* and following their example.

The Apostle of God said, 'Cursed be the Jews who took the graves of their prophets as places for kneeing [in prayer].'[57] But our community has taken the grave of our prophet as a mosque in accord with the *sunna* of the Israelites and following their example.

God has spoken of: 'Those who were driven from their homes without right, except that they say: "Our Lord is God"' [Q 22: 40]. In the same way our community drove from their homes without right him who was truer in devotion than he whose origin was the green lands and whom the dusty sands bore, loathing him for his resolve to speak the bitter truth. This is yet another example.

God has said: 'And of cattle and sheep We forbad them from their fat except for that on their backs or the entrails or mingled with bones' [Q 6: 146]. So, they pounded it and melted it and sold it and consumed its cost and said, 'The only thing forbidden us is its solid state.' In the same way wine was forbidden to this community. The Apostle of God said, 'Wine is what befuddles the mind and what intoxicates; both a little and a lot of it is forbidden.'[58] Watered wine is forbidden. But then

[57] See Bukhārī, *Ṣaḥīḥ* (#1330): '`Ā'isha said, "The Prophet in his fatal illness said, 'God cursed the Jews and the Christians because they took the graves of their Prophets as places for praying.'"' See also Muslim #529.

[58] For several versions of a similar *ḥadīth* quoted from the Imams, see al-Qāḍī al-Nu`mān, *Da`ā'im al-Islām*, tr. Asaf A. A. Fyzee, completely revised by Ismail K. Poonawala as *The Pillars of Islam* (New Delhi, 2002–2004), vol. 2, pp. 112–115.

the Murjiʾa produced a drink that intoxicates. They claimed, 'This is allowed and is not wine' and they called it *nabīdh*. They said, 'If it becomes vinegar, the name of wine no longer applies to it.' The Apostle of God said, 'People from my community will drink wine and call it by another name.'[59] So they permitted wine in cooking and cooked it, just as the Jews rendered fat and removed thus the name of fat and called it instead oil. So these people cook the wine and called it *nabīdh*. Then they said, 'Only wine is forbidden us and wine is what has not been cooked', just as the Jews said, 'Only the solid flesh is forbidden to us', all in accord with their *sunna* and in imitation of them.

The Christians regard as permitted carrion and the flesh of swine and they cite for that that it is so in the Psalms. In the same way the Murjiʾa[60] regard as permitted eating predators and foxes.

. . .

. . . ['and God took the covenant of the Israelites] and raised twelve among them as chieftains' [Q 5: 17] and God the Exalted said: 'Surely I am with you truly if you perform prayers, pay the alms tax and believe in My messengers and support them and lend to God a good loan. I will absolve you of your evil actions and I will admit you to the gardens underneath which flow rivers. So whoever disbelieves after that has surely deviated from the proper way. Thus, for their breaking of their covenant, We have cursed them and hardened their hearts' [Q 5: 12–13]. In the same way, God took the covenant of our community and the Apostle of God took it on the day they pledged allegiance to him, that surely they would protect his children as they would protect their own children. And so when they broke their

59 The prophet said: 'Verily and undoubtedly, there will appear people among my followers who will drink wine (*khamr*) and call it by another name' (al-Nasāʾī, *Sunan*, 'Ashriba', 41; Ibn Majāh, '*al-fitan*', 22, #4020).

60 The Murjiʾa are here and later in this text those who allowed the postponing of the recognition of ʿAlī as Muhammad's immediate successor, which means, in effect, all non-Shiʿa.

covenant, God cursed them and hardened their hearts. They kept al-Ḥusayn and his household away from the Euphrates and they swore, 'You will surely taste death before you taste the water, O Ḥusayn.' They claimed that they would not acknowledge a close relationship between him and the Apostle of God and they would kill him as he was dying of thirst. God said: 'And some among them had heard the word of God but then perverted it even after they understood it and were fully aware' [Q 2: 75]. In the same way the opponents of ʿAlī said, 'Al-Ḥasan and al-Ḥusayn are not two sons of the Apostle of God' and they interpreted the statement of God: 'Muhammad is not the father of any of your men but is rather the Apostle of God and the seal of the prophets' [Q 33: 40]. He, the Exalted, had him marry Zaynab in order that there be no restriction on the believers in regard to wives of their adopted sons, and after that He forbade the believers to say, 'Zayd is the son of Muhammad.' So He said: 'Call them after their fathers; that is the more just with God; so if you do not know their fathers, they are your brethren in religion and they are clients of yours' [Q 33: 5]. So they denied both his sons, al-Ḥasan and al-Ḥusayn, and they did not believe God and His Messenger when He called them the two sons of the Apostle of God on more than one occasion: Say O Muhammad: 'Come, let us call our sons and your sons, our women and your women, ourselves and yourselves, and pray asking for the curse of God on those who lie' [Q 3: 61]. God would not have ordered him to call his sons if he had had no sons. His sons at that time were al-Ḥasan and al-Ḥusayn. He had no other son than these two. The Apostle of God called them his two sons on more than one occasion.

In the same way they spoke about the verse of purification. They said that it was revealed solely in regard to the wives of the prophet. But they forgot what God mentioned about His prophet Moses: 'Appoint for me a minister from among my family Aaron my brother, thus strengthening me through him' [Q 20: 29–31]. And when God revealed to His prophet: 'Command for your people prayers' [Q 20: 132], he used to come for six months to the door of ʿAlī and Fāṭima and call out to them,[61] '[Time for] prayer, O People of the House, "God wants to remove impurity from you, O People of the House, and to cleanse you by purification" [Q 33: 33].' If this address were to women, He would have mentioned them in the feminine form as when He mentioned them: 'Stay at home, and do not decorate yourselves ostentatiously, as in the early days of pagan ignorance, perform prayers and pay the alms tax' [Q 33: 33]. But when He reached the subject of purification, He used the masculine form for them and stopped using the feminine. So He said instead: 'God only wants to remove impurity from you (masc.), O people of this house and to cleanse you by purification' and did not say: 'to cleanse you (*yuṭahhirukunna* with the feminine object pronoun) by purification.' The feminine form was not used in the testimony of the Apostle of God about them when he said, 'This verse was revealed in regard to five individuals: me, ʿAlī, Fāṭima, al-Ḥasan and al-Ḥusayn.' 'God only wants to remove from you impurity' (to the end of the verse).[62] Umm Salama[63] related from him that he gathered them in her house under a Khaybarī cloak. Then he said, 'These are my family and the people of my house. So remove from them impurity and cleanse them by purification.' So I said, 'Am I a member of your household?' He said to her, 'There is good for you but this is something special for them.' Similarly, ʿĀʾisha related and al-Nawwās b. Samʿān[64] related the same. He said, 'Then he wrapped around them a cloak while I was sitting nearby. He said, "'God wants

[61] Anas b. Mālik says about this verse that the prophet stopped at Fāṭima's house on the way to the mosque and proclaimed it for six months every day before morning prayers. Al-Maqrīzī, *Faḍāʾil ahl al-bayt*, ed. Muḥammad ʿĀshūr (Cairo, 1973), p. 21.

[62] '. . . O member of the family, and to make you pure and spotless.'

[63] Umm Salama was second only to ʿĀʾisha among the female sources of *ḥadīth;* on her see R. Roded, 'Umm Salama Hind', *EI2*.

[64] Al-Nawwās b. Samʿān al-Kilābī was a Companion who related a number of *ḥadīth*. See ʿAbd al-Barr, *al-Istīʿāb*, vol. 4, p. 1534.

only to remove from you impurity . . . and to cleanse you by purification' [Q 33: 33]. O God, these are most truly the people of my house." So I said, "Am I not a member of your household?" He replied, "You are a member of my people."'[65] Al-Nawwās said, 'Truly she is the one who hopes what I hope.' So they took it out of its proper context and said, 'It was revealed in regard to the wives of the prophet.' They perverted it after having known it and fully understood, exactly as the Jews had done.

God said: 'Woe to those who write the Book with their own hands and then claim that this is from God'[66] [Q 2: 79]. In the same way some of the Companions said, 'We used to recite in the time of the Apostle of God, "If the son of Adam had two valleys of money, he would seek a third one, but the belly of the son of Adam will not be filled with anything but earth and God will forgive him who repents."'[67] 'Stone [even] the elderly man and woman as a punishment for committing adultery'[68] and the like of it. God said about the likes of them: '"But when they leave you" O Muhammad, "At night a group of them discuss things that are other than those you say and God records what they discuss"' [Q 4: 81], that is, He records what they intend, in exactly the same manner.

God has said: 'When We saved you from Pharaoh's people who were inflicting on you harsh punishment, they slaughtered your sons

[65] The two *ḥadīth*s, or version thereof, as related above from Umm Salama and ʿĀʾisha respectively, are both fairly well known even in Sunni sources.

[66] The verse continues 'in order to sell it for a profit.'

[67] From the *Ṣaḥīḥ* of Bukhārī, vol. 8, book 76, #445: narrated from Ibn ʿAbbās: 'I heard God's Apostle saying, "If the son of Adam had money equal to a valley, then he will wish for another similar to it, for nothing can satisfy the eye of Adam's son except dust. And God forgives him who repents to Him."' Ibn ʿAbbās said: 'I do not know whether this saying was quoted from the Qurʾan or not.' ʿAṭāʾ said, 'I heard Ibn al-Zubayr saying this narration while he was on the pulpit.' (*Ṣaḥīḥ Bukhārī*, #6437). From the same source (vol. 8, book 76, #446): as narrated by Sahl b. Saʿd: 'I heard Ibn al-Zubayr who was on the pulpit at Mecca, delivering a sermon saying, "O men! The Prophet used to say, 'If the son of Adam were given a valley full of gold, he would love to have a second one; and if he were given the second one, he would love to have a third, for nothing fills the belly of Adam's son except dust.'"' (*Ṣaḥīḥ Bukhārī*, #6438).

[68] This was a statement of the caliph ʿUmar.

and spared your women; in that there was a tremendous trial from your Lord' [Q 2: 49]. Next He said: 'Then We caused the people who were considered weak to inherit the east of the land and its west which We had blessed and thus the good word of your Lord was fulfilled for the Israelites because they had been patient, and We destroyed what Pharaoh and his people had been making and what they were erecting' [Q 7: 137]. The oppressors of Muhammad's family acted in the same way. They slaughtered their sons and spared their women. And He promised them that He would surely destroy their enemies, save them from their enemies and cause them to inherit the land, like the Israelites. He said: 'God has promised those of you who believe and do the righteous things that He will continually make you successors in the land as He had made those who came before them successors; and He will surely establish for them their religion He approved for them, and exchange in them previous fear for security. They will worship Me and not associate Me with anything' [Q 24: 55]. And He said: 'God's promise, God never fails in His promise' [Q 30: 6]; and He said: 'In the heavens is your provision and what you are promised' [Q 51: 22]. The Mahdī is the one of Muhammad's family who will rise, in exactly the same manner.

The Jews said: 'The fire will not touch us save for a few days' [Q 2: 80] on account of their evil deeds. God said: 'And the lies they invented have deceived them in their religion' [Q 3: 24]; in answer to them. God has said: 'Yes, whoever acquires evil and is encompassed by his transgression, they are the inhabitants of hellfire; in it they shall remain forever' [Q 2: 81]. In a similar way a group among our community have resembled the Jews in their saying, 'The fire will not touch us save for a few days, and none of us will remain forever in the fire.' They tell a lie about our prophet Muhammad in mentioning that he said, 'If this Qur'an were in a skin, fire would never touch it.' Thus, they claim that whoever recites the Qur'an, fire will never touch him, even though he commits a mortal sin. God has said, and He has no partner: 'Faces on that day will be contrite, labouring, worn out, roasting in the fire' [Q 88: 2–4], and He said: 'Those who consume the funds of orphans unjustly, will surely taste fire in their bellies and will certainly roast in a blaze' [Q 4: 10]. And He said: 'Whoever kills a believer intentionally his recompense will be hellfire, there to remain forever' [Q 4: 93]. Yet the Murjiʾa insist that none of the people of the *qibla* will remain in the fire and that the last person from this community to exit from it will be a man who has abided in the fire seventy thousand years and seventy thousand numbered years, as had said the Jews. God said: 'O Muhammad: "Say, have you taken thus a pledge from God, for God will never rescind His pledge; or do you impute to God what you have no knowledge of? Yes, whoever acquires evil and is encompassed by his transgression they are the inhabitants of hellfire; in it they shall remain forever"' [Q 2: 80–81]. And He, the Exalted, said: 'It is neither by your wishes nor the wishes of the people of the book, but whosoever does an evil act will be punished for it' [Q 4: 123], and God said: 'Only they who feel secure against the plan of God are the people certain of being ruined' [Q 7: 99]. They felt secure from God's plan and slandered the Apostle of God by attributing to him the saying: 'If this Qurʾan were in a skin fire would never touch it' and they claimed that no one could remain in the fire for seventy thousand years and seventy thousand years more. And that al-Ḥajjāj b. Yūsuf,[69] Abu'l-ʿĀdiya,[70] ʿUbayd Allāh b. Ziyād, ʿUmar b. Saʿd, Yazīd b. Muʿāwiya, Ibn Muljam,[71] and others like

69 He was the Umayyad governor of Iraq. On him see A. Dietrich, 'al-Ḥadjdjādj b. Yūsuf', *EI2*.

70 Abu'l-ʿĀdiya al-Fazārī was a Companion, who was later responsible along with Ibn Ḥawā al-Saksakī for killing ʿAmmār b. Yāsir at the Battle of Ṣiffīn. Together they, along with Muʿāwiya and his supporters, are the *fiʾa bāghiya* cited in a statement of the prophet that ʿAmmār would be killed by a *fiʾa bāghiya*. See note 71 below.

71 The five men mentioned here were all involved in crimes against ʿAlī, his son Ḥusayn and their descendants and supporters and thus are considered particularly evil by the Shiʿa. Ibn Muljam was the murderer of ʿAlī; Yazīd b. Muʿāwiya was the second Umayyad caliph and the one ruling at the time of Ḥusayn's death at Karbalāʾ; ʿUmar b. Saʿd was the commander of the Umayyad army that confronted Ḥusayn and his family at Karbalāʾ; ʿUbayd Allāh b. Ziyād was governor of Kufa on behalf of the Umayyads at the time; Abu'l-ʿĀdiya killed ʿAmmār, and al-Ḥajjāj was the governor of Iraq on behalf of the Umayyads.

them of the accursed, would one day emerge from hellfire and enter paradise with written on their faces 'these inhabitants of hell were freed by the Most Merciful'. The Apostle of God once said, 'The most wretched of the ancients was Qudār b. Sālif;[72] and 'Abd al-Raḥmān b. Muljam, your murderer, O ʿAlī, will be the most wretched offspring of Adam of the ancient and later generations.' Shall the most wretched creature exit from the fire and someone better than he will be left in it?

And God has said: 'As for those who are wretched, they will be in the fire moaning and sobbing, abiding in it as long as the heavens and earth exist unless your Lord wills otherwise' [Q 11: 106–107]. 'As for those who are happy, they will be in paradise, dwelling there forever as long as the heavens and earth exist' [Q 11: 108]. How could the name of happiness come to an end for them when they enter the fire but their destination is paradise; or, how could the name of wretchedness leave them when they will be in the fire that only a wretch in disgrace and unbelief enters? God is high above dishonouring His threat and promise. God has said: 'The day God will not put the Prophet to shame and those who believe with him' [Q 66: 8] and He said: 'Shame today and evil surely are for the unbelievers' [Q 16: 28], and He said: 'Our Lord, whoever You cast into the fire, You surely disgrace, and the transgressors will have no supporters' [Q 3: 192], and He said: 'Hell will surely surround the unbelievers on all sides' [Q 9: 49]. Thus, whomsoever hell surrounds, that person is an unbeliever, an unbeliever either by polytheism or by ingratitude. To whomsoever the name unbeliever applies is forbidden the felicity of paradise. [God] said, speaking about the inhabitants of hellfire who will ask the people of the Heights (Aʿrāf): 'Pour down some water on us or give us some of what God has provided you; they will reply God has forbidden these things to those who disbelieve' [Q 7: 50]. And to whomever neither aspect of this name applies at all, they 'will be far removed from it and

[72] Qudār b. Sālif was the person responsible for hobbling the camel of the prophet Ṣāliḥ, an incident related in the Qurʾan (Q 7: 73–77; 11: 61–65; and 26: 155–157).

will not hear its whisper and will live forever in what their souls desire' [Q 21: 101–102].

As for the meaning of the *ḥadīth* that has come down in regard to intercession and exiting from the fire and the succession of stations in the course of the reckoning and the fire that will take them on the bridge, among them there will be those the fire will take to his ankles, some to his knees, some to his groin, his navel, his neck. As for whom hell surrounds and his transgression surrounds him, he will dwell in the fire forever, eternally and endlessly, in the absence of death in it and without end to its torture. Similarly, not only will those admitted to paradise abide there forever with an absence of death and without end to their felicity, but 'they will be eternally in what their souls desire, and the greatest terror does not cause them grief; and the angels commune with them: "This is your day which was promised to you" [Q 21: 102–103] and they will say: "Peace be upon you; you are the good ones, so enter here to live forever" [Q 39: 73].' It is not like the doctrine of those whom the lies they forged misled them in the religion so much so that the community acts insolently towards their Lord with the words of the scholars of evil, in accord with the *sunna* of the Israelites and in imitation of them.

The Israelite worshippers, when the corruption in their community became obvious to them, separated themselves from them and adopted for worship hermitages at the heads of mountains. They ceased the jihad and enjoining the good and prohibiting the bad. God said: 'They invented a monasticism that We had not prescribed for them except if it was for seeking the pleasure of God but they did not observe it as it should have been' [Q 57: 27], that is, We did not impose it on them nor order that. In a similar way a monasticism was established by our community in which they ceased to enjoin the good and prohibit the bad as they have been described: 'A day will come to the people when some people will follow foolish youths who are not satisfied with enjoining (the good) or prohibiting bad except when they themselves are safe from harm. They will follow the mistakes of the scholars and the irregularities of their scholarship. They will eagerly engage in prayer and fasting and whatever will not hurt them (*yaklumuhim*) in regard to themselves or their property. If the prayer and fasting and the rest of what they did, harmed their monies and their bodies, they will abandon these just as they abandoned the most basic of obligations and the most noble: enjoining the good and prohibiting the bad.' At that the wrath of God against them will reach completeness and He will inflict on them His total punishment. So the pious will perish along with the profligate and the weak with the powerful. It was as Muʿādh b. Jabal related from the Apostle of God, he said, 'There will be peoples at the end of time who confine themselves in the mosques; they will invent doctrines not taken from the Book nor from the *sunna*. So beware of them.' In another *ḥadīth* related of the Apostle of God, he said, 'They will wear the skins of sheep but their hearts are like the hearts of wolves, their tongues sweeter than sugar, and it will overcome the community, torn apart by the innovations in their doctrines that have no basis in the Book or in the *sunna*.'[73] He (God) admonished His servants by the tongue of His prophet enough as to spare them the exhortations of Shaqīq, Ḥātim, Muʿādh, Ibn Karrām and the rest of the monks

[73] It is reported that Abu'l-ʿĀliya said: 'There will come upon the people a time when their hearts will be derelict of the Qurʾan; they will find neither sweetness nor pleasure by it. If they fall short of doing what they have been commanded to do, they will say: "God is most forgiving, merciful (He will forgive us)", and if they do what they have been forbidden from doing, they will say: "We will be forgiven, we have not committed any *shirk* with God." Their affairs will all be based on [false] hope, having no truth and sincerity with it. They will wear the skins of lambs over hearts of wolves. The best of them in his religion will be someone who compromises.' Aḥmad b. Ḥanbal, '*al-Zuhd*' #1741: 'Muʿādh b. Jabal – God be pleased with him – used to say: "Ahead of you are times of trials (*fitan*) in which there will be much wealth and in which the Qurʾan will be opened and taken (read) by believers and hypocrites, men and women, young and old and freemen and slaves. At that time it is likely that there will be people who will say, 'Why aren't the people following me when I have read the Qurʾan? They will not follow me until I invent something else.' So, beware of everything that is innovated (in religion), for those things that are innovated are misguidance."'

of the community.[74] But they were not satisfied with the exhortations of God and so they devised their own. God has said: 'There has come to them of recitations what should restrain them' [Q 54: 4]. Surely, for whosoever is not restrained by the restraint of God, what the monks, who have invented what God has not imposed on them, say will not suffice, in accord with the *sunna* of the Israelites and in imitation of them.

Then God tested the Israelites about the day of their Sabbath. God said: 'We said to them do not break the Sabbath and We took a solemn pledge from them' [Q 4: 154]. But, when the time grew long for them, a group of them violated the Sabbath. Thus they split into three factions: one faction preying on a faction that left their midst when they saw their enmity and were unable to change them away from it; a faction that could not be restrained; so He changed the two factions into monkeys, and the third He saved. God has said, and to Him belongs the ultimate example: 'We saved those who prohibited evil but inflicted on those who perpetrated wickedness a dreadful punishment' [Q 7: 165]. Then God tested our community through their obedience to their guardian [*walī*]. A faction of the community transgressed against them like the Jews did in the matter of the Sabbath. They were the unjust (*qāsiṭūn*); another faction separated themselves; they did not prohibit them from their transgressions. They were the first Muʿtazila but they would not kill the transgressor of the two [other] groups. God has said: 'If two groups of believers fight each other, promote accord between them; then, if one of them transgresses against the other, fight the transgressor until it reverts to the command of God' [Q 49: 9]. So they claimed that the matter was ambiguous for them and they did not know which one of them was the transgressor.

74 The four men named here as being 'among the monks of the community' are Shaqīq al-Balkhī, an early preacher of asceticism, and his student Ḥātim al-Aṣamm (d. 237/852), Muʿādh b. Jabal (d. 18/639) a Companion of the prophet who was sent by him to teach Islam in the Yemen, and Abū ʿAbd Allāh Muḥammad b. Karrām (d. 255/869), like the rest, a famous advocate of Sufi-like ascetic piety, but also the founder of the Karrāmiyya.

Yet they all have heard the Apostle of God say, 'Woe to ʿAmmār, the transgressor faction will kill him.'[75] And they have heard the Apostle of God say, 'Two immense factions will fight one another claiming the same thing: a renegade faction will depart from them both, fighting the most worthy of the two by right', besides what they heard from the Apostle of God who said, 'ʿAlī is in the right, and the right is with ʿAlī.' They will never part until they arrive at the Pool. For sure ʿAmmār was killed at the side of ʿAlī and the renegades strayed away from his army. They were those who had listened to his words. There are similar indications in what the most truthful had said to them. The unjust and the Muʿtazila were like those who broke the Sabbath, and God described the Muʿtazila as a faction of the hypocrites: 'They said: "If we had known of the fighting, we would have followed you"; they were nearer that day to unbelief than faith' [Q 3: 167]. They wavered between them, neither for these nor for those. They did not know what was right to follow and did not reject what was useless so that they would not follow it. They were in the position of whoever among the Israelites did not prohibit the reprehensible. Those who supported the guardian were in the position of whoever separated from the profligates of the Israelites because of their hostility. Two commands from God only are obligatory. God said to them: 'Do not break the Sabbath' [Q 4: 154] and He said to us: 'Obey the Messenger and those in command among you' [Q 4: 59]. Thus, the two factions did not obey God in regard to the guardian of their affairs, in accord with the *sunna* of the Israelites and in imitation of them.

75 As related in Ibn Hishām, the prophet's prediction of ʿAmmār being killed was a result of the latter's complaining that the builders of the mosque were killing him by overloading him with bricks. Umm Salama said that, at that, the prophet ran his fingers through ʿAmmār's hair and said: 'Alas, Ibn Sumayya! It is not they who will kill you but a wicked band of men.' 'A wicked band of men' is the *fiʾa al-bāghiya* mentioned here. Ibn Isḥāq, ed. Wüstenfeld, p. 337, tr. Guillaume, p. 229. Cited also by Ibn al-Haytham, see Wilferd Madelung and Paul E. Walker ed. and tr., *The Advent of the Fatimids: A Contemporary Shiʿi Witness* (London, 2000), pp. 71–72; several citations of versions of this *ḥadīth* are found in al-Qāḍī al-Nuʿmān, *Sharḥ al-akhbār* (Beirut, 1994), pp. 93–96.

God has said: 'Have you not seen notables of the Israelites after Moses how they said to a prophet of theirs: "Send us a king so that we fight in the way of God." He replied: "Is it possible that if fighting was decreed for you that you not fight?" They said: "Why would we not fight in the path of God when we have been driven from our homes and our families?" But when fighting was decreed for them, they turned away except for a few of them. But God knows full well the iniquitous' [Q 2: 246]. In a similar manner it was said to the Apostle of God on the day of the truce of al-Ḥudaybiyya,[76] 'Are we not in the right and they in the wrong?' He answered, 'Certainly.' They said, 'So why are we given infamy on account of our guardian and someone who does not judge between us and them?' They asked him to resume fighting and turn away from the truce. But, when fighting the iniquitous was decreed for them, 'they turned away except for a few of them. But God knows full well who are the iniquitous' [Q 2: 246]. And concerning the Israelites, God said: 'Behold Their prophet told them that God had sent to them Saul as king. They said: "How can he be king over us when we have more right to the kingship than he and he does not possess great wealth." He said: "God has chosen him over you and supplied him with vast knowledge and prowess, and God grants His dominion to whomsoever He wishes and God's knowledge is vast indeed"' [Q 2: 247]. 'And their prophet told them that, as a sign of his authority, there shall come to you the Ark in which is security from your Lord and relics left behind by the family of Moses' [Q 2: 248]. Just like that, some of his Companions said to the prophet, 'By God, we do not know what will happen to us. Will you not let us know about your successor among us so that our refuge will be in him?' So the prophet said, 'As for me, I know him, but I see his place and if I did that, you would separate from him, like the Israelites separated from Aaron . . .'

[76] A truce between Muhammad and the Meccan Quraysh, concluded in Dhu'l-Qaʿda of the year 6 (March 628), in which among other provisions he agreed not to enter the sanctuary that year but return a year later. For further details see M. Watt, 'al-Ḥudaybiya,' *EI2*.

. . . [And Moses said, as described by the Omnipotent and Glorious, to the Samaritan: 'Yours, in what remains of the life you have, is for you to say "Don't touch me", and for you it is a promise that will not fail' [Q 20: 97]. Likewise, the Samaritans of the community said, 'No fighting.' And the Apostle of God was asked on the day he mentioned that they were of the religious community of the Samaritans. They asked, 'O Apostle of God, do they say: "Do not touch me?" He said, 'No, but "no fighting"', in exactly the same way.

God said: 'Remember We took your covenant not to shed any of your blood and not to evict from their homes any of yourselves; then you confirmed it and so testified' to His words 'And God is not unmindful' [Q 2: 84–85].[77] In a similar manner, God took the covenant of this community through the tongue of His prophet on the day they pledged allegiance to him to protect the sons of the Apostle of God from what they protected their own sons. Then they deserted them and surrendered them to the bastard son of the bastard.[78] So he killed them and took them prisoner. So when Yazīd, may God curse him, sent them to Medina, he commanded its people not to allow them to enter Medina. God had obligated them, if brought to them as prisoners, to ransom them but their expulsion was forbidden. So God requited them with disgrace in the present life, the application of blame, the loss of their share of the *fay*ʾ (booty), the government over them of those who mete out evil punishment 'and on the day of judgment they will be consigned to the most grievous penalty' [Q 2: 85], in exactly the same manner.

77 The full verse 2: 85 says: 'After this it is you the same who fight among yourselves and banish a party of you from their homes, assisting against them in guilt and animosity; and if they come to you as captives, you ransom them; although it is not lawful for you to banish them. Thus is it only a part of the Book that you believe and reject the rest? But what is the reward for those among you who behave like this except disgrace in this life and on the Day of Judgment they will be consigned to the most grievous penalty, for God is not unmindful of what you do.'

78 The 'bastard son of the bastard' refers to ʿUbayd Allāh b. Ziyād who was the son of Ziyād b. Abīhi ('Ziyād the son of his father').

God commanded the Israelites to enter the gate submissively and to say, '*Ḥiṭṭa*';[79] they will be forgiven for their mistakes and we will increase the reward of those doing good deeds. But they entered the gate with their heads raised and saying, '*Ḥinṭa* (wheat)'. God said: 'But those who transgressed changed the words from what they had been told; so We sent down upon those who transgressed a plague from the heavens for their having acted unlawfully' [Q 2: 59]. The plague was a torment in which they drowned. God ordered our community to love their prophet. God said: 'Say, I ask nothing of you as reward except love of kin; whosoever does a good deed We increase him in it with a good' [Q 42: 23]. Then they repudiated his family after loving them; thus they diminished his reward and reduced his rank. They opposed his commands and treated him as a weakling 'those who transgressed changed the words from what they had been told; so We sent down upon those who transgressed a plague from the heavens for their having acted unlawfully'. Temptation spread so greatly that even the prudent became confused. God said: 'Let those who oppose his commands beware lest some trial fall upon them or they come to suffer a painful punishment' [Q 24: 63]. God has said: 'Relate to them the story of him to whom We sent Our signs but he passed them by; so Satan followed him and he became one of those astray. If We had so intended We should have raised him with them but he preferred the earth and followed his whims. His like is the dog who hangs out his tongue when attacked and hangs out his tongue even if you leave him alone' [Q 7: 175–176].[80] He did not benefit from the signs God provided him with:

[79] A word which the children of Israel were allegedly commanded to say to gain forgiveness for their sins. But they changed it to say, '*Ḥinṭatan shumqāyā*' meaning good wheat. See Lane under ḥ-ṭ-ṭ.

[80] It is in the nature of a dog to hang out its tongue, which it seems to do whatever the circumstances. Thus it is compared here to a person who persists in the wrong path, not being able to benefit from faith or comprehend what they are being called to. So this example is that of a dog which pants whether it was driven away or left alone. The person described here does not benefit from the advice or the call to faith, just as if the advice and call never occurred.

that God would cause his donkey that he tied to him to be swallowed by the earth. It was like that with al-Zubayr; God favoured him to recognize the right of him whose right He imposed upon him. So he fought on behalf of his pledge of allegiance. But then his son and Ṭalḥa ensnared him. So he turned away from it and Satan followed him. He became one of those astray and, if God had so intended, He would have raised him because of his friendship with the one whose friendship God has made obligatory. But he preferred the earth, and he sought selfishness and was not pleased with the paragon. 'His like is the dog who hangs out his tongue when attacked and hangs out his tongue if you leave him alone.' That which the Apostle of God had warned him of was mentioned to him, 'You surely will make war on him and you will be wronging him.' It was as if he forgot the words from his childhood. He did not support the one whose support God made obligatory.[81]

Ṣafrāʾ bint Shuʿayb rebelled against Yūshaʿ b. Nūn after Lāwī, peace be upon him. Seventy-thousand were killed between them.[82] God said

[81] Al-Zubayr b. al-ʿAwwām, a Companion, was with ʿAlī in Fāṭima's house when ʿUmar attacked it. He came out to fight the aggressors but lost his sword and was carried off. Only later was he an opponent of ʿAlī during the lead up to the Battle of the Camel, although he did not join in that fighting. Ṭalḥa b. ʿUbayd Allāh was also a Companion and he was commander of ʿĀʾisha's army at the Battle of the Camel.

[82] This event is cited in al-Majlisī's *Biḥār al-anwār* (13: 266–268, 445) in several slightly different versions. One (p. 445) says,

> After Moses, Joshua bin Nun was in charge of affairs, patiently waiting through agonies, hardships, strife and turmoil [to enter the holy lands] until three giants (*ṭawāghīt*) among them passed away and Joshua's position grew stronger. Two hypocrites among Moses's own people revolted against him along with Moses's wife, Ṣafrāʾ the daughter of Shuʿayb, with one hundred thousand men [of the Israelites] and they fought against Joshua bin Nun, but Joshua killed a great number of them and defeated the others by the grace of God. He captured Ṣafrāʾ the daughter of Shuʿayb and he said to her: 'I'll forgive you this for now waiting until we meet the Apostle of God Moses, and I will then complain to him about what I faced because of you.' Then Ṣafrāʾ said: 'Woe to me, and God, if paradise were permitted to me I would be ashamed that I would see in it the apostle of God having broken his covenant and fought against his viceroy after him.'

The source continues: 'About that God revealed, "Remain in your houses and do not make the display that was displayed in the previous time of ignorance" [Q 33: 33], referring here to Ṣafrāʾ bint Shuʿayb.'

Another, perhaps much earlier, source, in Ibn Bābawayh's *Kamāl al-dīn wa tamām al-niʿma* (pp. 26–27), says, in part, of a *ḥadīth* from the prophet:

to the Ḥumayrā'[83]: 'O wives of the Prophet, you are not like any other wives; if you fear God do not be submissive in speech such that the one in whose heart is disease should conceive a desire. Instead speak what is well known. Remain in your houses and do not make the display that was displayed in the previous time of ignorance' [Q 33: 32–33], meaning here Ṣafrā' bint Shu'ayb. The address [in this verse] is to the nine,[84] but the meaning concerns among them one only on account of God's prior knowledge about her that she would be the mistress of the dogs of Ḥaw'ab[85] and the instigator of fighting against the believers and the one who tore apart the veil of the Apostle of God. It is as He has said: 'Admonish your nearest kinsmen' [Q 26: 214]. The address was to forty men of the clan of 'Abd al-Muṭṭalib apart from the whole community that they shall have precedence in the religion of God before the others. The one among them meant was 'Alī b. Abī Ṭālib since God knew that no one other than him would respond to him on the day.

God has said: 'Indeed a sign of his kingship is that he will bring you the Ark in which is security from your Lord and the relics of the legacy of the family of Moses and Aaron, carrying it . . .'

> Yūshu' b. Nūn, the *waṣī* of Moses, lived for thirty years after Moses. Ṣafrā' bt Shu'ayb, the wife of Moses, rebelled against him, saying: 'I have more right to command than he.' So he fought her, killed her fighters and captured her, but he treated her captivity with favour. And to be sure the daughter of Abū Bakr will rebel against 'Alī with so and so thousands of my community. He will fight her, kill her fighters and capture her but he will treat her captivity with favour.

A closely similar report in the *Biḥār al-anwār* (13: 367–368) adds specifically, 'In regard to this God revealed Q 33: 32–33, "Remain in your houses and do not make the display that was displayed in the previous time of ignorance"', meaning here a reference to Ṣafrā' bt Shu'ayb.

83 Ḥumayrā', meaning little red-faced one, refers to 'Ā'isha.

84 Meaning the nine wives of the prophet.

85 According to Umm Salama, the prophet mentioned the revolt of one of his wives, that being 'Ā'isha, in the following words: 'It seems to me that the dogs will bark at you in Haw'ab when you are revolting unjustly against 'Alī.' Just prior to the Battle of the Camel, accordingly, the dogs of Haw'ab will bark at her as she approaches. A better source here is Ibn al-Haytham who reports this in the following words: 'The Apostle of God . . . said to 'Ā'isha, "You will fight with 'Alī, at which time you will be so wrong towards him that even the dogs of al-Ḥaw'ab will bark at you."' (*Advent of the Fatimids*, p. 71).

. . . And the Apostle of God said, 'The night I was made to travel to the heavens and saw men whose lips had been cut off by scissors of fire. So I said, "O Gabriel, who are these men?" He replied: "These are the preachers of your community who order justice but forgot themselves and they recite the Book, but they did not have knowledge."'[86] Surely when the Israelites disobeyed the Apostle of God, God was angry with them. They wandered about the land for forty years. Every time they moved on, the land around them became farther as a punishment for when they had said to their prophet: 'Go, you and your Lord, and fight while we sit here' [Q 5: 24]. And when our community disobeyed the legatee of the Apostle of God, God became angry with them, so that they wandered in the land for eighty years confused about the religion as their punishment for having contravened the order of their guardian. The time of the Umayyads was for this community like the wandering in the wilderness of the Israelites, exactly the same.

'And the Jews said: "The hand of God is tied up"; but their own hands are tied up and cursed are they for what they said' [Q 5: 64]. In the same way their brethren among the Murjiʾa say, 'Hell will be filled by the Most Merciful, Exalted and Blessed, when the fire will say, "Enough, enough,"' meaning enough is enough, God is indeed high above what they describe except for God's most sincere servants. Thus they described God just as the Jews had described Him, in exactly the same manner.

When the Jews and the Christians saw the error of the people of various religions and that the book was with their prophets, they became conceited about themselves saying: 'None shall enter paradise except for Jews and Christians' [Q 2: 111]. God said: 'These are their vain hopes; say; "Produce your proofs if you are truthful"' [Q 2: 111]. And yet, previously, some of them testified against others about being in error. 'The Jews said the Christians have nothing to stand on and

[86] Almost identical versions of this *ḥadīth* are related by Ibn Abī Dunyā, Ibn Ḥanbal, Ibn Ḥibban and others.

the Christians say the Jews have nothing to stand on' [Q 2: 113]. So when our community split apart, one faction began cursing the other. So God detached the Ḥarūriyya[87] through their deviation from religion; and the Muʿtazila for their withholding assistance; and the Jahmiyya[88] for their error; and the rest of the sectarians for their heretical tendencies and innovations. Two related factions remained. One of them claimed that it was communal and the other claimed that it was *sunnī*. The obscenity of the doctrine of the rest of the sects and their error was obvious to them and they became conceited about themselves, saying, 'None will enter paradise except the one who has chosen to fight al-Ḥusayn.' So al-Ḥusayn fought until he was killed and his head was sent to the Accursed son of the Accursed[89] and he put it into a basin of gold, in exactly the same manner.

The profligates of the Israelites in their time burned the best of the people of that era, who commanded them to be just and he summoned them to the Most Merciful. They ill-treated them for no reason except that they believed 'in God the highest in power and praise; he to whom belongs the dominion of the heavens and the earth' [Q 85: 7–8]. God said: 'The inhabitants of the pit were killed, fuel of fire supplied profusely when they were seated over it and they were witnesses to what they did to the believers and they took revenge on them solely because they believed in God who is highest in power and praise' [Q 85: 4–7]. Similarly, the profligates of the Umayyads burned the best of the people of their time. They took revenge on them solely because they believed in God, Highest in Power and Praise, and the offspring of their prophet in the community, and in upholding the Book and reviving the *sunna*, like Zayd b. ʿAlī, may the blessings of

87 Ḥarūriyya is an alternative name for the Khārijīs.

88 The Jahmiyya was a sect that claimed as its founder Jahm b. Ṣafwān, an early theologian who was killed by the Umayyad authorities in 128/746. They believed, among other things, that the Qurʾan was created. See, W. Montgomery Watt, 'Djahmiyya', *EI2*.

89 'Accursed son of the Accursed' is a Shiʿi way of referring to Yazīd son of Muʿāwiya who is damned by them for his involvement in the murder of al-Ḥusayn at Karbalāʾ.

God be upon both. They burned him in the fire,[90] roasting, like had been done to the believers among the inhabitants of the pit. Zayd b. ʿAlī said to them, 'Do not worship the pharaohs of the Umayyads', that is, do not obey them in their disobedience to the Creator. So their pharaohs became angry and said, 'Burn him and support your gods.' It was like the anger of the unbelievers among the people of Abraham because of their idols. They said, 'Burn him and support your gods', in exactly the same manner.

God said: 'Among the people of Moses there is a community that guides to the truth and acts with justice' [Q 7: 159]. They are towards the east beyond China at the sunrise. God said: 'We broke them up into communities, among them some are righteous' [Q 7: 168]. They are beyond the river Dahal(?) 'and some among them are much less so' [Q 7: 168], meaning the Jews you see here. So, like that, among the community of Muhammad, there is 'a community that guides to the truth and acts justly' [Q 7: 159]. They are towards the west, as the people of Moses were towards the east, in the territory of the descendant of Idrīs b. Idrīs;[91] the rule of the Book is manifest among them and apportioning is equitable, and justice for the subjects prevails; the opposite of what is right here among the Murjiʾa in the justice of their imams and their conduct, in exactly the same manner.

When Pharaoh knew that the birth of Moses son of ʿImrān would occur in his kingdom, that his kingdom would be made to disappear and his opinion be declared foolish and his religion would be destroyed by this man's hand, he slaughtered the sons of the Israelites

90 Zayd b. ʿAlī was a grandson of al-Ḥusayn who led a revolt against the Umayyads in 122/740. Though not immediately upon his death, Zayd's body was eventually burned by the Umayyads some four years later in 126/743–744. On Zayd himself, see W. Madelung, 'Zayd b. ʿAlī b. al-Ḥusayn', *EI2*. On his crucifixion in more detail see Sean Anthony, *Crucifixion and Death as Spectacle*, pp. 46–51.

91 The descendant of Idrīs b. Idrīs would be a later ruler of the Idrīsid dynasty in the Maghrib, centred at Fez, quite likely Yaḥyā b. al-Qāsim al-Miqdām (269–292/883–905), but possibly Yaḥyā b. Idrīs b. ʿUmar (r. from 292/905 until the Fatimid takeover).

and spared their women. He delegated agents over their pregnant women in order to ward off the decree of God. 'And the decree of God became manifest and they were loath' [Q 9: 40] to be humiliated. For surely, the tyrants of our community, when they learned that there would occur among them the birth of the righteous servant, the person who would take their kingdom away from them, belittle their opinions, and through whom and by whose hand God would revive the Book and the *sunna*, they killed the sons of the family of Muhammad and spared their women. They appointed agents over the women of the family of Muhammad, as Pharaoh had done in the days of the birth of Moses over the women of the Israelites, so that he [Pharaoh] said to kill the sons of those who believe with him and spare 'their women for we have over them dominant power' [Q 7: 127]. God will manifest His religion at the hands of His vicegerent, the Mahdī, may the blessings of God be upon him, while they will be loath. God has said: 'God promised those among you who believe and act righteously that He will surely make them vice-regents in the land as He had made vice-regents before them and that He will certainly establish for them their religion that He approves for them and that He will surely substitute security after they previously were in fear; they will be worshipping Me and not associating Me with any thing' [Q 24: 55]. And God has said: 'And that day the believers will rejoice in the succour of God who supports whoever He wills' [Q 30: 4–5]. And God the Exalted said: 'The promise of God and God does not fail in His promises' [Q 39: 20]. And He said: 'O you who believe, whoever among you turns back from his religion, God will bring forth a people He loves and who love Him, lowly with the believers but powerful against the unbelievers, who will strive in the path of God unafraid of the slander of the slanderers' [Q 5: 54]. The Pharaoh of Moses in his unbelief and tyranny duped his people by preaching religion. He said to his followers: 'I have you see only what I see and I guide you not but to the path of the right guidance' [Q 40: 29] and he said: 'I fear that he will change your religion or make corruption appear in the land' [Q 40: 26]. He made light of his people but they obeyed him. So he made war against Moses out of fear that he would change their religion which they approved for themselves. Likewise the pharaohs of our community caused fear over the manifestation of the family of Muhammad through the tongues of their friends: 'Truly we fear that the family of Muhammad will gain ascendency over you and so will change your religion which you manifest, since God made them forefathers and models for those who will come later.' So that community believed jihad against the family of Muhammad was an obligation out of fear that any change and deviation from what is sound would alter their religion, as happened with the customs of the family of Pharaoh, in accord with their *sunna* and in imitation of them.

Seventy men from the family of Pharaoh believed in Moses and Aaron and rejected Pharaoh. So Pharaoh called them the Rejecters (*rāfiḍa*).[92] God inspired Moses to record their names in the Torah as al-Rāfiḍa because of their rejection of evil and their following of the good. Then God honoured their brethren in the words of Muhammad in the Qur'an. So he said: 'Men who have been true to what they commit themselves to God. Of them some have redeemed their vow and some of them still wait' [Q 33: 23]. The vow was to be killed. They redeemed their vow [of being killed] on the basis of love for the family of Muhammad. And some are still alive, awaiting the reign of truth. They have not substituted for the family of Muhammad any substitution. The most evil people according to Pharaoh and his followers were the party of Moses and Aaron and, according to the Jews, they were the party of Jesus and Simon whom they labelled

[92] A term applied abusively to the early Imāmiyya. See E. Kohlberg, 'al-Rāfiḍa', *EI2*.

al-Rāfiḍa and Disciples.[93] They were only called Disciples on account of their white clothing. Similarly, the most evil of the community according to those who imitated them were the party of Muhammad whom they labelled Rejecters (Rāfiḍa) and Mubayyiḍa, as their associates were labelled in past communities and bygone generations. They are the disciples of the community who reject evil and follow the good and its people, just as the partisans among the people of Pharaoh had done [in following] Moses in the days of Moses, and the Disciples in the days of Jesus. They were the fewest of the few in number and only a few in the community took up their ways. Truly God censured the majority of the Israelites. He said to His prophet: 'O People of the Book, do you disapprove of us for other than that we believe in God and what has been revealed to us and what was revealed previously, and that most of you are iniquitous' [Q 5: 59] and He said: 'Among them is a community on the right course but many of them commit evil acts' [Q 5: 66]. And He said: 'And indeed before them most of the previous peoples went astray' [Q 37: 71]. And He said: 'Their messengers had come to them with explanations but, even after that, many of them committed atrocities' [Q 5: 32]. And He said: 'So their hearts were hardened and many of them were profligates' [Q 57: 16] and He said: 'You will see many among them who rush into sin and wickedness and devour unlawful gain, how evil are the things that they do' [Q 5: 62]. And He said: 'We did not find many of them who are faithful to a commitment but rather We found most of them to be profligates' [Q 7: 102] and He said:

93 The Arabic term for Disciples is *ḥawārī* from a root that can mean white or to be white, wear white, and thus the author here can claim that this term indicates that Jesus's Disciples were known as such because they wore white clothing. That then allows him to also equate them with the Mubayyiḍa (*abyaḍ, bayḍā'*, means 'white'). However white was the colour chosen by many of the supporters of the Family of the Prophet. Those actually called the Mubayyiḍa were the followers of the anti-ʿAbbasid rebel in Transoxania known as al-Muqannaʿ who wore white in opposition to the black of the ʿAbbasids, but were usually condemned by the Shiʿa as extremists. On the latter, see W. Madelung and P. E. Walker, *An Ismaili Heresiography, The 'Bāb al-Shayṭān', from Abū Tammām's Kitāb al-shajara* (Leiden, 1998), text, pp. 76–79, tr., pp. 74–77.

'Every time they made a commitment, a group of them pushed it aside but most of them do not believe' [Q 2: 100]. He did not praise but a few of them. He said: 'You will never cease to hear of treachery on their part except for a few of them' [Q 5: 13]. And He said: 'But God cursed them for their unbelief; they did not believe except for a few' [Q 4: 46]. And He, the Exalted, said: 'So those who believed but only a few believed with him' [Q 11: 40] and He said: 'Remember when We took a covenant of the Israelites not to worship . . .' [Q 2: 83]

. . . parts(?) so that his perpetration will transfer him to another form of the varieties of abomination in it or that the doctrine of the Jews makes him taste the evil of his affair. God has said: 'There is a ban on any town that We have destroyed that they will not return' [Q 21: 95] and He said: 'Twice You made us die and twice You made us live' [Q 40: 11]. Its explanation is in another verse: 'You were dead so He gave you life, then He will have you die then bring you back to life' [Q 2: 28]. The Commander of the Believers has said, 'We found that God arranged His creation in nine stages that He mentioned in His book when He said: "We have created mankind from an extract of clay, then We placed him as a drop of sperm in a firm and settled place, then We fashioned the drop into a clot, then We created out of the clot a tissue, then We created out of the tissue bones, then We clothed the bones in flesh, then We produced him as another creature. So blessed be God, the best of creators, then after that you will surely die and then on the day of resurrection you will be raised up" [Q 23: 12–16].' God did not mention a tenth period among these periods of the creation of man from an extract of clay to the day of raising which they claim is their being moved from the last form to the final form. However, God has said about whosoever seeks guidance in a book other than His: 'Whoever is blind to the remembrance of the Most Merciful, to him We assign him a satan as his companion' [Q 43: 36] to the end of this verse.[94] The Jews killed the prophets without right and they killed those of the people who ordered justice. So when God sealed prophecy with Muhammad, and there inevitably occurred in this community what occurred among the Israelites, the Jews of our community killed whoever's blood was equivalent to the blood of the prophets, who were God's proofs in their time, as had the prophets been in their time. They were the progeny of the Chosen One, the offspring of the prophets and descendants of the Pure Ones. God delayed [their punishment] as those taken as responsible for the blood of the progeny who were killed before them, from the time of al-Ḥusayn son of ʿAlī, up to our own day, like the Jews of the time of the prophet. God held them responsible for the blood of the prophets whose blood was shed in their era but before them alike with whoever wetted his sword with their blood, since they are the ones who affirm the views of their fathers. God said: '"Say", O Muhammad, "Why have you been killing God's prophets previously if you are in fact believers?"' [Q 2: 91]. So the Murjiʾa imitated the *sunna* of the Israelites in killing the sons of the prophets and those among the people who command the just and their affirmation of the obligation of allegiance to their killers as a duty imposed on them, in exactly the same manner.

The blood of the prophets has so abundantly been shed among the nations for God to take revenge for the blood of a prophet in the lower world such as... ['and they speak lies against God] and do so knowing it' [Q 3: 75]. In a similar way, some of those who claim the Imamate have regarded as lawful, they hold supporting of the tyrannical rulers to be rightful. They (the Kharijites) say, 'This abode is an abode of unbelief; our taking the monies of those who repudiate the rights of the Imam is not a guilt upon us.' 'And they speak lies against God and

[94] This is unclear since the verse in the Egyptian codex ends with the word 'companion' (*qarīn*) and there is no more of it. The codex used by Abū ʿAbd Allāh al-Shīʿī evidently had a different numbering of the *āyāt*.

do so knowing it' [Q 3: 75], in accord with the *sunna* of the Israelites and in imitation of them.

Among the Christians, the Jacobites[95] said that Jesus, son of Mary, is God. He appeared as long as he intended. So, when he was taken away, he was concealed and became hidden. God said about them: 'Those who say that God is the Masīḥ, the son of Mary, are unbelievers' [Q 5: 17]. A faction of the heretics[96] who embrace the Shiʿa say about ʿAlī a doctrine like that of the Jacobites among the Christians, in accord with the *sunna* of the Israelites and in imitation of them.

Among the Christians, the Melkites said that the lamp does not light without oil, a wick and fire, and the divine is three, two hidden and one apparent. God has said about them: 'Do not say He is three; refrain from this for your own good' [Q 4: 171] and 'Those who say that God is the third of three are unbelievers' [Q 5: 73]. Among the heretics who embrace the Shiʿa, the Bashīriyya[97] say that ʿAlī is God, because the Executors[98] are the flame and the flame in Hebrew is the female companion of the divinity and they insist, 'We do not worship a god we cannot see.' And they claim that God wanted to show His creatures His power so as to not have the servants apprehend Him other than in the heart. They say that ʿAlī dug the rivers, planted the trees and built the mountains. They seek to prove this by the Qurʾan.

95 The Jacobites were and are the Syrian Orthodox church of Syria, Iraq and India, recognizing the Syrian Orthodox patriarch of Antioch as its spiritual head. It was founded in the 6th century AD as a Monophysite church in Syria by Jacob Baradaeus. It is thus analogous in position to the Coptic Church, the Monophysite church of Egypt. However, although its Christological doctrine is essential to its identity, exactly how what is claimed in our text about them fits with that doctrine is not at all clear.

96 It is likely that our author is thinking here of the quite early Islamic sect of the Sabaʾiyya, followers of ʿAbd Allāh b. Sabaʾ, who are said to have held that ʿAlī did not die but rather was God and had ascended to heaven in occultation (*ghayba*).

97 The information given here on this early Shiʿi Wāqifī sect is mostly new; it does not appear in any of our other sources about them. On the Bashīriyya, who followed a certain Muḥammad b. Bashīr and held that Mūsā b. Jaʿfar was either the last Imam, now in occultation, or is the divinity (with Ibn Bashīr himself as a prophet) see, in general, Hamed Khani, 'Bashīriyya', *Encyclopaedia Islamica*, vol. 4, pp 489–492.

98 The Executors, *al-awṣiyāʾ* in Arabic.

They say: *naḥnu* ('we'), *innā* ('verily we'), *arsalnā* ('we sent'), *awḥaynā* ('we revealed') and if expressions like these were in the singular, it would be as you say. However, these are in the plural and are evidence proving what we maintain. So they were cursed for what these imitators of the Melkites among them said. The Commander of the Believers said, 'Two will perish on account of me: an excessive lover and a lying loather.' And he said, 'My likeness in this community is like that of Jesus among the Christians. Some people loved him excessively so they perished; and some people hated him such that they perished.' Thus, just as the Jacobites and Melkites among the Christians exceeded the proper bounds, these two were excessive in regard to ʿAlī.

The Jews said, 'We have seen the sorcerers and diviners doing the like of what Jesus did.' They claimed that Mary was a prostitute and that Jesus was not properly guided when he learned sorcery and divination. And thus he became a sorcerer. God has said about them: 'Their statements about Mary are monstrous calumnies as is their claim that we have killed Jesus the son of Mary the apostle of God, but they did not kill him nor did they crucify him but so it was made to appear to them' [Q 4: 156–157]. So the Jews denied him his rightful place and his own claim that he was a servant of God and His messenger and they denied his prophethood. The Jews of our community said, 'The prophet did not designate ʿAlī as commander, and he was not the closest to the believers after the Apostle of God.' They declared his being a brother of the Apostle of God a lie as was ʿAlī's being his minister and executor in his family and vicegerent in his community, just like the Jews denied the prophethood of Jesus, in accord with the *sunna* of the Israelites and in imitation of them.

The Jews assert that their faith in God and in Moses and the prophets before him absolves them from having faith in Muhammad, and that they recognize him as they recognize their own sons. But they rejected him out of envy on their part. The Jews of our community claim that their faith in Muhammad spares them from having to recognize the Imam of the God-fearing and leader of those with a radiant white spot on the forehead,[99] the Commander of the Believers and the brother of the lord of messengers, and obedience to him. They reject the guardian out of envy on their part and they say, 'this is that which ... he responded to the summons of the prophet,' and they called ʿUthmān the possessor of two lights.[100] Al-Ḥasan and al-Ḥusayn were the two lights of the Apostle of God. Their father was ʿAlī and their mother was Fāṭima, the daughter of the Apostle of God. And they called Khālid b. al-Walīd the sword of God which he unsheathed against the polytheists and the hypocrites. The sword of God never misses. But Khālid b. al-Walīd did to the tribe of Jadhīma what did not please God and His Apostle, so that the prophet of God went out dragging his cloak and said, 'O God, I absolve myself to You from what Khālid b. al-Walīd has done.' Then he dispatched ʿAlī to them and he rectified the matter. He returned their slain to them even including the rope of the dog. And there remained with him seven hundred or five hundred. He said, 'This is yours for the terror of the women and the children.'[101] So they esteemed the Apostle of God highly and ʿAlī was the sword of God that he unsheathed against the polytheists and hypocrites. He exterminated with it their battle heroes and their duellers. He was called Commander of the Believers only because the believers used to draw knowledge from him like from the deliverer of food. The Apostle of God said to him, 'O ʿAlī, the people of the heavens name you Commander of the Believers.' Umm Salama

[99] The Arabic *Qāʾid al-ghurr al-muḥajjalīn* as here is a standard way the Shiʿa have of referring to ʿAlī. At the resurrection the pious (Shiʿa) will have a radiant white light at the spot on their foreheads where they once touched the ground in prayer.

[100] 'Uthmān was called 'the possessor of two lights' (*Dhu'l-nūrayn*) because he married two of Muhammad's daughters, first Ruqayya and, when she died, Umm Kulthūm. He thus was said to possess two lights.

[101] On Khālid, who was an important early commander of Muslim armies see, in general, P. Crone, 'Khālid b. al-Walīd', *EI2*. In the incident cited here, Khālid had been sent by the prophet to the Banū Jadhīma as a missionary not to fight, but when they surrendered to him, he ordered a number of them to be killed. The prophet was mortified and sent ʿAlī to make amends. A fuller version of this event can be found in Ibn Isḥāq, *Sīra*, ed. Wüstenfeld, pp. 833–836, tr. Guillaume, pp. 561–562.

said, 'The Apostle of God said to me, "When the Commander of the Believers ascends my pulpit and then descends, he will ask you for this book. So hand it to him."' She continued, 'When Abū Bakr ascended, I waited for him to ask me for it, but he did not do it. Then ʿUmar ascended and I waited for him to ask me for it, but he did not do it. Next ʿUthmān ascended, so I waited for him to ask me for it, but he did not do it. Then ʿAlī ascended and descended. He said, "O Umm Salama, where is the book that the Apostle of God handed over to you?"' She continued, 'So I gave it to him. For he is the Commander of the Believers in truth.' It was asked, 'O Commander of the Believers, what was in the book?' He said, 'The knowledge needed by the community until the day of resurrection.' Abū Dharr[102] was told, 'Would you appoint as executor of your will the Commander of the Believers?' meaning ʿUthmān b. ʿAffān. He replied, 'I have named as executor of my will the true Commander of the Believers' meaning ʿAlī. So they competed with him for these names.

God has made the blood of Jesus the greatest bloodshed. And the Apostle of God said, 'The most wretched of the older and later generations was the hobbler of the she-camel, and the most wretched of the later and earlier generations will be your killer, O ʿAlī.'[103] They passed on this great sanctity to the blood of each one among us on whom God bestows His grace. Is not God the most knowledgeable as to whom the grateful are? God, blessed and exalted is His mention, said: 'Or do the people envy what bounty God conferred on them? We provided the family of Abraham with the Book and wisdom, and We conferred on them great dominion' [Q 4: 54]. And Muhammad said, 'ʿAlī is the lion of those who are envied whom God provided with what He provided the family of Abraham, the Book and wisdom.' Then the Murjiʾa rejected them. God has said: 'Do you believe in a

[102] Abū Dharr al-Ghifārī, a Companion of the prophet, was cited earlier.
[103] The author has mentioned this event previously, see note 72 above.

part of the Book and disbelieve in a part' [Q 2: 85]. The meaning of this is: they believed in the prophet, and they disbelieved in the guardian and the legatee. By their own claim they believed in the Apostle and rejected the guardian. The Apostle of God has said, 'I am the city of faith and ʿAlī is its gate. So whoever wants to find the way to faith, let him come through the gate.' God has said: 'Enter the houses by their doorways' [Q 2: 189]. It means: 'Come to the prophets through the gateways of the executors.' But they rejected him even while they knew him as they know their children, in accord with the *sunna* of the Israelites and in imitation of them.

The Jews claimed that God tormented Nebuchadnezzar's spirit with many kinds of the vilest animals and vermin, such as monkeys and pigs . . .

Kitāb mafātīḥ al-niʿma

The Book of the Keys to Grace attributed to Abu'l-ʿAbbās

In the name of God the Merciful the Compassionate

Thanks be to God, the dispenser of good fortune, and may the blessings of God be upon our lord Muhammad and his family, the people of truth and verification.

May God aid you, O brother, in obeying Him and provide you with His safekeeping, felicitate you with His approval, make you suitable for His guidance, have you discern the way markers of His religion without a veil between you and His friends. May He put you among those who strive in the land of His sanctity as a person who possesses a heart with which he understands His parables and ears with which he hears His command and prohibition. Truly there is no power or strength save through Him. We ask Him that He bless the one chosen out of His creation, the one trusted with His revelation, Muhammad, His prophet, and to bless his family, the luminaries of guidance and the caves of refuge for mankind, God's proofs to His servants, lords of His religion, interpreters of His book, the ships of salvation on which he who sails is saved and he who stays behind drowns and is lost.

Furthermore: Our brother Abu'l-Ḥasan al-Baghdādī,[1] may God strengthen him, has conveyed to us what God the Exalted has

1 Neither of the two al-Baghdādīs who are prominent in our sources for this time have the *kunya* Abu'l-Ḥasan. One is Abū Jaʿfar Muḥammad b. Aḥmad b. Hārūn, appointed by the Imam-caliph al-Mahdī to the Dīwān al-Barīd, and the other is Abu'l-Yusr Ibrāhīm b. Muḥammad, known as al-Riyāḍī, a poet and man of letters in Qayrawan.

implanted in you and has granted you of a subtle mind, superbly piercing intelligence and the quest for the noble sciences and remarkable refinements. It was such as to make us long for your acquaintance, to form an attachment to you, and to mingle with you in the love of God. What confirmed that for us was your being prompted to join us in our region, which is known as Silyāna,[2] but you came to us, may God grant you honour, while we were unable to obtain our desire from you or what we hope for you since I was away from my residence. So I wrote to my brother Abū ʿAbd Allāh with news of you and I appraised him of your position and I advised him to reveal to you some of what you were seeking, until [such time as] God facilitates our getting together with you and meeting so as to confer together about what you require, God the Exalted willing. My opinion of you was good because of what I had heard concerning the amplitude of your knowledge and the superiority of your understanding, and that you know the objective that you seek and the goal you wish to attain, especially since you have reached the source and are aware of the matter, and have read from books, even if you are not aware of the entire matter, and you have only read in the guarded books what deals with the people who have attained high rank. The extent you reached and recognized and read, made it obligatory for you to consider it and use some of it as testimony for the other, its exterior and interior. And, if you found in that a disagreement, you [should have] asked about it. Yet there is no disagreement. And, whatever was difficult for you and impossible or incomprehensible, when you encountered it, and it seemed unlikely, it was incumbent on you to refer it to those designated to explain it. You ought not to have reviled it, nor to have rejected what was problematic. The Veracious (al-Ṣādiq),[3] peace be upon him, has

[2] Silyāna is a region (a governorate) of modern Tunisia. Its capital Silyāna was founded only in 1905, the region, however, may have been known by that name in Fatimid times.

[3] Al-Ṣādiq generally refers to the Shiʿi Imam Jaʿfar al-Ṣādiq, the great great grandson of ʿAlī and the father of Ismāʿīl but may also refer to an anonymous Imam.

said, 'What of our knowledge is difficult for you, refer it to us and do not turn it against us by calling it a lie. That is to say, bring it to us so that we can demonstrate for you its proof and make you acquainted with its explanation. Do not turn it against us by calling it a lie and rejecting it.' Upon my life, whoever begins a trade and offers his goods to those who are not suited for it, and does not understand its value and does not distinguish between its benefits and its loss, he values himself lightly and is described as being reckless in his affairs.

Abū ʿAbd Allāh has had me read your letter asking what I have quoted about God's guardian, even though All-Powerful and Mighty God had rendered him needless of the ephemeral effects of this passing world. However, his acceptance of it [the offering] is for the cleansing of souls and the purification of wealth. You yourself initiated the payment by that without having being forced or compelled. However, when my brother, Abū ʿAbd Allāh, informed you in regard to what is required of you in respect to God's guardian, the person who renders that offering out of the goodness of his own self, God will cleanse thereby his spirit and purify his money, and thus it will be lawful for his *dāʿī* and mentor to reveal to him the interpretive (*taʾwīlī*) sciences and make known to him the truths hidden from the enemies of God's religion. Verily does God the Exalted try the people with severe ordeals. Those who can bear it patiently, and those who cannot perish. There is in the world nothing more dear to a human being than himself and his possessions. God tries the people in regard to the two together, as He has said: 'Truly God has purchased of the faithful their souls and possessions in exchange for paradise; they fight on behalf of God and kill and are killed, a promise incumbent on Him, as in the Torah, the Gospels and the Qurʾan' [Q 9: 111]. Thus, He commanded them to perform the jihad with their souls and ordered them to turn over their money for various aspects and within fixed limits. I will hereafter explain to you some of what God made obligatory on the believers with respect to turning over their monies to God's guardian in order that, since God has proscribed alms for him as a means to keep him above the filth of the community, he expend it solely for the amelioration of things in general. So do not let it enter your mind that this is a trick your *dāʿī* perpetrates in order to take your money or the money of anyone else. God forbid that! But the religion of God, both the outward and inward, exists so that His unique oneness, both outwardly and inwardly, leads to three conditions and three benefits. One of them is the worship of God. The second of them is that by means of which the world flourishes, that is, by His commandments and judgments. The third is that it points to the inner meaning of the law, the interpretation of the revelation, and to the spiritual and the physical hierarchy. The surface [*ẓāhir*] of the law is that by which it is determined, fixed and set, leading thereby to those who are the causes of salvation and through whom there is the ascent to the abode of the Return.

God, may His praise be glory, said: 'By the night enshrouding and the day in splendour and what created male and female, truly your efforts are to diverse ends' [Q 92: 1–4], that is, in respect to the religion of God and your seeking the approval of His friends. If it were not for an aversion to long-windedness, I would provide you with an explanation of the meaning of 'night and day', 'male and female'. Rather I will produce for you the meanings that indicate what God has made obligatory on His creatures. Also, the pure interpretation is only set forth to him who searches out of desire and does not reject or oppose obstinately. Next the Exalted said: 'As for him who gives and fears God and affirms goodness' [Q 92: 5–6], that is, he who gives what is incumbent on him according to what is commanded of him concerning his property, who is on his guard against there being in it [i.e. the giving] confusion and error, and who affirms the good in what he hears in the way of explanation and proof. 'We will ease for him the way to good fortune' [Q 92: 7], that is facilitation of prosperity. The meaning of this is that property is of two kinds: property God provides for the maintenance of bodies and the amelioration of worldly affairs; and property God provides for the maintenance of spirits and the benefits pertaining to matters of the Hereafter, which are the knowledge God provided for the maintenance of the souls in the abode of the Return. And He said: 'Thus We will ease for him the way to good fortune' if he gives what he is ordered to give by his *dāʿī* and guards against that in which there are the people of confusion and discord who do not know the interpretation of the books of God. If he does that, the way is made easy, his knowledge increases and his prestige rises with the believers and with God's guardian. His rank increases and his station rises. 'But the one who is miserly, keeps for his own self, and considers the good to be false' [Q 92: 8–9], that is, he who is miserly in respect to the obligation he has been commanded to observe and does not produce it, regarding himself as above having to pursue that in which there is his very life, and who declares false the interpretation God set forth to give comfort to the believers, 'So for him We will ease the way to adversity' [Q 92: 10] and to poverty, thus cutting off for him the substance of the knowledge by means of which is his salvation. He is thus kept from good fortune and attachment to the guides of the time and adherents of the Speaking prophet (*nāṭiq*) and the Proof (*ḥujja*). Next God censures him, saying: 'His possessions will not suffice him when he perishes, surely to Us belongs the guidance, to Us is the first and the last' [Q 92: 11–13]. Then He cautions: 'So I have warned you of the blazing fire in which none but the most wretched are burned, those who rejected the truth and turn away' [Q 92: 14–16]. Then He praises the one who hastens to that [duty]: 'but the most God-fearing will avoid it, he who devotes his wealth to purifying himself and confers no favour on anyone for reward but only by seeking the face of His lord most high, he will be favoured' [Q 92: 18–21]. So, consider the *sūra* to its end; do you find in it any meaning other than this?

And His statement, glorious is the Sayer: 'Did We not give him two eyes, a tongue and two lips, and guided him along the two highways'

[Q 90: 8–10], meaning by the two eyes, the Speaker and the Foundation,[4] since they are the eyes of God on earth; the tongue is the Proof[5] because he proves for the believers the science of the interpretation and the revelation; and by the two lips the *dāʿī* and the *maʾdhūn*[6] because they are the gates to the Proof and they are the ones who strive for the religion of God. 'We guided him along the two highways' means the two paths, the exoteric and esoteric, 'Yet he has not scaled the steep ascent' [Q 90: 11]. Then He explained this saying: 'What will make you grasp what is the steep ascent? The freeing of a slave' [Q 90: 12–13]. The meaning of 'freeing' is for the novice to produce what his *dāʿī* has commanded of him, because he made that a trial for him. Hence patience during that trial is the scaling of the steep ascent so that God can discern the vicious from the good, 'so that he who was to die might perish after a sign and he who was to live might live after a sign' [Q 8: 42].

With this meaning God has said: 'Those your right hands own who seek emancipation, make a contract with them if you know of some good in them, and give them some of the wealth that God has granted you' [Q 24: 33], that is, free them from the covenant and release them for being broken and persuaded by argument. Provide them with some of the knowledge that God has granted you. Do that after freeing

4 The two terms Speaker and Foundation are specific to the Ismailis. The first, in Arabic *nāṭiq* (plural *nuṭaqāʾ*), denotes those prophets who have brought or issued a Law or Scripture. They are Adam, Noah, Abraham, Moses, Jesus, Muhammad and the expected Messiah (the *Qāʾim*). The Foundation, in Arabic *asās*, indicates the position of the one who initiates (or founds) the interpretation (*taʾwīl*) of that Scripture. For the era of Islam that means ʿAlī. For a complete review of these terms in various Ismaili contexts and sources, consult F. Daftary, *The Ismāʿīlīs: Their History and Doctrine*, index s.v. *nāṭiq* and *asās*.

5 Proof, here, is the Arabic *ḥujja,* a term with slightly differing meanings in various Shiʿi contexts, but in general for the Ismailis it refers to a high rank in the *daʿwa* coming just below that of the Imam. It can also indicate the Imam himself, as it seems to do in this passage. On the terms and its various usages, see F. Daftary, *Ismāʿīlīs*, index s.v. *ḥujja*.

6 *Maʾdhūn* means 'the one who has a license, a permit' to teach or propagate doctrine on behalf of the *daʿwa*, in some contexts a person who acts as the assistant of the *dāʿī*. For a complete review of this term in Ismaili sources, see F. Daftary, *Ismāʿīlīs*, index s.v. *maʾdhūn*.

them from their slavery and their having rendered what is incumbent upon them. I will reveal to you the meaning of emancipation lest you say: When was I a prisoner so that I was in need of emancipation? Know that God ordered the jihad against the infidels in all lands. Those of them that were abducted became slaves in the Abode of Islam until they were released or freeing his own self by his soul. Likewise, in the inner meaning [*bāṭin*] of the law, the one for whom the *dāʿī* breaks the external on which he relies because he does not know the interpretation or its meanings, he is in the position of someone from the land of ignorance, being hauled to the land of knowledge. If the *dāʿī* intends to raise his rank and to reveal to him the secrets of the law, he will command him to render what is incumbent on him in order to test him thereby and reveal what is in his heart. He does not provide him with any knowledge except in accord with the value of his rank and certainty, following the saying of God the Exalted: 'When believing women come to you as emigrants, test them; it is God who knows their faith' [Q 60: 10]. This is, in the outward meaning of the law, the coming of a woman from the abode of polytheism to the Abode of Islam. So, they are asked to swear that they have not come except out of love for Islam. This is its explanation in exoteric terms. As for the interpretation of it in this verse, it is that the women who believe in the religion of God are the students, since the male is like the teacher and the student is like the female. The meaning of emigration is the departure by the student from the threshold of ignorance to the state of seeking to understand and knowledge of the light and explanation. His saying: 'Test them, it is God who knows their faith best', that is, because their hearts are in the hand of God and no one else can know what is in them. The *dāʿī* knows of humans only what is apparent on the surface. Thus, God orders him to examine the believers who seek the benefits of the religion to test out their secrets. If they bear the trial with patience, it is licit for the teacher to initiate them and educate them in the interpretive sciences. Initiation is forbidden to anyone who breaks and perishes and does not bear up during the trial and ordeal. 'God knows their faith best' meaning that it is He who has access to their consciences. 'So if you find that they are believers' [Q 60: 10], that is, if they bear up during the trial and testing, 'do not return them to the infidels' [Q 60: 10], that is, to the people of the outward meaning which they previously upheld. Do not cut off from them the desire for knowledge.

Consider carefully His statement: 'Forbidden to you are carrion, blood, the flesh of pigs, what has been offered up to other than God, the strangled animal, an animal killed by a blow or by falling, an animal mauled by animals, or one eaten by wild beasts except what you have duly sacrificed, and what is sacrificed to idols' (to the end of the verse) [Q 5: 3], in order that you understand that what is meant by this is the prevention of initiating someone whose initiation is not licit. The outward meaning of carrion, in which there is no movement, is the search for wisdom, interpretation and the benefits of proof. The meaning of blood is the man who was a member of the *da'wa* but who revealed the explanation and interpretation without the permission of his *dā'ī*. The meaning of pigs is he who affirms all the ranks and what he hears of the explanation and wisdom, yet denies the position of the Imam. That is because the cloven hoof of the pig resembles the hoof of the sheep devoid of its head because it is deformed. That is like his disavowal of the Imam of the time who is the head of the believers. What has been offered up to other than God means the one on whose neck is pledged to another than the true Imam since God has made only the oath to the true Imam obligatory. Thus, one from whom the pledge to someone else was taken is not permitted to be initiated. The strangled animal is one who breaks the oath at the moment it is taken from him, so that he says: Give me time and have patience with me. The animal killed by a blow is the one the shepherd has beaten to death. The shepherd is like the *dā'ī* and beating with a staff is like putting him to the test. The sheep is like the novice. When the *dāʿī* puts the novice to the test and the novice bears up patiently through the ordeal, he is allowed to initiate him in the keys to knowledge. If he flees and does not bear patiently the ordeal, initiation in knowledge is forbidden. The one killed by a fall is the person who cannot bear the interpretation nor embrace its understanding. He may have once reached one of the ranks but then reverted to the outward meaning and its people. The one mauled by wild animals is he who argues with the *dāʿī* and debates without any understanding or insight. Then he does not cease from that when he is forbidden. The animal eaten by a wild beast, and not [an animal] you have been able to slaughter properly, means him whom someone from the people of the outward meaning has corrupted and who has turned his face from the *daʿwa* of the truth. He is not to be initiated, unless he has been properly purified, meaning someone who has renewed the oath of covenant. What has been sacrificed on a stone altar is he from whom a pledge has been taken to an Imam who appointed himself without having been chosen for it by God, and even so he puts himself in the position of God's guardian and summons the people to himself. Initiation by means of explanation and interpretation is forbidden to all these people.

The Exalted said: 'Take the offerings they make of their property thereby to purify and cleanse them' [Q 9: 103]. It is only called an offering (*ṣadaqa*) because it constitutes a confirmation by the believers of what they have been allowed to hear of the interpretation and explanation. God makes it a trial in the inner meaning of the law, testing the believer through it in order to indicate, by that means, the truth of their conviction to the *dāʿī*. Then He said: 'and invoke blessing on them, truly your blessings are a comfort for them' [Q 9: 103]. That means, when you collect that from them, appeal for them, for truly the blessedness of your appeal is a bond for them and a quieting of their apprehension and dismay. He the All-Powerful and Glorious said: 'O you who believe, when you take counsel with the prophet in private bring an offering before him for the conversation; that is best for you and appropriate' [Q 58: 12]. It is reported that when this verse was revealed, the Commander of the Believers, ʿAlī b. Abī Ṭālib, at once sold his armour for forty dinars and sat down in front of the prophet and began asking him question after question and producing dinar after dinar. But the people then refrained from it. So, God revealed: 'Are you hesitant about making offerings while conferring; if you do not do so and God forgives you, maintain prayers and pay alms' [Q 58: 13]. That means that, surely you hesitated to donate your wealth upon each and every question, [but] He forgives you and lifts off you the burden of that. So, maintain prayers and pay the alms tax, meaning here purification and cleansing. Had He not said: 'If you hesitate about making offerings while conferring; if you do not do so and God forgives you' every believer would have had to produce an offering for the consultation with each question. However, by His favour and benefaction, He approved that they pay once only for each time and occasion.

You mentioned in your letter, may God ennoble you, that God says: 'And He will not ask of you your property' [Q 47: 36]. So, consider the whole verse, may God ennoble you, for surely the argument in it is against you, not for you. The meaning of His saying: 'He will not ask of you your property', meaning, all of what you own, is that 'if He were to ask for all of it, and press you for it, you would withhold it' [Q 47: 37]. This means, if He asked for it and insisted on the request, your hypocrisy would be evident and you would withhold payment. He has forgiven you for that as a favour and ordered a payment of only some of your wealth in order that it be expended in the way of God at the hand of God's guardian and for the benefit of the believers. He, the Exalted, has said: 'Look then, you are those invited to spend in the way of God; some among you will withhold but he who withholds only withholds it at the expense of his own soul' [Q 47: 38]. This verse is parallel to the verse concerning the confidential discourse, which is His statement: 'When you have a private consultation with the prophet make offerings before doing so', that is, at each question. But then He was merciful to His servants and exempted them from that, and instead ordered the payment of only some of their wealth. Thereafter, He announced that He is in no need of your wealth except as a testing and a means of determining the true state of your affairs. Thus, some of you are of those who bear the test patiently, others of you are of those who turn away. God has said: 'God has no needs but it is you who are poor; if you turn away He will substitute others than you who are not like you' [Q 47: 38]. Then He ruled on the payment of that and the urgency of doing so. He said: 'Pay something out of what We have provided you before death comes upon one of you and he says, O Lord, would only that You would grant me a delay until a time near, I would give an offering and then be one of those who do good' [Q 63: 10].

And the Exalted has said: 'Pay something out of what We have provided you with before the day arrives in which there is no commerce, nor friendship and intercession, and those who reject the faith they are the evil doers' [Q 2: 254]. At that He ordained payment from the good things in one's property. He said: 'Pay out of the good things you have acquired and of what We have brought forth for you from the earth; do not resort to the bad things in it for donations' [Q 2: 267]. He commanded that you produce that out of the goodness of your souls. He said: 'Do not invalidate your charitable offerings by seeking benefit or harm' [Q 2: 264]. Then He ensured blessedness and purification for the souls of those who spend. He said: 'The like of those who expend their wealth in the way of God is that of a grain of corn which grows into seven ears, each with a hundred grains; God grants a manifold increase to whomsoever He wishes' [Q 2: 261]. And He said: 'The like of those who expend their wealth seeking the approval of God and the steadying of their own souls are the like of a garden high and fertile, heavy rain falls on it and its harvest is doubled' [Q 2: 265]. He also said: 'Those who spend of their wealth night and day, in secret and openly, for them is a reward with their Lord; they have no fear nor will they grieve' [Q 2: 274]. He made the giving of that a purification and cleansing of their souls and their wealth. He said: 'He will prosper who purifies himself and glorifies the name of his Lord and prays' [Q 87: 14–15]. Then He also said: 'He succeeds who purifies it; he fails who corrupts it' [Q 91: 9–10].

Then He disciplined His prophet and restrained him from going after those who fled from the trial, failed to purify themselves, and held back from listening to the explanation. He said: 'As for him who considered himself self-sufficient, you attended to him although it is not upon you that he did not purify, but of him who came to you earnestly seeking with fear you were neglectful, that should not be; this is a reminder for him who remembers it' [Q 80: 5–12]. Next, He alluded to His saints and the Imams of His religion, saying: 'In honoured scriptures kept raised and pure' [Q 80: 13–14]. Then He pointed to the Proofs who are the gates to the Imams, saying: 'By the hands of scribes noble and pious' [Q 80: 15–16] because the Proofs disclose the secrets of the interpretation and the revelation and provide the community with proofs for the meanings of all things.

Then He ordered the payment of charitable offerings to the people of the *daʿwa* of the Interpretation [*taʾwīl*]. He, the Exalted, said: 'Alms offerings are for the poor' [Q 9: 60], that is, the Speakers since there is no one in the world who benefits them; so they are in need of the spiritual benefits that come to them. 'And the needy', meaning the Foundations because the people rely on their interpretation and proofs, and 'those employed in this work', meaning the Imams, since they have inherited the knowledge of the revelation and the interpretation; thus they are those who employ it and urge the community to adhere to it. 'And those whose hearts are reconciled', that is, the Proofs because God has reconciled their hearts, so that they are like one soul with no disagreement between them. 'And those in bondage', meaning the *dāʿīs*, since the service of the *daʿwa* falls on them. It is they who break down the people of the outward meaning and place the oath of the covenant on the necks of those of the believers who respond to the appeal of truth. 'And those in debt', that is, the *maʾdhūns* because training in the interpretive sciences falls to them without them [having to take] an oath to do so. So, they are the wet-nurses who raise those whom they have not borne. 'And in the way of God' that is, the limited *maʾdhūns* who have achieved the knowledge they need and who have been permitted to educate the novices and instruct them, but do not break down any of the people of the outward meaning. The authentic *maʾdhūns* are the ones who both break down and instruct while these instruct but do not break down any of the people of outward meaning. 'And the wayfarer' refers to the believing students seeking the benefits of religion. These are eight kinds [religious ranks] whom God made the pillars of His religion and the treasurers of its science. He made it a duty for the people to know them and obligated them to obey them and ordered that offerings and alms be paid to them and put in their proper place with them, so that those of them who are not an Imam can convey it to the Imam who will expend it for the benefit of religion.

It is reported of the Apostle of God, that he was in the process of dividing up the charitable offerings when a man said to him, 'Give me some of it.' He replied, 'If you were one of the eight; otherwise they are a disease in the belly and an ache in the head.' He thus let the community know that it was not allowed to give that except to those eight who are the lords of the religion. On that score, the Veracious one (al-Ṣādiq), upon whom be peace, said, 'Give alms to those it belongs to. I am the one who guarantees what you give.' If the people of the outward meaning are questioned as to what the difference is between the poor and the miserable and those God mentioned in His book in this verse, you would find them in disagreement. Some would say that the poor person is he who has nothing. As for the miserable person, that is he who has something to which he has recourse. If the matter is thus, arriving at knowledge of these eight types is precluded except through research and investigation. But that is not in the ability of anyone through the exterior of a matter or its interior except through the guidance of God's friends [*awliyāʾ*].

Know that sound practice in the religion of God is that the Speaker pays out from all that he possesses and he devotes to God from his least and his largest property at every turn of the year; he cannot do otherwise. As for the Foundation, he pays on half of what he possesses every two years because he is the partner of the Speaker and has only one of the two ranks of the Speaker. As for the Imam, he pays on a third of what he possesses every three years. As for the Proof he pays on a fourth of what he possesses every four years. As for the *dāʿī* he pays on a fifth of what he possesses every fifth year. As for the believer, he pays what he pays on the measure of his sincerity and in accord with what his *dāʿī* determines for him in order to test him. If he pays that once, he has fulfilled the basic requirement of the religion and thus fulfilled the necessary obligation, by his fulfilment of which he distinguishes himself from the people of outward meaning and he departs from their ranks. If he pays a second time, his *dāʿī* knows the goodness of his intention and the firmness of his certainty and then he reveals to him the secrets of the interpretation. If he pays out a third time, his status with God's guardian rises and his rank similarly rises among the believers. The Apostle of God has explained this meaning in respect to the ritual ablution and Prayer. That is, he performed the ablution and washed his limbs time after time. Then he said, 'This is the ablution of him whose prayer God does not accept without it.' The prayer is obedience and the ablution is the purification and the cleansing that God made obligatory on every believer as a payment. He said, 'The obedience of a man is not acceptable except along with payment of what is incumbent on him, because his purification depends on that.' Then he washed his limbs twice each time and he said, 'This is the ablution of the one for whom God doubles the reward twice over', meaning by this that the believer, if he pays out what is required of him one time, he has purified himself since fulfilling that constitutes his purification. If he pays out a second time, God doubles his reward twice and his *dāʿī* knows the goodness of his intention and firmness of his certainty. Next, he washed his limbs three times each time. And he said, 'This is my ablution and the ablution of the prophets before me.' That means that the believer, if he pays his obligation three times, his position with God's guardian rises, as does his status with his *dāʿī*, and he achieves a rank among the ranks of religion.

The Apostle of God, may God bless him, has explained this meaning in the grades of prayer. That is, he assigned prayer three grades: obligatory, customary and supererogatory. The obligatory allows no leeway and it is not permitted to abstain from it. The worshipper either performs it or is an unbeliever. He meant by that the payment of the obligation once is incumbent on the novice; no shortcoming is allowed him in that. When he fulfils it, he is a believer, and, if he does not do it, he is a person of outward meaning excluded from initiation to the explanation. As for the second grade, which is the customary, if he does it after the obligatory prayer, he is God-fearing. Should he permit himself some leeway, he would be remiss, but not an unbeliever. The meaning here is that the novice, if he pays the obligatory amount a second time, his soul is cleansed and his guardian knows thereby the soundness of his intention and the firmness of his certainty. If he should fall short in that and not pay, he does not become a person of outward meaning[7] but rather comes up short in seeking superiority, loftiness and nobility before God and His guardian. As for the third grade, which is the supererogatory, if the servant does it after the

[7] 'A person of outward meaning', a *ẓāhirī*, is a strict literalist with respect to understanding and applying the meaning of the Law and Scripture. The doctrine of our author, in contrast, holds that a true believer must know and apply both the literal outward meaning and the inner esoteric truth to which it refers. They are equally essential.

customary and obligatory, his faith becomes perfect, meaning here that the novice, if he pays his due amount three times, his position with respect to God's guardian rises, as does his rank among the believers. Thus, purification of the soul and cleansing of properties, may God ennoble you, consist in the payment of what I have just explained in regard to these three grades. The first of them is a test by which the novice is examined. Therefore, it is incumbent on him to pay what accords with what his *dāʿī* imposes on him. It might happen that *dāʿī* orders that his wealth be divided into two parts, or he might order him to pay out a third or a fourth, or some other amount. Sometimes he may be satisfied to say to him, 'Pay such and such.' Yet again the *dāʿī* might look at what has passed of the novice's life, that is, the amount of his years, and deduct from it for his age or boyhood and command him, in respect to what is left over, to pay an amount he deems appropriate each year. On occasion he might impose the obligation to pay an amount equal to the number of Speakers, Foundations and Imams from the time of Adam to the *Qāʾim* of the Resurrection, in cash or specie, and that is seven eras and in each era there is a Speaker, a Foundation, an Imam, an Adjutant,[8] a Wing,[9] and twelve Proofs, the sum of which is seventeen.[10] For that reason seventeen *rakʿa*s are required in the obligatory prayer. If seventeen is multiplied by seven, the result of that is one hundred and nineteen. Therefore, the *dāʿī* orders paying, for each one of these ranks, a specific amount as a test and does not tolerate any holding back from that. Thus, the believer's paying his obligatory due a second and third time

8 'Adjutant' is the Arabic *lāḥiq* (pl. *lawāḥiq*) and it denotes a rank in the *daʿwa* between the Imam and the individual *dāʿī*s. For more see F. Daftary, *Ismāʿīlīs*, index, s.v. *lāḥiq*,

9 'Wing' is the Arabic *janāḥ*, a rank in the *daʿwa* equivalent to *dāʿī*. The term itself was used much less often and mainly by Ismailis in the East. For sources see F. Daftary, *Ismāʿīlīs*, pp. 219 and 231 and the citations given there.

10 Our author appears clearly to separate here the rank of Adjutant (*lāḥiq*) from that of Proof (*ḥujja*). He would have a single Adjutant and a single Wing (*janāḥ*) along with twelve Proofs at one time. However, in other Ismaili writings, the Adjutants are equivalent to the Proofs, simply another term for the same office, and thus there would be twelve of them. A Wing is a *dāʿī* of which there are many more than one.

is an initiative on his part in accordance with his good will. However little or great that may be, it is accepted from him.

God's Apostle has explained this meaning in the actions of prayer by ordering men during the bowing (*rakʿa*s) to keep their backs so straight that, should water fall on the back of one of them, it will not divide in two because of the level straightness of his back. For women it is permitted for them to complete their bowing simply by their tilting heads and inclining their chests. The meaning here is that men are the teachers and that women the students. The meaning of bowing is maintaining obedience to God and to His guardian. That is because obedience was originally prostration because of God's saying: 'And behold We said to the angels prostrate to Adam and they bowed down except Iblis' [Q 2: 34]. Then the bowing became obedience because of His saying: 'O you who believe bow down and prostrate yourselves' [Q 22: 77]. So, prostration corresponds to the rank of the Imam, on whom be peace, indicating thus that the Imam originally initiated the explanation for the believer. Then, when he set up for himself a gate, namely the Proof, God ordered the bowing down and then the prostration. That is, you must render obedience to the Proof, and then from him enter into the knowledge of the Imam since the former is his gate. For this reason, God said: 'Enter houses by their doors and fear God' [Q 2: 189]. And straightness in bowing down for men means that the scholars who teach are not allowed any negligence or that any imperfection or mistake enter their actions. For the student that is allowed in some of his acts even if he should fall short because of the paucity of his knowledge or the weakness of his resolve. Excellence in carrying out the obligation has the believer do so according to his ability. For this reason, God has said: 'They ask you what they are to give, say, whatever you can spare' [Q 2: 219], meaning here obedience and tolerability.

There are people who pay that with malice in their soul and weak resolve. Because of that God said: 'Some of the desert Arabs regard their payments as a penalty and watch out for fortune to turn against you; on them be the disaster of evil' [Q 9: 98]. Among them are also some who pay with good will in their hearts, strength of conviction, and affirmation of the truth. For that reason God said about them: 'But some of the Arabs . . . look upon what they give as bringing them closer to God and the blessings of the Apostle, surely it is a means of bringing them nearer' [Q 9: 99]. The bedouin are those of outward meaning who seek the benefits of religion. The indication of that is the statement of the Apostle of God, 'Let not the bedouin Arab be the Imam of an Emigrant in prayer.' He meant by 'bedouin Arab' the person of literal meaning and, by the Emigrants, the believer, because he has emigrated from the domain of ignorance, confusion and discord to the domain of pure interpretation, proof and explanation. He says, 'The believer is not allowed to take any of the people of literal meaning as Imam, whom he follows and adheres to for his guidance towards salvation.'

God's Apostle has explained the meaning of the obligation that is emancipation in the pilgrimage and its rituals. I will explain this for you briefly as I have reached mention of the religious laws and what is in them pointing to the sacrificial offerings for which God has no need. Rather they are the purification of souls and the cleansing of wealth in order that the virtue of the believer, during the days of his life, be good rather than wicked, and that he be, in his afterlife, saved and not doomed to perish. God says: 'It is not its flesh or its blood that reaches God but the piety of yourselves that reaches Him' [Q 22: 37]. Similar to this statement, there is in the Torah: 'By the action will you be blessed, not by the sacrifice itself.'[11] And the Exalted said: 'Whatever good you

[11] A careful examination of this purported quotation from the Bible and also the one that follows has not uncovered an exact match but this one appears to hint at the message of Samuel 15: 22 which reads 'And Samuel said, Whether the Lord will burnt sacrifices, either slain sacrifices, and not more, *rather*, that men obey to the voice of the Lord? (And Samuel said, Desireth the Lord burnt sacrifices, and slain sacrifices, or *rather*, that people obey his voice?) Forsooth obedience *to him* is better than sacrifices, and to take heed *to his word* is more than to offer the inner fatness of rams.'

put forward on your part, you will be fully compensated and no wrong will be done to you' [Q 2: 272]. God also said: 'Whatever good you give benefits yourselves and you will do so seeking the face of God' [Q 2: 272]. And the Almighty said: 'Whatever good you put forth for yourselves, you will find it with God . . . truly God is most forgiving and merciful' [Q 2: 110 . . . Q 73: 22]. Parallel to this in the Gospels: 'Place your sacrifices and your treasures where no one else can eat it nor a thief gain access to it'[12] meaning here '[place it] with God.'

Know that God the Exalted gave this world with all that is in it to His Apostle, may God bless him and his pure family. Thus, it belongs to the Guardian of the age and, that being so, he is, by virtue of God's command, more dear to them than their own selves. So, all that is in the hands of the believers and others is his. Some understand that, and some fail to understand that. God says: 'The Prophet is dearer to the believers than they are to themselves' [Q. 33: 1]. That being so and he being dearer to them than themselves by God's command, he has even more right to their wealth than they themselves. The Imam is in every age and time the successor of God's Apostle and is thus dearer to the believers than their wealth and themselves. If it were not for [my] concern not to go on too long, I would explain, from the perspective of the composition of the world, that the Imam, who is master of the age, is the essence of the world and its contents. Everything that is in the world of animals and plants is an instrument for him and a container, like the shell that surrounds things that have shells. His essence is like the heart in the body. Every limb and component is an instrument for it and a protection. He puts them to use, commands and prohibits them, since there is no difference between the human who is the microcosm and the macrocosm itself. Since he is in this position in the world, he is dearer to the believers or others than their wealth and themselves.

12 Again, it seems that no exact match exists but Matthew 6: 19–20 comes close. It states: 'Lay not up for yourselves treasures upon earth, where moth and rust doth corrupt, and where thieves break through and steal; But lay up for yourselves treasures in heaven.'

So, the believer knows that his wealth and his self belong to God's guardian. He is thus certain and acutely aware of that. He is not subject to doubt about what he pays to God's guardian because he knows this because of God's having said: 'Truly God buys from the believers their selves and their wealth so that they have paradise; they fight in the way of God; they fight and are killed, a promise on Him by right in the Torah, the Gospels and the Qur'an; none are more faithful to a promise than God; then rejoice in your bargain that you have made and that is a great achievement' [Q 9: 111]. All that is in the hands of the believers belongs to God and what belongs to God belongs to His guardian. However, by the grace of God and His mercy, he commanded them to pay out only a portion of what they possess to God and to His Apostle and to the Guardian of the age after him. God has said: 'And know that out of the booty you seize a fifth belongs to God and to the Apostle' [Q 8: 41]. And the Veracious (al-Ṣādiq) said, 'God gave to His Apostle a fifth of the earth. What belongs to God belongs to His Apostle, and what belongs to His Apostle belongs to us. Thus whoever acquires a single dirham or more that is booty, and who pays it to us as our right, he has paid what he was obligated to pay; and he who withholds it, on him God puts a collar of fire. And our followers escape from that because we have exempted them from it.' Then he said, 'God has given the booty to us.' Someone asked him, 'What is the booty?' He replied, 'Mines of gold, silver, gems, mountains, caverns and all lands lacking an owner.'

Sudayr al-Ṣayrafī, the Kufan,[13] went to see al-Ṣādiq one day and with him were the alms of the believers, their offerings and gifts. He placed them before him. Al-Ṣādiq said to him, 'What is this?' He replied, 'The alms of your servants and their gifts.' He responded, 'Surely we will accept that from them, although we have no need for it.

[13] On this Sudayr al-Ṣayrafī al-Kūfī, who was a companion of the Imams al-Bāqir and al-Ṣādiq, see al-Qāḍī al-Nuʿmān, *Daʿāʾim al-Islām*, trans. Asaf A. A. Fyzee, completely revised by Ismail K. Poonawala (Oxford, 2002), vol. 1, pp. 66–67 and n. 177 with citation of additional sources.

However, [we accept it] it in order to purify them in accord with the words of God: "Of their wealth take an offering to purify and cleanse them thereby" [Q 9: 103].' Alms' payments are a purification of sins and transgressions. God said to Moses: 'Go to Pharaoh for he has transgressed; and say to him: "Would you like to be cleansed and have me guide you to your Lord so that you come to fear Him?"' [Q 79: 17–19]. There cannot be any purification without patiently bearing the trial and test. God said: 'And We will put you to the test until We know among you those who strive and are patient and thus verify reports about you' [Q 47: 31].

Observe here how God tested the two sons of Adam: 'When each of them offered a sacrifice it was accepted from one of them but not accepted of the other' [Q 5: 27]. In envy 'he said: "I will surely kill you"; he replied: "God only accepts from those who are righteous"' [Q 5: 27]. The reason for this was that Abel, because of the goodness of his intentions and the firmness of his conviction, paid, as an offering, out of all he possessed, the most excellent, finest and best. Cain paid as offering, because of the badness of his intentions and his disdain for the commands of God, out of all he possessed, the worst, least and most detestable. The outcome of their affair is as you have heard. Also observe Abraham. God tested him with the sacrifice of his son, ordering that he offer him up to God as a sacrifice. Do you not see that He only wished by that to test him and not because He had any need for Abraham's sacrifice of his son? Observe how God commanded the people of Israel to offer and sacrifice in the temples [*kanāʾis*] the best that they had available, the finest and most excellent of it, and that they put the fat of the sacrifice on the altar and stain the altar with the blood in front of the priest and the curtains of the temple. The sacrifice was accepted when the fire descended, consumed the fat and the blood splattered the curtains of the temple in front of the priest. If the fire did not come down and did not do what we mentioned here, they knew the sacrifice had not been accepted and that the conscience of the one who made the sacrifice was bad while the intention of the other, for whom the fire came down and did as we have mentioned, was good. So, they would order [the former] to repent of that to God. Observe in this matter how it is a trial for the servant. The sacrifice is a trial by which the servant is tested in order to ascertain his true secrets and his conviction and intention.

Observe the *sunna* of God's Apostle in respect to the *fiṭra* offering of fasting[14] as he made it obligatory on the small and the great, male and female, free and slave, present and absent. He indicated by it payment of the obligatory, the redemption and the appeal to interpretation. Moreover, he ordered it to be carried out speedily, hastening to the congregational mosques before the rising of the sun. If it was paid prior to the rising of the sun, it was the *fiṭra* offering; if it was paid after the rising of the sun, it was a charitable offering. The meaning of fasting is secrecy, concealment and silence; the meaning of *fiṭra* is the payment of the obligation to God and to His guardian in the way of redeeming a pledge and sacrifice; the meaning of the rising of the sun is the rising of the Imam and his unveiling of the *daʿwa*. A man's paying the *fiṭra* offering before the rise of the sun[15] has the meaning of affirming the Imam prior to his advent. Thus, paying of the obligation is an affirmation, being devoted and redeeming a pledge. Paying the *fiṭra* after the rising of the sun has the meaning of affirming the Imam after his having appeared, and thus paying the redemption without pious devotion. The meaning of paying it to the congregational mosques is to pay it to the *dāʿī* who is the locus of your obedience and your prostration. In regard to hastening and seeking an elevation in ranks through actions, God has said: 'Then

[14] The *fiṭra* offering is an alms' payment paid on the day of the breaking of the fast of Ramaḍān. It becomes due after sunset on the eve of the Feast, which commences the following day. The offering, which is paid by the head of the household, applies to all members of it including women, children, slaves and guests.

[15] The normal rule here dictates payment only prior to the moment of the *ʿīd* prayer, without reference to sunrise. However, Abu'l-ʿAbbās may regard the time of the prayer as itself coming just after sunrise.

whoever has done an atom's weight of good shall see it and whoever has done an atom's weight of evil will see that' [Q 99: 7–8]. And He, exalted is His name, said: 'For all there are ranks in accord with their actions' [Q 6: 132] and He also said: 'Be in haste for the forgiveness of your Lord' [Q 3: 133]. Observe here the *sunna* concerning the newborn. When he leaves the belly of his mother, a dinar is paid on his behalf. He is anointed, swaddled, his head rubbed with honey and aloe, then made to drink milk after that. He is given a name on the seventh day and the middle of his head is shaved. An offering is given for it and his hair weighed in silver and a sacrifice slaughtered for him. The meaning of the new-born is the novice; the meaning of paying a dinar on his behalf is what is required of the novice in fulfilment of the private consultation; the meaning of swaddling is the oath by which he swears allegiance. The meaning of honey and aloe is what is revealed to him of the explanation and interpretation and what patience is required of him in keeping that secret. The meaning of his being named on the seventh day is revealing to him the Imam of the age because the Imam, who is the master of the age, is one of the seven Imams. The meaning of shaving the middle of his head is disclosing the matter of his chief who is the Imam of the age. The offering for him by the weight of his hair has the meaning of redemption, and the sacrifice for him has the meaning of breaking him, that is, the novice by another novice and the taking from him of the oath. That is because, when he reaches maturity, he is then able to educate another. About that God has said: 'Test the orphans until they reach the age of marriage; if you find sound judgment in them, turn over to them their property and do not consume it' [Q 4: 6]. In this sense God says: 'and what you taught the hunting animals to catch in the manner directed by God; eat what they catch for you' [Q 5: 4], that is, take the oath from the one they have broken and control him, 'and mention the name of God', that is, call upon him, when taking the oath of him, to maintain obedience to the Imam and the Proof. At the moment of the sacrifice, it is said: 'In the name of God'. 'In the name of' (*bism*) consists of three letters, indicating thus the Proof (*ḥujja*); *Allāh* has four letters, pointing to the Imam. For this reason God says: 'And when the children reach the age of puberty, let them ask for permission just as those before them asked for permission' [Q 24: 59].

Thus, all that I have cited from the Book of God, its exterior is firm and acted upon. But it leads to three conditions and three meanings, as I mentioned to you at the beginning of this treatise. One of them is that it constitutes worship of God. A second is discipline, rules and stipulations for the prospering of this world. The third points to the hierarchy of God's religion and the links [*asbāb*] mentioned in the book of God by means of whom there is a rising up towards the abode of the Return. He who knows them knows them; he who ignores them ignores them. 'But only those who have wisdom take heed' [Q 3: 7].

And take note of the actions at the pilgrimage and its rituals and the obligation God imposed on every believer of proffering a sacrifice by which he seeks to draw closer to God. God the Exalted says: 'A duty owed to God is the pilgrimage to the House for whoever has the means to do it' [Q 3: 97]. Having the ability to do it involves provisions, a mount, a secure passage, and expenditures for one's dependents. A person who has that must make the pilgrimage. There is no latitude in that for any Muslim by unanimous agreement. The meaning here of provisions is knowledge which is the nourishment of souls; the meaning of riding animal is the *dāʿī* who moves you on in God's religion from rank to rank until he causes you to attain your place of safety and security and makes you understand what is obligatory, both for you and against you. He who finds a *dāʿī* is obliged to seek the Imam, until reaching him and accepting obedience to him, acknowledging the ranks of God's religion from the time of Adam to the Resurrection. The meaning of discarding the sown cloths you wore previously is your discarding knowledge of every Imam of literal meaning that you had previously adhered to. Your putting on the covering and cloak is your entering into obedience to the Imam and the Proof. Your purification with water is your accepting the knowledge by which you are purified. Your saying, 'Here I am, O God, here I am' is your responding to the Imam of the age when he sends the *dāʿī* to you to summon you to God and to knowledge of His religion, and you answer him with compliance, that is, affirmation. Your acceptance of the Proof is your acceptance of the knowledge and your acknowledgment that he is the gateway to the Imam, on whom be peace. Your circumambulation seven times is your affirmation of seven Imams. Your standing at al-Ṣafā and al-Marwa is your acknowledgment of the Speaker and the Foundation and your running back and forth between them is your seeking your learning from them both. Your coming to Minā is your coming to the one who bestows on you understanding and he is your *dāʿī*. Your prayer at Minā is your establishment of obedience to your *dāʿī* and submitting humbly to him. Your standing at ʿArafat and combining the prayers of midday and afternoon there is your maintaining obedience to the Speaker and the *Qāʾim* and affirming both. Your ascending after that to al-Mawqif is your rising to understand the heavenly spiritual ranks and your praying at al-Muzdalifa the sunset and last evening prayer (*al-ʿishāʾ al-ākhira*) is your affirmation of the Founder and the Imam and those Imams who were concealed.[16] Your gathering of pebbles to the number of seventy is your affirmation of seventy ranks who are the elect of God who assemble with every Imam. Your throwing twenty-one pebbles is your repudiating the opponents of the seven Speakers (i.e. speaking prophets – *nuṭaqāʾ*), the seven Executors and

[16] Those 'Imams who were concealed' is a fairly standard Ismaili Fatimid way of citing the Imams who immediately preceded the first caliph al-Mahdī. The usual enumeration would have three Imams between Muḥammad b. Ismāʿīl b. Jaʿfar and al-Mahdī, all of whom went into concealment as a protection against ʿAbbasid persecution. Typically, their names are not given.

the seven Imams.[17] Your burying the rest of those pebbles is your protecting of the ranks of God's religion who are the seven heptads. Your driving of your sacrificial animal is your hastening to pay what God has made incumbent on you and every believer as a redemption. That is your sacrifice by means of which you draw closer to God by purifying your soul. Your shaving your head is your disclosing your chief who is the Imam of your time and the recognition of him. Your breaking the fast on three days is your enunciation of the explanation and revealing what you used to keep secret of the knowledge of the Speaker, the Foundation and the Imam. Your returning to Mecca is your returning to your *dāʿī* in order to seek to learn from him what remains that you do not know and that you do not abide with the people of literal meaning and do not put their learning in a position treasured or valued by you since they are mere shells having no saving value in them.

So this, may God ennoble you, is the meaning of the pilgrimage and its rituals. I have summarized it for you. I hoped by doing that to reveal what God has imposed on you and on every believer concerning the sacrifices by which you draw closer to God. As for your saying at the moment of making your sacrifice [which] draws you closer, 'O God, accept it from me as You accepted it from Abraham the Friend', that is its literal meaning. It indicates what your *dāʿī* has ordered you to do in respect to paying what God requires of you as a mercy from God to you and a bestowal of benefit on you and on the believers in

[17] 'Executors' (or alternately 'Legatees') is the Arabic *waṣī* (pl. *awṣiyāʾ*) referring here to what would otherwise be called the Foundation (*asās*). The term Executor however emphasizes his role as the executor of the prophet's legacy by inheritance. Each Speaker-prophet has one and thus there are, at least potentially, seven in all, if the final Speaker, the seventh, has one. The Messiah, the *Qāʾim*, would be the seventh and it is not clear how he would have a Foundation (*asās* or *waṣī*) let alone seven Imams after his advent, since he normally heralds the end of time. Is our author projecting a future event? Or, as specified in some early Ismaili texts, has the seventh speaker already appeared once, thus commencing a special era in which there is (or will be) an executor and a set of seven Imams, even though he will reappear again later? For more on this problem and its variations, see F. Daftary, *Ismāʿīlīs*, index under the term *waṣī*.

order to purify their souls. It is as I have informed you in the words of God: 'And were it not for the grace and mercy of God to you not one of you would ever have been pure, but God purifies whomsoever He wishes' [Q 24: 21]. Were I to fully account to you the explanation of what God has made obligatory on you and on the believers in respect to this matter in the Book of God and the *sunna* of His Apostle and what there is in the laws as indications of that, this book would run on at length. What I have mentioned of that is sufficient for him who possesses a heart to think with and ears with which to hear. Certainly, the sights are not blind but rather the hearts that are in chests are blind. If you consider well part of the indications I have mentioned to you and apply to them research and investigation or by questioning and drawing inferences, you would not attribute trickery to your *dāʿī* and the one obedience to whom God imposed on you in respect to taking what belongs to you and others. God forbid that! Do you suspect that even a single grain of it goes to him? Certainly not; that could never be the case! I have arranged to have sent back to you what he took from you if the letters and their reading be not successful with you. This is for the likes of you out of concern to you. So, turn back if you wish that. If you seek wealth by it, friends have no need for it. Peace be on you and the mercy of God and His blessings. May God bless His Apostle, our lord Muhammad, and his family, give them peace.

Bibliography

EI2 = *The Encyclopaedia of Islam*, ed. H. A. R. Gibb et al. New edition, Leiden, 1960–2004.

EI = *Encyclopaedia Islamica*, ed. W. Madelung and F. Daftary. London, 2008–.

Abel, A. 'Baḥīrā', *EI2*.

Anthony, Sean. *Crucifixion and Death as Spectacle: Umayyad Crucifixion in its Late Antique Context*. New Haven CT, 2014.

Ayoub, Mahmoud. *Redemptive Suffering in Islam*. The Hague, 1978.

Cortese, Delia. *Ismaili and Other Arabic Manuscripts. A Descriptive Catalogue of Manuscripts in the Library of The Institute of Ismaili Studies*. London, 2000.

Crone, P. 'Khālid b. al-Walīd', *EI2*.

Daftary, Farhad. *The Ismāʿīlīs: Their History and Doctrines*. 2nd edn, Cambridge, 2007.

Gacek, Adam. *Catalogue of Arabic Manuscripts in the Library of The Institute of Ismaili Studies*, vol. 1. London, 1984.

Ghalib, Muhtadī Muṣṭafā, ed., *Mafātīḥ al-niʿma*. Salamiyya, 1982.

al-Ḥākim al-Naysabūrī, Muḥammad b. ʿAbd Allāh. *al-Mustadrak ʿalā al-ṣaḥīḥayn fi'l-ḥadīth*.

Ibn ʿAbd al-Barr al-Numayrī, Abū ʿUmar Yūsuf b. ʿAbd Allāh. *al-Istīʿāb fī maʿrifat al-Aṣḥāb*. Cairo, n.d.

Ibn Bābawayh, Abū Jaʿfar Muḥammad b. ʿAlī al-Ṣadūq. *Kamāl al-dīn wa tamām al-niʿma*, ed. ʿAlī Akbar al-Ghafārī. Qumm, 1362/1983.

Ibn Ḥanbal, Aḥmad b. Muḥammad. *Kitāb al-Zuhd*. Various editions.

Ibn ʿIdhārī al-Marrākushī, Abu'l-ʿAbbās Aḥmad b. Muḥammad. *al-Bayān al-mughrib fī akhbār al-Andalus wa'l-Maghrib*, vol. 1, ed. G. S. Colin and É. Lévi-Provençal. Beirut, 1948.

Ibn Isḥaq, Muḥammad. *Sīrat rasūl Allāh* (The Life of Muhammad), ed. F. Wüstenfeld as *Das Lebens Muhammed* (1st edn Stuttgart, 1864), trans. A. Guillaume. London, 1955; rpr. Karachi, 1997.

Ibn al-Haytham, Abū ʿAbd Allāh Jaʿfar b. Aḥmad al-Aswad. *Kitāb al-munāẓarāt*, ed. and tr. Wilferd Madelung and Paul E. Walker as *The Advent of the Fatimids: A Contemporary Shiʿi Witness*. London, 2000.

Khani, Hamed. 'Bashīriyya', *EIS*, vol. 4, pp. 489–492.

al-Kirmani, Ḥamīd al-Dīn Aḥmad b. ʿAbd Allāh. *al-Maṣābīḥ fī ithbāt al-imāma*, ed. and tr. Paul E. Walker as *Master of the Age: An Islamic Treatise on the Necessity of the Imamate*. London, 2007.

Madelung, W. 'Zayd b. ʿAlī b. al-Ḥusayn', *EI2*.

al-Majdūʿ, Ismāʿīl b. ʿAbd al-Rasūl. *Fahrasat al-kutub wa'l-rasāʾil*, ed. ʿAlī Naqī Munzavī. Tehran, 1966.

al-Majlisī. *Biḥār al-anwār*.

al-Maqrīzī, Taqī al-Dīn Aḥmad b. ʿAlī. *Faḍāʾil ahl al-bayt* (*Kitāb fīhi maʿrifat mā yajību li-āl al-bayt min al-ḥaqq ʿalā man ʿadāhum*, ed. Muḥammad ʿĀshūr. Cairo, 1973.

al-Nuʿmān b. Muḥammad, al-Qāḍī Abū Ḥanīfa. *Daʿāʾim al-Islām*, ed. Asaf A. A. Fyzee. 2 vols, Cairo, 1951–1961. English trans. Asaf A. A. Fyzee, completely revised by Ismail K. Poonawala as *The Pillars of Islam*. 2 vols, New Delhi, 2002–2004.

—. *Iftitāḥ al-daʿwa wa ibtidāʾ al-dawla*, ed. Wadād Qāḍī. Beirut, 1970; ed. Farhat Dachraoui. Tunis, 1975; English trans. *Founding of the Fatimid State: The Rise of an Early Islamic Empire*, tr. H. Haji. London, 2006.

—. *Sharḥ al-akhbār fī faḍāʾil al-aʾimma al-aṭhār*, 3 vols. Beirut, 1994.

Poonawala, Ismail K. *Biobibliography of Ismāʿīlī Literature*. Malibu, CA, 1977.

Pregill, Michael. 'Measure for Measure: Prophetic History, Qur'anic Exegesis, and Anti-Sunnī Polemic in a Fāṭimid Propaganda Work (BL Or. 8419)', *Journal of Qur'anic Studies*, 16 (2014), pp. 20–57.

Reynolds, G. S. 'The Muslim Jesus: Dead or Alive?', *Bulletin of the School of Oriental and African Studies*, 72 (2009), pp. 237–258.

Steingass, F. *A Comprehensive Persian-English Dictionary*. London, 1892, rpr., 1977.

Vacca, V. 'Usāma b. Zayd', *EI2*.

Watt, W. M. *Muhammad at Medina*. Oxford, 1956.

—. *Muhammad at Mecca*. Oxford, 1953.

—. 'ʿAbd al-Muṭṭalib b. Hāshim', *EI2*.

—. 'Hāshim b. ʿAbd al-Manāf', *EI2*.

—. 'al-Ḥudaybiya', *EI2*.

Index

Aaron, 5–6, 29, 30–1, 32, 34, 35, 39
al-ʿAbbās, 22, 41–2
ʿAbd Allāh b. ʿUmar, 17
ʿAbd al-Muṭṭalib, 20, 64
ʿAbd al-Raḥmān b. Muljam, 55
ʿAbd Shams, 18
Abel, 99
ablutions, ritual, 92–3
Abraham, 31, 99
Abū ʿAbd Allāh, 4, 5, 9, 81
Abū ʿAbd Allāh al-Shīʿī, 1, 2, 3, 4
Abū ʿAbd Allāh Muḥammad
 b. Karrām, 58n74
Abū Bakr, 41–2
Abū Dharr al-Ghifārī, 40
Abū Lahab, 28
Abū Sufyān b. Ḥarb, 23
Abu'l-ʿAbbās, 1–2, 3
Abu'l-ʿAbbās Muḥammad, 9, 10–12
Abu'l-ʿĀdiya, 54–5, 57n73
Abu'l-Ḥasan al-Baghdādī, 9, 79–80
Adam, 95
Advent of the Fatimids: A Contemporary Shiʿi Witness, The, 1
ahl al-bayt, 4
 importance, 6
aim, 5
ʿĀʾisha, 35, 48n57, 51, 52n65, 64n85,
ʿAlī b. Abī Ṭālib, 2, 4, 5, 59
 Bashīriyya and, 73–4
 consolation of for the Prophet, 37–8
 denial of succession, 6, 41–2
 first male believer, 28–9
 as God's plot, 36–7
 Muhammad appoints successor, 32–4
 Muhammad on, 76–7
 relationship with Muhammad, 5–6
 sells armour, 88
 the sword of God, 75–6
alms, 10–2, 82, 89–90
 payments, 92–5, 98–9, 100–1
 payments with good will, 96
 payments with malice, 95–6
 recipients, 12, 90–2, 94
ʿAmmār b. Yāsir, 40n53, 59
ʿAmr b. ʿAuf b. Ṭalḥa al-Muzanī, 15–6
angels, 38, 95
al-Aqraʿ b. Ḥābis al-Tamīmī, 24–5
audience, 5, 8, 12
authorities, hierarchy of, 11
authorship, 1, 2–3, 6–7, 8–9

Baḥīrā, 23
Bashīriyya, the, 73–4
BL OR4819, 3–8
 aim, 5
 audience, 5–6
 authorship, 2, 4, 6–7
 characteristics, 5
 date, 4–5
 editions, 13
 historical incidents, 5–6
 manuscript, 2
 message, 5
 polemical purpose, 4
blessedness, 89–90
British Library, 2

Cain, 99
charity, 89–90
Christians, 16, 17, 65–6
 dietary laws, 49
 feast days, 47–8
 Jacobites, 73
 Melkites, 73–4

neglect of the Book of God, 42–3, 45, 47–8
Confederates, Battle of the, 35–8
confidential discourse, the, 89
creation, 71

David, 41, 42, 47
debt, 91
dietary laws, 48–9, 86–7
disunity, warning against, 15
dues, 10–2

emancipation, 84–5
end of time, the, 57
Esau, 18
evil, 53–5
rejection of, 70
evil people, 69–70
Executors, 104

factions, 66
faith, 16, 39
fasting, 100–1
Fāṭima, 29–30, 75
Fatimid caliphate, 1, 3
fees, 10–2
finery, 24
fiṭra, 100–1
Flood, the, 39–40
Foundation, the, 84, 92, 94, 103

Gabriel, 16, 38, 65
God
censure of Israelites, 70–1
covenant with, 49–50, 61–3
eyes of, 83–4
gift of knowledge, 22–3
gift of water, 21–2
law of, 17–8
love of, 79–80
on messengers, 19–21
obligatory commands, 59
oneness, 82
plot, 36–7
promise of, 53, 68–9
proofs regarding his brother, 72
and property, 88–9
punishments with hellfire, 53–6
to the Quraysh, 21
restraint of, 58
support for Muhammad, 62–3
testing of Abraham, 31
testing of Muhammad, 31–2
testing of the Israelites, 26, 58–9
tries the people, 81–2
on unbelievers, 55
vengeance, 21
God's guardian, 81, 81–2, 83, 88, 93–4, 98
goodness, 82
Gospels, the, 16, 42–3
guarded books, the, 80

Ḥabīb b. ʿAbd Allāh, 26
ḥadīth, 5, 16–7, 43, 44n55, 56, 57
al-Ḥajjāj b. Yūsuf, 54–5
happiness, 55
Ḥarūriyya, 66
al-Ḥasan, 29, 30, 50, 75
Hāshim b. ʿAbd al-Manāf, 18
Ḥātim al-Aṣamm, 58n74
hellfire, 53–6
al-Ḥudaybiyya, truce of, 60
al-Ḥusayn, 29, 30, 50, 66, 75
Ḥudhayfa b. al-Yamān, 16–7, 43

Ibn ʿAbbās, 38
Ibn al-Haytham, 1, 3
Ibn ʿIdhārī al-Marrākushī, 4
Ibn Muljam, 54–5
idols, 34–5, 67, 86
Idrīs b. Idrīs, 67
Imams, 4, 90, 92, 94, 97, 101–2, 103, 104
initiation, 85–6
interpretive sciences, training in, 91
Ismāʿīl, 31
Ismaili caliphate, 1
Ismaili doctrinal writings, 5

Ismaili manuscript tradition, 2
Israel, family of, 18
Israelites, 53, 65–6
  break their covenant, 49
  censure, 70–1
  covenant, 60–2
  and the Golden Calf, 38–9
  imitation of, 41
  kings, 60
  monasticism, 56
  oaths of allegiance, 45–6
  profligates, 66
  rule of the Book, 67
  Sabbath, 58–9
  testing of, 26, 58–9
  unbelievers, 25
  in the wilderness, 21–2, 23

Jacob, 18
Jaʿfar al-Ṣādiq, 80–1, 98–9
Jaʿfar b. Abī Ṭālib, 29
Jersualem, 37
Jesus, son of Mary, 20, 20–1, 22–3, 37, 47, 73, 74, 76
Jews, 16, 17–8, 72, 77
  feast days, 47–8
  and Jesus, 74
  neglect of the Book of God, 42–8, 53
  oaths of allegiance, 45–6
  rejection of Muhammad, 74–5
jihad, 6, 69, 81
Joseph, shirt of, 36
Journal of Qur'anic Studies, 4

Karbalā, Battle of, 39n51
Keys to Grace, The, 8–12
  audience, 8, 12
  authorship, 8–9
  compiler, 10
  date, 10
  editions, 13
  extraneous material, 8
  language, 8, 12
  and the Mahdī, 10
  misattribution, 8
  preservation, 1–2
  principal message, 12
  recipient, 9
  themes, 10–2
Khadīja, 28–9
Khālid b. al-Walīd, 75
knowledge, gift of, 22–3
Kutāma Berbers, 4

law, of God, 17–8
luxuries, 24

maʾdhūn, 91
al-Mahdī, Caliph, 10
Mahdī, the, 5, 10, 39, 53
  rise of, 6–7
al-Majdūʿ, 8
mankind, creation of, 71
Mary, mother of Jesus, 74
Maryam, 29, 30
Mecca, 28
Medina, 27, 28
messengers, God on, 19–21
Miqdād Aswād al-Kindī, 40
miracles, 19, 20
modesty, 64
monasticism, 56–8
Moses, 5–6, 18–9, 21, 23, 26–7, 28, 29
  and Aaron, 30–1, 32, 34, 35
  birth of, 67–8
  and the Golden Calf, 38–9
  and oaths of allegiance, 45–6
  proposes fight for Jerusalem, 37
  purification, 99
  questioning of, 34
  and Samaritan, 61
  staff, 35
  war against, 69
  words distorted, 40–1
mosques, 45
Mount Sinai, 40–1, 45–6
Muʿādh b. Jabal, 57, 58n74
Mubayyiḍa, 70

Muhammad, 15–6
 on ʿAlī, 76–7
 breaks canine tooth, 27–8
 confidential discourse with, 89
 covenant of Companions, 46–7
 covenant, 49–50, 61–3
 death of, 38
 family of, 28–31
 fear of family ascendency, 69
 flees Mecca, 28
 gift of knowledge, 22–3
 on idols, 34–5
 Jews rejection of, 74–5
 in Medina, 27
 miracle of water, 21–2
 miracles, 5, 19, 20
 and the miserable person, 91–2
 oppressors of family, 52–3
 and the poisoned lamb, 22
 and prayer, 93
 predicts victory, 23–4
 prediction of ʿAmmār being killed, 59
 proofs regarding his brother, 36–7
 relationship with ʿAlī, 5–6
 revelation, 16–7
 ridiculed, 21
 role as prophet, 5
 sacrifice, 37
 on sin, 45
 sons of family killed, 68
 and status, 25
 succession, 32–4, 38–42, 60
 suffering, 18–9
 support for, 62–3
 testing of, 31–2
 warnings against seditions, 40
 on wine, 48–9
 wives, 64
 words distorted, 41
Muhtadī Muṣṭafā Ghālib, 8
al-Muʿizz, Caliph, 8
Murjiʾa, the, 49, 53–4, 65
al-Mustawrid b. Shaddād, 16
Muʿtazila, the, 59

al-Nawwās b. Samʿān, 51–2
Nebuchadnezzar, 76–7
newborn, the, 101
Night of the Cave, 36–7
Noah, 24, 25, 39–40

obligation, 11, 93–4, 102, 105
offerings, 87–8
ordeals, 81–2
orphans, 101

paradise, 56
pilgrimage, the, 96–7
 rituals of, 102–4
Poonawala, Ismail, 8
poverty, 83
prayer, 51
 actions of, 95
 grades of, 93
Pregill, Michael, 3–4
profligates, 66–7
Proof, the, 84, 92, 95, 101–2, 103
property, 82–3, 88–9
Prophets, killing of offspring, 72–3
purification, 83, 87, 89–90, 92–3, 94, 96–7, 105
 and alms giving, 98–9
 the verse of, 50–2
 with water, 103

al-Qāḍī al-Nuʿmān, 2, 4, 8
qiṣaṣ al-anbiyāʾ (stories of the prophets), 2, 4
Qudār b. Sālif, 55
Quraysh, the, 19, 20–1, 23–4, 25–6, 28, 35–8

recipients, alms, 12, 90–2, 94
redemption, 104
Rejecters, the, 69, 70
religious hierarchy, 5, 12

Ṣafrāʾ bint Shuʿayb, 63–4
Sabbath, the, 58–9
sacrifices, 96n11, 99–100, 101–2, 104–5
saints, 90
Salmān al-Fārisī, 40
salvation, ship of, 40
Samaritans, 61
Satan, 62–3
seditions, 40
self-sufficient, the, 90
Shaqīq al-Balkhī, 58n74
Shiʿa, 73
Silyana, 80
sin, 45
slaves, emancipation, 84–5
sorcery, 18–9, 20, 26, 35
sources, 1–3
Speaker, the, 84, 90, 92, 94, 103
spiritual benefit, 10
status, 25
Sudayr al-Ṣayrafī al-Kūfī, 98–9
Sunni Muslims, 4–5, 66

testing, 89, 99–100
Torah, the, 16, 42–8, 96

ʿUbayd Allāh b. Ziyād, 54–5, 61n78
Uhud, Battle of, 27n32
ʿUmar b. Saʿd, 54–5
Umayyad caliphate, 65, 66–7
Umm Maʿbad al-Khuzāʿiyya, 27
Umm Salama, 51, 75–6
unbelievers, 19, 20–1, 25–6, 28, 55
ʿUsāma b. Zayd, 33
ʿUthmān b. ʿAffān, 75, 76
ʿUyayna b. Ḥiṣn al-Fazārī, 24–5

wealth, 83, 89–90, 98
wine, 48–9
women, 46–7
  prayer, 95
  purification, 51–2
  testing, 85
worldly life, 24

Yazīd b. Muʿāwiya, 54–5
Yūshaʿ b. Nūn, 63–4

Zakariyāʾ, 30
Zayd b. ʿAlī, 66–7
al-Zubayr b. al-ʿAwwām, 63
Zaynab bt al-Ḥārith, 22n22

رسالة بدون عنوان منسوب إلى
أبي عبد الله الشيعي
(مخطوطة ٨٤١٩ OR المكتبة البريطانية)

رسالة بدون عنوان منسوب إلى أبي عبد الله الشيعي

..."(﴿يَاَهْلَ الْكِتٰبِ قَدْ جَآءَكُمْ رَسُوْلُنَا يُبَيِّنُ لَكُمْ عَلٰى فَتْرَةٍ مِّنَ الرُّسُلِ اَنْ تَقُوْلُوْا مَا جَآءَنَا) مِنْ بَشِيْرٍ وَّلَا نَذِيْرٍفَقَدْ جَآءَكُمْ بَشِيْرٌ وَّنَذِيْرٌ وَاللّٰهُ عَلٰى كُلِّ شَيْءٍ قَدِيْرٌ﴾ [المائدة ٥: ١٩] فعمُوا بعد البيان، وجحدوا بعد الإيقان، واختلفوا بعد البيّنات والهُدَى بغيًا منهم وحسدًا من عند أنفسهم، كما ذكر الله سبحانه عن الأمم الماضية والقرون الخالية ﴿فَمَا اخْتَلَفُوْٓا اِلَّا مِنْ بَعْدِ مَا جَآءَهُمُ الْعِلْمُ بَغْيًا بَيْنَهُمْ﴾ [الجاثية ٤٥: ١٧] وقال ﴿يُرِيْدُ اللّٰهُ لِيُبَيِّنَ لَكُمْ وَيَهْدِيَكُمْ سُنَنَ الَّذِيْنَ مِنْ قَبْلِكُمْ﴾ [النساء ٤: ٢٦] وقال: ﴿وَلَا تَكُوْنُوْا كَالَّذِيْنَ تَفَرَّقُوْا وَاخْتَلَفُوْا مِنْ بَعْدِ مَا جَآتهُمُ[1] الْبَيِّنٰتُ﴾ [آل عمران ٣: ١٠٥] وقال ﴿مَا[2] كَانَ اللّٰهُ لِيُضِلَّ [b1] قَوْمًا بَعْدَ اِذْ هَدٰىهُمْ حَتّٰى يُبَيِّنَ لَهُمْ مَا يَتَّقُوْنَ﴾ [التوبة ٩: ١١٥] فأنذر رسولُ الله صلى الله عليه وسلم وآله أمّته الفُرقة والاختلاف وأعلمهم أنهم سيركبون ما ركبت الأمم الذين من قبلهم، فقال عليه وعلى آله أفضل السلام: لتركبَنّ سنّة بني إسرائيل حَذْوَ النعل بالنعل والقُذّة بالقُذّة، فقال عمرو بن عوف

[1] جاءتهم: في المصحف العثماني: جاءهم.

[2] ما: في المصحف العثماني: وما.

بن طلحة المُزَني: كنا قاعدين عند رسول الله صلى الله عليه وآله في مسجده، فجاءه جبريل عليه السلام بالوحي، فتغشّى رداءه،[٣] فمكث طويلًا، ثمّ سرى عنه فكشف رداءه، فإذا هو يعرق [a٢] عرقًا شديدًا، وإذا هو قابضٌ على شيء، فقال: أيّكم يعرف ما يخرج من النخل؟ قالت له الأنصار: يا رسول الله بأبينا أنت وأمّنا ليس شيء من النخل إلّا نحن نعرفه، نحن أصحاب النخل، ثمّ فتح يده فإذا فيها نوى، فقال: ما هذا؟ فقالوا: يا رسول الله هذا نوى، قال: نوى أيّ شيء؟ قالوا: سنه، قال: صدقتم، جاءكم جبريل عليه السلام يتعاهد دينكم لتسلكنّ سُبل الذين قبلكم حَذْوَ النعل بالنعل ولتأخذُنّ أخذهم إن شبر فشبر وإن ذراع فذراع [b٢] وإن باع فباع حتّى إن دخلوا بجحر ضبّ دخلتم فيه.

وروى عُبادة بن الصامت قال: كيف فرّت[٤] قرّاؤكم وعلماؤكم إلي رؤوس الجبال خشية أن يُقتَلوا بكم؟ قالوا: نعم، قال: أولم تكن التوراة في اليهود فضيّعوها والإنجيل في النصارى فضيّعوه؟ إنما الشرّ يتبع بعضه بعضًا. وقال المستورد بن شدّاد: قال رسول الله صلى الله عليه وآله: لا تذرُ هذه الأمة من سُنن الأوّلين حتّى قاد هذه الإبهام التي تلتها، وقال حُذيفة بن اليَمان: لا يكون في بني إسرائيل شيء [a٣] إلّا وكان فيكم

---

[٣] رداءه: رداؤه، الأصل.

[٤] .فرّت: قرب، الاصل.

مثله، فقال رجل: نكون قردة وخنازير؟ قال: وما يريبك[٥] من ذلك لا أمّ لك؟ وفي حديث آخر عنه أنه قال: نِعم الإخوة لكم بنو إسرائيل كلّ حلوٍ لكم وكلّ مرّ لهم، وقال عبد الله بن عمر: قال رسول الله صلى الله عليه وآله: لتسلكنّ سنن الذين من قبلكم شبرًا لشبر وذراعًا لذراع حتى لو دخلوا جحر ضبّ لتبعتموهم، قالوا: يا رسول الله مِن اليهود والنصارى؟ قال: من اليهود والنصارى. قال الله سبحانه وله الحمد ﴿الٓمٓ أَحَسِبَ النَّاسُ أَنْ يُتْرَكُوٓا [b٣] أَنْ يَقُولُوٓا ءَامَنَّا وَهُمْ لَا يُفْتَنُونَ وَلَقَدْ فَتَنَّا الَّذِينَ مِنْ قَبْلِهِمْ فَلَيَعْلَمَنَّ اللَّهُ الَّذِينَ صَدَقُوا وَلَيَعْلَمَنَّ الْكَٰذِبِينَ﴾ [العنكبوت ٢٩: ١-٣] في أيمانهم، ثمّ قال الله تعالى ﴿سُنَّةَ اللَّهِ الَّتِي قَدْ خَلَتْ مِنْ قَبْلُ وَلَنْ تَجِدَ لِسُنَّةِ اللَّهِ تَبْدِيلًا﴾ [الفتح ٤٨: ٢٣] و﴿لَنْ تَجِدَ لِسُنَّتِ اللَّهِ تَحْوِيلًا﴾ [فاطر ٣٥: ٤٣] وقال عزّ وجلّ ﴿فَاسْتَمْتَعُوا بِخَلَٰقِهِمْ كَمَا اسْتَمْتَعَ الَّذِينَ مِنْ قَبْلِكُمْ بِخَلَٰقِهِمْ[٦] وَخُضْتُمْ كَالَّذِي خَاضُوٓا﴾ [التوبة ٩: ٦٩] وقال جل ذكره: ﴿كُبِتُوا كَمَا كُبِتَ الَّذِينَ مِنْ قَبْلِهِمْ﴾ [المجادلة ٥٨: ٥] وقال تعالى ﴿كَذَٰلِكَ قَالَ الَّذِينَ مِنْ قَبْلِهِمْ مِثْلَ قَوْلِهِمْ تَشَٰبَهَتْ قُلُوبُهُمْ﴾ [البقرة ٢: ١١٨].

---

[٥] يريبك: يرابك، الأصل.

[٦] بخلاقهم: خلاقهم، الأصل.

[a٤] لقد كان يعقوب وعيصا تؤمين، فعصى الله عيصا في يعقوب إسرائيل[٧] وبغى عليه، فبارك الله على نسل إسرائيل وجعل منهم الأنبياء والأصفياء، كذلك هاشم وعبد شمس تؤمين، فعصى أميّة في هاشم مُضر، فبارك الله في بني هاشم، فجعل منهم سيّد الأنبياء وخاتم الأوصياء، وكان اسم إسرائيل يعقوب، فلما سار بالليل سمّي إسرائيل، فغلب اسمه حتّى لو قيل: بني يعقوب، لم يُدْرَ إلا أن يقال: بنو إسرائيل، كذلك كان اسم هاشم عمرًا، فلما هشم الثريد لقومه [B٤] سمّي هاشمًا، فغلب هاشم حتّى لو قيل: بني عمرو، لا[٨] يدرى حتى أن يقال بنو هاشم، حَذْوَ النعل بالنعل.

ولقد لقي رسول الله صلى الله عليه وآله من كفّار قومه ما لقيت الرسل من كفّار قومهم من التكذيب والرمي بالسحر والبهتان، فإنّ فرعون وملأه قالوا لموسى ﴿مَهمَا تَأتِنَا بِهِۦ مِنۡ ءَايَةٍ لِتَسۡحَرَنَا بِهَا فَمَا نَحۡنُ لَكَ بِمُؤۡمِنِينَ﴾ [الأعراف ٧: ١٣٢] وقال ﴿قَالَ إِن كُنتَ جِئۡتَ بِـَٔايَةٍ فَأۡتِ بِهَآ إِن كُنتَ مِنَ ٱلصَّٰدِقِينَ فَأَلۡقَىٰ عَصَاهُ فَإِذَا هِيَ ثُعۡبَانٌ مُّبِينٌ وَنَزَعَ يَدَهُۥ فَإِذَا هِيَ بَيۡضَآءُ لِلنَّٰظِرِينَ﴾ [الأعراف ٧: ١٠٦-١٠٨] ثمّ قال الملأ

[٧] إسرائيل: بهيا(؟)، الأصل.

[٨] لا: ولا، الأصل.

﴿ اِنَّ هٰذَا [a٥] لَسٰحِرٌ[٩] عَلِيْمٌ ﴾ [الأعراف ٧: ١٠٩] و ﴿قَالُوْا هٰذَا سِحْرٌ مُبِيْنٌ﴾ [النمل ٢٧: ١٣] كذلك قالت كفرة قريش للنبيّ صلى الله عليه وآله: شقّ لنا هذا القمر، فدعا ربّه فانشقّ القمر بنصفين، فلمّا رأوه قالوا: سحر محمد القمر، قال الله تبارك وتعالى ﴿اِقْتَرَبَتِ السَّاعَةُ وَانْشَقَّ الْقَمَرُ وَاِنْ يَّرَوْا اٰيَةً يُّعْرِضُوْا وَيَقُوْلُوْا سِحْرٌ مُّسْتَمِرٌّ﴾ [القمر ٥٤: ١-٢] وقال معرّفًا لنبيّه صلّى الله عليه وآله وسلّم: ﴿وَلَقَدْ كُذِّبَتْ[١٠] رُسُلٌ مِّنْ قَبْلِكَ فَصَبَرُوْا عَلٰى مَا كُذِّبُوْا وَاُوْذُوْا حَتّٰى اَتٰىهُمْ نَصْرُنَا﴾ [الأنعام ٦: ٣٤] ﴿وَقَالُوْا مَالِ هٰذَا الرَّسُوْلِ يَاْكُلُ الطَّعَامَ وَيَمْشِيْ فِى الْاَسْوَاقِ﴾ [الفرقان ٢٥: ٧] وقال الله جلّ ثناؤه ﴿وَمَآ اَرْسَلْنَا قَبْلَكَ مِنَ الْمُرْسَلِيْنَ اِلَّآ اِنَّهُمْ [b٥] لَيَاْكُلُوْنَ الطَّعَامَ وَيَمْشُوْنَ فِى الْاَسْوَاقِ﴾ [الفرقان ٢٥: ٢٠] ثمّ قال عزّ وجلّ ﴿ مَا يُقَالُ لَكَ اِلَّا مَا قَدْ قِيْلَ لِلرُّسُلِ مِنْ قَبْلِكَ﴾ [فصلت ٤١: ٤٣] وقال سبحانه: ﴿وَمَا مَنَعَ النَّاسَ اَنْ يُّؤْمِنُوْٓا اِذْ جَاۤءَهُمُ الْهُدٰى وَيَسْتَغْفِرُوْا رَبَّهُمْ اِلَّآ اَنْ تَاْتِيَهُمْ سُنَّةُ الْاَوَّلِيْنَ اَوْ يَاْتِيَهُمُ الْعَذَابُ قُبُلًا﴾ [الكهف ١٨: ٥٥] وقال تعالى ﴿وَلَوْ نَزَّلْنَا عَلَيْكَ كِتٰبًا فِيْ قِرْطَاسٍ فَلَمَسُوْهُ بِاَيْدِيْهِمْ لَقَالَ الَّذِيْنَ كَفَرُوْٓا اِنْ هٰذَآ اِلَّا سِحْرٌ مُّبِيْنٌ﴾ [الأنعام ٦: ٧].

---

[٩] لساحر: ساحر، الأصل.

[١٠] كذّبت: كذّب، الأصل.

قال الله سبحانه ﴿وَاِذۡ قَالَ عِيۡسَى ابۡنُ مَرۡيَمَ يٰبَنِىۡۤ اِسۡرَآءِيۡلَ اِنِّىۡ رَسُوۡلُ اللّٰهِ اِلَيۡكُمۡ مُّصَدِّقًا لِّمَا بَيۡنَ يَدَىَّ مِنَ التَّوۡرٰىةِ وَمُبَشِّرًا ۢ بِرَسُوۡلٍ يَّاۡتِىۡ مِنۡۢ بَعۡدِى اسۡمُهٗۤ اَحۡمَدُ‌ فَلَمَّا [a٦] جَآءَهُمۡ بِالۡبَيِّنٰتِ قَالُوۡا هٰذَا سِحۡرٌ مُّبِيۡنٌ﴾ [الصف ٦١: ٦] وإن رسول الله صلّى الله عليه وآله وسلّم قال لبني عبد المطّلب يوم أُنزل عليه ﴿وَاَنۡذِرۡ عَشِيۡرَتَكَ الۡاَقۡرَبِيۡنَ﴾ [الشعراء ٢٦: ٢١٤] يا بني عبد المطّلب إني أتيتكم بآيات بيّنات أتيتكم بعزّ الدين وشرف الآخرة، فكونوا في هذا الأمر رؤساء ولا تكونوا أذنابًا، فلمّا جاءهم بالبيّنات من إطعام أربعين رجُلًا من رجْل شاة وصاع من شعير وعُسّ من لبن، وكان الرجل منهم يأكل الجذع ويشرب الفرق، فقالوا: لقد سحركم صاحبكم، ثمّ تضاحكوا وقالوا لأبي طالب [b٦]: أمَركَ أن تسمع وتطيع لهذا الغلام، كفرعون وملئه، قال الله عزّ وجلّ ﴿فَلَمَّا جَآءَهُمۡ بِاٰيٰتِنَاۤ اِذَا هُمۡ مِّنۡهَا يَضۡحَكُوۡنَ﴾ [الزخرف ٤٣: ٤٧] وقال سبحانه لا شريك له ﴿وَلَـقَدِ اسۡتُهۡزِئَ بِرُسُلٍ مِّنۡ قَبۡلِكَ فَحَاقَ بِالَّذِيۡنَ سَخِرُوۡا مِنۡهُمۡ مَّا كَانُوۡا بِهٖ يَسۡتَهۡزِءُوۡنَ﴾ [الأنبياء ٢١: ٤١] وقالت بنو إسرائيل لعيسى بن مريم: سل ربّك ﴿اَنۡ يُّنَزِّلَ عَلَيۡنَا مَآئِدَةً مِّنَ السَّمَآءِ﴾ [المائدة ٥: ١١٢]، كذلك قالت كفرة قريش لرسول الله صلى الله عليه وآله اسأل ربّك يا محمد أن يجعل لنا هذا الصفا ذهبًا، ولقد استهزأ كفّار [a٧] قريش برسول الله صلى الله عليه وآله ككفّار من كان قبلهم، قال الله جلّ وعزّ ﴿وَاِذَا رَاَوۡكَ اِنۡ يَّتَّخِذُوۡنَكَ اِلَّا هُزُوًا اَهٰذَا الَّذِىۡ بَعَثَ اللّٰهُ رَسُوۡلًا

اِنْ كَادَ لَيُضِلُّنَا عَنْ اٰلِهَتِنَا لَوْ لَآ اَنْ صَبَرْنَا عَلَيْهَا﴾ [الفرقان ٢٥: ٤١-٤٢] قال الله عزّ وجلّ لكفّار قريش ﴿وَلَقَدْ اَهْلَكْنَآ اَشْيَاعَكُمْ فَهَلْ مِنْ مُدَّكِرٍ﴾ [القمر ٥٤: ٥١] ثمّ ذكر القرون الأولى ممن كذّب الرسل فأنزل بهم من عذابه ونقمته وبأسه حتى ذكر آل فرعون فقال ﴿وَلَقَدْ جَآءَ اٰلَ فِرْعَوْنَ النُّذُرُ كَذَّبُوْا بِاٰيٰتِنَا كُلِّهَا فَاَخَذْنٰهُمْ اَخْذَ [b٧] عَزِيْزٍ مُقْتَدِرٍ﴾ [القمر ٥٤: ٤١-٤٢] ثمّ قال ﴿اَكُفَّارُكُمْ خَيْرٌ مِنْ اُولٰٓئِكُمْ اَمْ لَكُمْ بَرَآءَةٌ فِى الزُّبُرِ﴾ [القمر ٥٤: ٤٣] ولقد دعا رسول الله صلى الله عليه وآله على أهل مكّة فقال: اللهمّ سنين كسني يوسف، فكانوا يأكلون العظام والجيف.

وإن الله سبحانه وتعالى لما ابتلى بني إسرائيل في التيه لمعصيتهم استسقى بنو إسرائيل وكان [موسى] يحمل معه حجرًا، قال الله عزّ وجلّ ﴿فَقُلْنَا اضْرِب بِّعَصَاكَ الْحَجَرَ فَانْفَجَرَتْ مِنْهُ اثْنَتَا عَشْرَةَ عَيْنًا﴾ [البقرة ٢: ٦٠] لاثنتى عشرة قبيلة عطيّة من الله سبحانه ونعمة عظيمة [a٨] وإكرامًا وزيادة في برهان نبوّته، كذلك عطش أصحاب رسول الله صلى الله عليه وآله في بعض غزواتهم ونفد ماؤهم، فاستسقوا رسول الله صلى الله عليه وآله، فوجد ماءً قليلًا في جلدة رجل، فملأ فاه ماءً ومجّ فيها، ثمّ سقى منها عسكرًا عظيمًا عطيّةً من الله تعالى ونعمةً وإكرامًا وزيادةً في برهان نبوّته، فأراهم بركة لعابه وريقه حَذْوَ النعل بالنعل.

وإن الله تعالى أعطى روحه وكلمته لعيسى أن كان يحيي الموتى وينبئهم بما يأكلون [b٨] وما يدّخرون في بيوتهم، وإن الله تعالى كذلك أعطى نبيّه محمّدًا صلى الله عليه وآله العلم، فرنّت بين يديه جذعة مشوية على الذعف (كذا) فقالت: لا تأكل منّي يا محمد فإني مسمومة، وتفدّت الأسارى بما كانوا ادّخروه في بيوتهم، فقال عليه السلام لعمّه العباس: أين الدنانير التي أخفيتها[١١] عند أمّ الفضل؟ فزاد في برهان نبوّته على برهان نبوّة عيسى أن أطلعه الله على الضمائر ولم يطلع الله تعالى عيسى على الضمائر إلا بما كانوا يأكلون وما كانوا يدّخرون في بيوتهم، فأطلع الله [a٩] تعالى سيّد رسله على الضمائر يوم أتاه أبو سفيان بن حرب مسلّمًا عليه، فلما أن بصر به رسول الله صلى الله عليه وآله قال في نفسه: لأعادينّ هذا الرجل، فقال له عليه السلام: إذاً بحربك؟ فقال: أشهد أنّك رسول الله حقًا. وكما[١٢] كانت بنو إسرائيل في التيه لا أكنان لهم تُظلّهم من حرّ الشمس الذي لا قوام معه لذي نفس إلا بكنّ يكنّه فمنّ الله عليهم من الأكنان بما جعله الله عزّ وجلّ آية وحجّة وزيادة في البرهان ومكرمة وشرفًا لهم في الذكر [b٩]، ظلّل الله لنبيّه صلى الله عليه يوم رجعت زُفّته لخديجة من الشام، فاطّلع عليهم بحيرا فرأى سحابة تُظلّهم،

---

[١١] التي أخفيتها: قراءة تقديرية، ونص الأصل ممحو.

[١٢] وكما: ولما، الأصل.

فدعاهم إلى طعامه، فخلّفوا رسول الله صلّى الله عليه في الرحل، فوقفت السحابة تظلّه، فدعاه فسارت السحابة معه حيث سار، جعلها الله عزّ وجلّ ظلًّا ظليلًا مكرمةً وشرفًا وأوّلَ برهان لنبيّه صلى الله عليه وآله.

وإن بني إسرائيل أطيروا بموسى ومن معه وقالوا: أوذينا من قَبل أن تأتينا ومن بعدما جئتنا، قال: عسى ربّكم أن يُهلك عدوّكم [١٠a] ويستخلفكم في الأرض، كذلك قالت قريش لرسول الله صلى الله عليه وآله: قد قامت حربنا بك على ساق، فقال: ليُتمّنّ الله هذا الأمر وليُظهرني على الدين كلّه ولو كره المشركون، ولتُنفَقنّ كنوز كسرى وقيصر في سبيل الله، ولو لم يبقَ من الدنيا إلا يوم واحد لطوّل الله عزّ وجلّ ذلك اليوم حتّى يُملكها رجلًا من عترتي، فيملأ الأرض قسطًا وعدلًا كما مُلئت جَوْرًا وظلمًا، وليفتحنّ الله عليه مشارق الأرض ومغاربها، فقالت [١٠b] المنافقون والذين في قلوبهم زيغ: ما وعدَنا الله ورسوله إلا غرورًا، يزعم محمّد أنه يملك مشارق الأرض ومغاربها وهو يخندق على نفسه، فأنزل الله عزّ وجلّ ﴿وَكَذَّبَ بِهِۦ قَوۡمُكَ وَهُوَ ٱلۡحَقُّ﴾ [الأنعام ٦: ٦٦].

وإن فرعون قال لقومه الذين يريدون زينة الحياة الدنيا ﴿أَمۡ أَنَا۠ خَيۡرٌ مِّنۡ هَٰذَا ٱلَّذِي هُوَ مَهِينٌ وَلَا يَكَادُ يُبِينُ فَلَوۡلَآ أُلۡقِيَ عَلَيۡهِ أَسۡوِرَةٌ[١٣] مِّن ذَهَبٍ أَوۡ جَآءَ مَعَهُ ٱلۡمَلَٰٓئِكَةُ مُقۡتَرِنِينَ فَٱسۡتَخَفَّ قَوۡمَهُۥ فَأَطَاعُوهُۚ إِنَّهُمۡ

---

١٣ أسْورة: اساورة، الأصل.

كَانُوا قَوۡمًا فٰسِقِيۡنَ﴾ [الزخرف ٤٣: ٥٢-٥٤] كذلك قال أحد[١٤] فراعنة [a١١] قريش لأتباعه الذين أُترفوا في الدنيا يوم قال رسول الله صلى الله عليه وآله: سألتُ ربّي مواخاة عليّ عليه السلام وموازرته، فأعطاني، فقال: لَشنّة فيها تمر أحبّ إليّ مما سأل محمّد صلى الله عليه وآله ربّه عزّ وجلّ، ألا سأل ملكًا يعضده أو كنزًا يُنفقه؟ فأنزل الله عزّ وجلّ ﴿فَلَعَلَّكَ تَارِكٌۢ بَعۡضَ مَا يُوۡحٰۤى اِلَيۡكَ وَضَآئِقٌۢ بِهٖ صَدۡرُكَ اَنۡ يَّقُوۡلُوۡا لَوۡلَاۤ اُنۡزِلَ[١٥] عَلَيۡهِ كَنۡزٌ اَوۡ جَآءَ مَعَهٗ مَلَكٌ ؕ اِنَّمَاۤ اَنۡتَ نَذِيۡرٌ﴾ [هود ١١: ١٢] حَذْوَ النعل بالنعل.

وقالوا لنوح عليه السلام [b١١] ﴿أَنُؤۡمِنُ بك[١٦] وَاتَّبَعَكَ الۡاَرۡذَلُوۡنَ قَالَ وَمَا عِلۡمِىۡ بِمَا كَانُوۡا يَعۡمَلُوۡنَ اِنۡ حِسَابُهُمۡ اِلَّا عَلٰى رَبِّىۡ لَوۡ تَشۡعُرُوۡنَ وَمَاۤ اَنَا بِطَارِدِ الۡمُؤۡمِنِيۡنَ﴾ [الشعراء ٢٦: ١١١-١١٤] كذلك جاء الأقرع بن حابس التّميمي وعُيينة بن حصن الفزاري فوجدا رسول الله صلى الله عليه وسلم قاعدًا مع عمّار وخبّاب وصُهيب في ناس[١٧]

---

[١٤] قال أحد: قالت، الأصل.

[١٥] أنزل: نزل، الأصل.

[١٦] بها: وفي المصحف العثماني لك.

[١٧] ناس: الناس، الأصل.

من الضعفاء من المؤمنين، فلما رأوهم استحقروهم وقالوا: ما يمنعنا من الجلوس معك إلا هؤلاء الأعبد وريح جبابهم، فنحّ هؤلاء عنك واجعل لنا منك مجلسًا تعرف لنا العرب القرب [a١٢] منك، فإن وفود العرب ستأتيك فنستحيي أن ترانا العرب مع هؤلاء الأعبد، فإذا نحن جئناك فأقمهم عنا، فإذا نحن قمنا فاقعد معهم إن شئت، فأنزل الله تعالى مجيبًا عن نبيّه صلى الله عليه ﴿وَلَا تَطْرُدِ الَّذِيْنَ يَدْعُوْنَ رَبَّهُمْ بِالْغَدْوةِ وَالْعَشِيِّ يُرِيْدُوْنَ وَجْهَهُ﴾ [الأنعام ٦: ٥٢] وقال تعالى ﴿وَاِذَا جَآءَكَ الَّذِيْنَ يُؤْمِنُوْنَ بِاٰيٰتِنَا فَقُلْ سَلٰمٌ عَلَيْكُمْ كَتَبَ رَبُّكُمْ عَلٰى نَفْسِهِ الرَّحْمَةَ﴾ [الأنعام ٦: ٥٤] وقال تعالى ﴿وَاصْبِرْ نَفْسَكَ مَعَ الَّذِيْنَ يَدْعُوْنَ رَبَّهُمْ بِالْغَدْوةِ وَالْعَشِيِّ يُرِيْدُوْنَ وَجْهَهُ﴾ [الكهف ١٨: ٢٨] [b١٢] وقال تعالى ﴿وَلَا تَعْدُ عَيْنٰكَ عَنْهُمْ تُرِيْدُ زِيْنَةَ الْحَيٰوةِ الدُّنْيَا﴾ [الكهف ١٨: ٢٨] وقال تعالى ﴿ وَ لَا تُطِعْ مَنْ اَغْفَلْنَا قَلْبَهُ عَنْ ذِكْرِنَا وَاتَّبَعَ هَوٰىهُ وَكَانَ اَمْرُهُ فُرُطًا﴾ [الكهف ١٨: ٢٨] يعني لا تجالس الأشراف كما قيل لنوح عليه السلام، حَذْوَ النعل بالنعل.

وقالت كفرة بني إسرائيل للتوراة والإنجيل ﴿ساحران[١٨] تَظَاهَرَا وَقَالُوْٓا اِنَّا بِكُلٍّ كٰفِرُوْنَ﴾ [القصص ٢٨: ٤٨] قال الله سبحانه ﴿قُلْ فَأْتُوْا بِكِتٰبٍ مِّنْ عِنْدِ اللّٰهِ هُوَ اَهْدٰى مِنْهُمَآ اَتَّبِعْهُ اِنْ كُنْتُمْ صٰدِقِيْ﴾

---

[١٨] سحاران: وفي المصحف العثماني سحران.

[القصص ٢٨: ٤٩] وكذلك قالت كفرة قريش ﴿لَن نُّؤْمِنَ بِهَٰذَا الْقُرْآنِ وَلَا بِالَّذِي بَيْنَ يَدَيْهِ﴾ [سبأ ٣٤: ٣١]، و﴿قَالَ الَّذِينَ كَفَرُوا لِلْحَقِّ لَمَّا جَاءَهُمْ هَٰذَا سِحْرٌ مُّبِينٌ﴾ [الأحقاف ٤٦: ٧] وذلك أنه كان قد بلغ من إخلاص [a١٥] بني إسرائيل حين امتحنهم الله عزّ وجلّ بعذاب فرعون وتوعّدهم و﴿قَالَ آمَنتُمْ بِهِ[١٩] قَبْلَ أَنْ آذَنَ لَكُمْ إِنَّهُ لَكَبِيرُكُمُ الَّذِي عَلَّمَكُمُ السِّحْرَ فَلَأُقَطِّعَنَّ أَيْدِيَكُمْ وَأَرْجُلَكُم مِّنْ خِلَافٍ وَلَأُصَلِّبَنَّكُمْ فِي جُذُوعِ النَّخْلِ وَلَتَعْلَمُنَّ أَيُّنَا أَشَدُّ عَذَابًا وَأَبْقَىٰ قَالُوا لَن نُّؤْثِرَكَ عَلَىٰ مَا جَاءَنَا مِنَ الْبَيِّنَاتِ وَالَّذِي فَطَرَنَا فَاقْضِ مَا أَنتَ قَاضٍ إِنَّمَا تَقْضِي هَٰذِهِ الْحَيَاةَ الدُّنْيَا﴾ [طه ٢٠: ٧١-٧٢] ولم يمسّهم ألم العذاب، فبلغ من محنة إخوانهم [في] أمّتنا أن صلبوا على الخشب وكسرت عظامهم بالدهق كعمّار وأصحابه [b١٥] وحبيب بن عبد الله، وقيل لحبيب وهو مصلوب: تودّ أنّ ما بك لمحمّد صلى الله عليه فنخلّي عنك، فقال: ولا شوكة شاكته، حَذْوَ النعل بالنعل.

قال الله عزّ وجلّ ﴿وَلَمَّا وَرَدَ مَاءَ مَدْيَنَ وَجَدَ عَلَيْهِ أُمَّةً مِّنَ النَّاسِ يَسْقُونَ وَوَجَدَ مِن دُونِهِمُ امْرَأَتَيْنِ تَذُودَانِ قَالَ مَا خَطْبُكُمَا قَالَتَا لَا نَسْقِي حَتَّىٰ يُصْدِرَ الرِّعَاءُ وَأَبُونَا شَيْخٌ كَبِيرٌ فَسَقَىٰ لَهُمَا ثُمَّ تَوَلَّىٰ إِلَى الظِّلِّ﴾ [القصص ٢٨: ٢٣-٢٤] وكانوا يسقون مع عصبة من الناس،

---

[١٩] به: وفي المصحف العثماني له.

فكان أحد براهينه وهو هارب إلى ربّه، فوصفت إحداهما أباها [a١٦] لما رأت هذه عنده من القوّة والأمانة ﴿يَآبَتِ اسْتَأْجِرْهُ اِنَّ خَيْرَ مَنِ اسْتَأْجَرْتَ الْقَوِيُّ الْاَمِيْنُ﴾ [القصص ٢٨: ٢٦] ولما توجّه رسول الله صلى الله عليه تلقاء المدينة نزل على أمّ معبد الخزاعية، فحلب شاتها العجفاء التي أصابها الضرّ والجهد، فدرّت له، فملأ القعب وشرب وسقى جماعة وخلّف عندها لبنًا كثيرًا، وكانت إحدى علامات نبوّته وهو هارب إلى ربه عزّ وجلّ، فأخبرت زوجها، ووصفت نوره وبهاءه، وأرته أثر بركته مثل [b١٦] ما وصفت ابنة شعيب أباها، فقال: واللهِ إنّ هذا صاحب قريش، فتفرّست في نبيّ الله صلى الله عليه وآله ما تفرست ابنة شعيب في موسى عليه السلام حَذْوَ النعل بالنعل.

ويوم كُسِرَت رَبَاعية رسول الله صلى الله عليه وآله همّ أن يدعو عليهم، ثمّ قال: رحمة الله على أخي موسى، لقد أوذي في الله أكثر من ذلك، فصبر على ذلك، فلم يدَع كفّار قريش من سنّة الأولين شيئًا إلا وقد أتوه[٢٠] رسول الله صلى الله عليه وآله، [a١٧] حتى أن أبا لهب بغى عليه من قومه كما بغى قارون من قوم موسى على موسى، وكان ابن عم موسى كأبي لهب عم رسول الله صلى الله عليه وآله، لقد خرج رسول الله صلى الله عليه وآله من مكة خائفًا يترقّب إلى الغار كما

---

[٢٠] أتوه: اتو، الأصل.

خرج موسى من مصر إلى مدْين خائفًا يترقّب، قال الله سبحانه وله الحمد ﴿وَإِذۡ يَمۡكُرُ بِكَ ٱلَّذِينَ كَفَرُوا۟ لِيُثۡبِتُوكَ أَوۡ يَقۡتُلُوكَ أَوۡ يُخۡرِجُوكَ وَيَمۡكُرُونَ وَيَمۡكُرُ ٱللَّهُ وَٱللَّهُ خَيۡرُ ٱلۡمَٰكِرِينَ﴾ [الأنفال ٨: ٣٠] ثمّ قال تعالى يُعلم نبيّه [b١٧] صلى الله عليه وآله أن هذه المحنة لم تزل كانت في سائر الأنبياء، فقال ﴿وَهَمَّتۡ كُلُّ أُمَّةِۭ بِرَسُولِهِمۡ لِيَأۡخُذُوهُ﴾ [غافر ٤٠: ٥] ورجع رسول الله صلى الله عليه وآله من المدينة على كفّار قومه كما رجع موسى عليه السلام من مدين على فرعون وقومه، وأنزل الله تعالى على أعداء موسى الغرق، كذلك أنزل على أعداء نبيّه السيف، وكذلك أورث أولياء رسول الله صلى الله عليه وآله أرض أعدائه يوم فتح مكة ما أورث بني إسرائيل من جنّات وعيون [a١٨] وكنوز ومقامٍ كريم، هذه سنّة الله في كفّار بني إسرائيل، حَذْوَ النعل بالنعل.

ثمّ إن الله عزّ وجلّ اصطفى من آل محمّد صلّى الله عليه وآله كما اصطفى من آل عمران على العالمين، لقد كانت خديجة قرينة آسية امرأة فرعون، كانت أول مؤمنة بمحمّد صلى الله عليه، ولقد كان علي عليه السلام [أوّل مؤمن]، فكان هارون أوّل من اتّبع موسى عليه السلام، وعلي عليه السلام أول من اتّبع محمّدًا صلى الله عليه وآله، فقال الله تعالى ذكره ﴿فَمَآ ءَامَنَ لِمُوسَىٰٓ إِلَّا ذُرِّيَّةٞ مِّن قَوۡمِهِۦ عَلَىٰ خَوۡفٖ مِّن فِرۡعَوۡنَ وَمَلَإِيْهِمۡ أَن يَفۡتِنَهُمۡ﴾ [يونس ١٠: ٨٣] وما آمن لمحمّد صلى

الله عليه إلا ذرية [b١٨] من قومه مثل جعفر وعلي عليهما السلام على خوف من فراعنة قريش أن يفتنوهم، وكان منزلته من نبيّنا صلى الله عليهما بمنزلة هارون من موسى إلا أنه لا نبيّ بعد نبيّنا صلى الله عليه وآله، ولقد كان محمّد النبي وعلي الوصيّ يصلّيان بمكة سبع سنين مخيفين كما مكث موسى عند شعيب ثماني حجج مخيفين[٢١] من قومه، كذلك[٢٢] قال رسول الله صلى الله عليه: لقد صلّت الملائكة عليّ وعليٍّ عليه السلام سبع سنين ولم يصلِّ[٢٣] معي ذكَر غيره.

[a١٣] ولقد كانت فاطمة عليها السلام قرينة مريم عليها السلام اصطفاها الله وطهّرها على نساء العالمين كمريم ابنة عمران عليهما السلام، أعاذها الله وذرّيتها من الشيطان الرجيم، ثمّ قال الله عزّ وجلّ ﴿إِنَّمَا يُرِيدُ اللَّهُ لِيُذْهِبَ عَنكُمُ الرِّجْسَ أَهْلَ الْبَيْتِ وَيُطَهِّرَكُمْ تَطْهِيرًا﴾ [الأحزاب ٣٣: ٣٣] قال رسول الله صلى الله عليه وآله: نزلت هذه الآية فينا خمس فيّ وفي عليّ وفاطمة والحسن والحسين، ألا إني وأهل بيتي مطهّرون من الرجس، فكانوا معصومين[b١٣] من الشيطان الرجيم، ولقد أنزل الله تعالى على فاطمة مائدة من السماء كما أنزل على مريم ابنة

---

[٢١] مخيفين: مخيفان، الأصل.

[٢٢] كذلك: فذلك، الأصل.

[٢٣] يصلّ: يصلي، الأصل.

عمران، يوم دخلت محرابها وصلّت ركعتين، ثمّ قالت: يا ربِّ هذا محمّد نبيّك، وهذا عليّ ابن عم نبيّك، وأنا فاطمة بنت نبيّك، وهاذان الحسن والحسين سبطا نبيّك، اللهمّ أنزل علينا مائدة من السماء كما أنزلتها على بني إسرائيل، فكفروا بها، ربّنا إن أنزلتها لا أكفر بها، فإذا هي بجانب المحراب بصحفة من ثريد، وعليها من لحم يفور منها رائحة المسك، [a١٤] فحملته فاطمة عليها السلام ووضعته بين يدي رسول الله صلى الله عليه وآله، فأقبل النبيّ صلى الله عليه وآله يأكل وعليّ عليه السلام ينظر، فقال: يا أبا الحسن كلْ ولا تسألْ، الحمد الله الذي أراني فيك وفيها ما رأى زكريّاء عليه السلام في مريم عليها السلام، ﴿كُلَّمَا دَخَلَ عَلَيۡهَا زَكَرِيَّا الۡمِحۡرَابَ وَجَدَ عِنۡدَهَا رِزۡقًا قَالَ يٰمَرۡيَمُ اَنّٰى لَـكِ هٰذَا قَالَتۡ هُوَ مِنۡ عِنۡدِ اللّٰهِ اِنَّ اللّٰهَ يَرۡزُقُ مَنۡ يَّشَآءُ بِغَيۡرِ حِسَابٍ﴾ [آل عمران ٣: ٣٧].

وإن هارون بن عمران لم يتخلّف عن أخيه موسى صلوات الله [b١٤] عليهما إلا مرّتين، يوم ﴿تَوَجَّهَ تِلۡقَاءَ مَدۡيَنَ﴾ [القصص ٢٨: ٢٢] ﴿فَخَرَجَ مِنۡهَا خَآئِفًا يَّتَرَقَّبُ﴾ [القصص ٢٨: ٢١] ويوم خرج موسى عليه السلام إلى الطور، فاستخلف أخاه هارون، وإن عليًّا عليه السلام لم يتخلف عن أخيه رسول الله صلى الله عليه وآله إلا مرتين، يوم توجّه تلقاء الغار، خرج منها خائفًا يترقّب، ويوم خرج رسول الله صلى الله عليه وآله إلى تبوك، فاستخلف أخاه عليًا عليه السلام، فخرج إليه علي

فقال: يا رسول الله زعَمت قريش أنك استثقلتني وكرهتَ صحبتي، فقال: أما ترضى[٢٤] أن تكون منّي بمنزلة هارون من موسى إلا [a١٩] أنه لا نبيّ بعدي، قال: بلى يا رسول الله، قال: ارجع فإنه لا يصلح هناك إلا أنا وأنت. ولقد كان الحسن والحسين عليهما السلام قريني شبير وشبر ابني هارون عليهم السلام، ويوم أمر النبيّ صلى الله عليه وآله بسدّ الأبواب التي كانت لهم شارعة في مسجده وترك بابه وباب علي عليه السلام، وقال: إن الله عزّ وجلّ أوحى إلى موسى وهارون عليهما السلام أن ﴿تَبَوَّآ لِقَوْمِكُمَا بِمِصْرَ بُيُوتًا وَٱجْعَلُوا بُيُوتَكُمْ قِبْلَةً﴾ [يونس ١٠: ٨٧] فقال: اللهمّ إنّي لا أحلّ لأحدٍ أن [b١٩] يدخل المسجد خائفًا ولا جُنُبًا إلّا لعليّ وفاطمة والحسن والحسين عليهم السلام.

قال الله عزّ وجلّ ﴿وَإِذِ ٱبْتَلَىٰٓ إِبْرَٰهِـۧمَ رَبُّهُۥ بِكَلِمَٰتٍ فَأَتَمَّهُنَّ﴾ [البقرة ٢: ١٢٤] كانت محنة منها ذبح أحبّ خلقه إليه ابنه إسمعيل، فقال: ﴿يَٰبُنَيَّ إِنِّىٓ أَرَىٰ فِى ٱلْمَنَامِ أَنِّىٓ أَذْبَحُكَ فَٱنظُرْ مَاذَا تَرَىٰ قَالَ يَٰٓأَبَتِ ٱفْعَلْ مَا تُؤْمَرُ سَتَجِدُنِىٓ إِن شَآءَ ٱللَّهُ مِنَ ٱلصَّٰبِرِينَ﴾ [الصافات ٣٧: ١٠٢] فوجده صابرًا بما وعد أباه عليهما السلام، قال الله تعالى ذكره ﴿وَٱذْكُرْ فِى ٱلْكِتَٰبِ إِسْمَٰعِيلَ إِنَّهُۥ كَانَ صَادِقَ ٱلْوَعْدِ وَكَانَ رَسُولًا نَّبِيًّا﴾ [مريم ١٩: ٥٤] وابتلى [a٢٠] محمّدًا صلى الله عليه وآله بأحبّ الخلق

[٢٤] ترضى: ترض، الأصل.

إليه أن قال له: يا عليّ إن كفّار قريش همّوا بقتلي الليلة، فهل أنت يا عليّ تنام على فراشي؟ قال: يا رسول الله تنجو بنفسك؟ قال: نعم، فنام على فراشه مستيقنًا بتلف نفسه، فأنجاه الله من القتل مثل ما أنجى إسمعيل عليه السلام وشكر سعيه، قال الله عزّ وجلّ ﴿وَمِنَ النَّاسِ مَنْ يَشْرِىْ نَفْسَهُ ابْتِغَآءَ مَرْضَاتِ اللّٰهِ وَ اللّٰهُ رَءُوْفٌ بِالْعِبَادِ﴾ [البقرة ٢: ٢٠٧] ولقد أحبّ رسول الله صلى الله عليه وآله أن يخلّف عليًا في أمّته [b٢٠] ويجعله وزيرًا من أهله ووصيّاً في قومه كما سأل موسى عليه السلام ربّه فقال: ربّ ﴿وَاجْعَلْ لِّىْ وَزِيْرًا مِّنْ اَهْلِىْ هٰرُوْنَ اَخِى اشْدُدْ بِهٖٓ اَزْرِىْ وَاَشْرِكْهُ فِىْٓ اَمْرِى﴾ [طه ٢٠: ٢٩-٣٢] وخاف تكذيب قومه، فأنزل الله عزّ وجلّ عليه[٢٥] هدايته وصحّة ولايته لأخيه من السفهاء، وأمره أن يبلّغ ذلك، فقال ﴿يٰٓاَيُّهَا الرَّسُوْلُ بَلِّغْ مَآ اُنْزِلَ اِلَيْكَ مِنْ رَّبِّكَ﴾ [المائدة ٥: ٦٧] أي بلّغ الولاية بعد الرسالة ﴿وَاِنْ لَّمْ تَفْعَلْ فَمَا بَلَّغْتَ رِسٰلَتَهُ وَاللّٰهُ يَعْصِمُكَ مِنَ النَّاسِ اِنَّ اللّٰهَ لَا يَهْدِى الْقَوْمَ الْكٰفِرِيْنَ﴾ [المائدة ٥: ٦٧] قال رسول الله [a٢١] صلى الله عليه وآله: فضقتُ به ذرعًا وعلمتُ أن الناس مكذّبيّ، فأوعدني ربّي تعالى لأبلّغها أو ليعذّبني، فقام بغدير خمّ، فأخذ بيد عليّ عليه السلام ونصبه مكان نفسه، فكان تصديقه إيمان وتكذيبه كفر وطغيان، وائتمنه على ما أدّي إليه من

---

٢٥ عليه: على، الأصل.

النصيحة والدعاء إلى الخير وإلى سبيل الرشاد كما نصبه جبريل عليه السلام بأمر ربّ العالمين تبارك وتعالى في أدائه ما أدّى إليه إسرافيل، فكان طاعته طاعة الله عزّ وجلّ وطاعة رسوله صلى الله عليه وآله [b٢١] حُجةً للخلق ورحمةً من الله عز ذكره لعباده، فأقامه تحت دوحتين وقال لأصحابه: ألستُ أولى بالمؤمنين من أنفسهم؟ قالوا: اللهمّ نعم، ثمّ قال: من كنتُ مولاه فعليّ مولاه، ومن كنتُ نبيّه فعليّ أميره ومن كنتُ أولى بنفسه من نفسه هذا أولى بنفسه من نفسه، اللهمّ والِ من والاه وعادِ من عاداه، وانصر من نصره واخذل من خذله، وأمر أصحابه أن يبلّغ الشاهد منهم الغائب، ثمّ قال: يا علي إنّ مثلك في هذه الأمّة كمثل: ﴿قُلْ هُوَ اللَّهُ أَحَدٌ﴾ [الإخلاص ١١٢: ١] في القرآن، من قرأها مرّة فكأنما [a٢٢] قرأ ثُلث القرآن، ومن قرأها مرّتين فكأنما قرأ ثلثي القرآن، ومن قرأها ثلاث مرّات فكأنما قرأ القرآن جميعه، فمن أحبّك يا علي وفاطمة كان له مثل أجر ثُلث هذه الأمّة، ومن أحبّك بقلبه وأعانك بلسانه كان له مثل أجر ثلثي هذه الأمّة، ومن أحبّك بقلبه وأعانك بلسانه ونصرك بسيفه كان له مثل أجر جميع هذه الأمّة.

فأنزل الله عزّ وجلّ ﴿الْيَوْمَ أَكْمَلْتُ لَكُمْ دِينَكُمْ وَأَتْمَمْتُ عَلَيْكُمْ نِعْمَتِي﴾ [المائدة ٥: ٣] أي لا أُنزل بعدها فريضة أبدًا، فقال رسول الله [b٢٢] صلى الله عليه وآله: الله أكبر على كمال الدين وتمام النعمة،

ووكّد رسول الله صلى الله عليه وآله الولاية لعلي بن أبي طالب عليه السلام، ولم يوكّد موسى عليه السلام على قومه أكثر من هذا في خلافة هارون عليه السلام، إنما كانت خلافته كلمة، قال ﴿اخْلُفْنِي فِي قَوْمِي وَأَصْلِحْ وَلَا تَتَّبِعْ سَبِيلَ الْمُفْسِدِينَ﴾ [الأعراف ٧: ١٤٢] ورسول الله صلى الله عليه وآله وكّد على قومه في خلافة علي عليه السلام ما وكّد بغدير خم ثمّ أخرج من المدينة جميع من خاف على منازعة [a٢٣] عليّ عليه السلام في خلافته وولايته بجعلهم تحت يدي أسامة بن زيد مولاه وأمرِهم أن لا يلبث أحد منهم بالمدينة، وهو صلى الله عليه وآله يوكّد حتّى يُصْفو الخلافة لعلي بن أبي طالب عليه السلام، فكان لا بدّ لهذه الأمّة أن تحذو حذو بني إسرائيل لما وعدهم رسول الله صلى الله عليه وآله أنهم سيركبون سنّة بني إسرائيل وما وعدهم الله عزّ وجلّ في الكتاب أنهم يُفتنون كما فُتن الذين من قبلهم، وقال رسول الله صلى الله عليه وآله: يا علي لو رجعتُ عند فتنتهم لآخذ برأسك ولحيتك ورددتَ عليّ ما ردّ هارون على موسى عليهما السلام أن القوم استضعفوني وكادوا يقتلونني، فلا تُشمت فيّ الأعداء، واعلم أنّ له ضغائن[٢٦] في صدور قوم لا يُبدونها له إلا من بعد موته صلى الله عليه وآله.

---

[٢٦] ضغائن: ضغائنا، الأصل.

ولقد سألوه عليه السلام فقالوا: من نفزع [إليه] بعدك يا رسول الله ومن خليفتك فينا؟ فلما أخبرهم ساءهم ذلك، قال سبحانه لا شريك له ﴿ يَٰٓأَيُّهَا ٱلَّذِينَ ءَامَنُواْ لَا تَسْـَٔلُواْ عَنْ أَشْيَآءَ إِن تُبْدَ لَكُمْ تَسُؤْكُمْ وَإِن تَسْـَٔلُواْ عَنْهَا حِينَ يُنَزَّلُ ٱلْقُرْءَانُ تُبْدَ لَكُمْ عَفَا ٱللَّهُ عَنْهَا وَٱللَّهُ غَفُورٌ حَلِيمٌ قَدْ سَأَلَهَا قَوْمٌ مِّن قَبْلِكُمْ [a٢٤] ثُمَّ أَصْبَحُواْ بِهَا كَٰفِرِينَ ﴾ [المائدة ٥: ١٠١-١٠٢] قال الله عزّ وجلّ لأصحاب نبيّه صلى الله عليه وآله ﴿أَمْ تُرِيدُونَ أَن تَسْـَٔلُواْ رَسُولَكُمْ كَمَا سُئِلَ مُوسَىٰ مِن قَبْلُ وَمَن يَتَبَدَّلِ ٱلْكُفْرَ بِٱلْإِيمَٰنِ فَقَدْ ضَلَّ سَوَآءَ ٱلسَّبِيلِ﴾ [البقرة ٢: ١٠٨] فسألوا رسول الله صلى الله عليه وآله: ما سأل أصحاب موسى عليه السلام حين جاوزهم البحر وأراهم العجائب فمرّ بقوم ﴿يَعْكُفُونَ عَلَىٰٓ أَصْنَامٍ لَّهُمْ قَالُواْ يَٰمُوسَى ٱجْعَل لَّنَآ إِلَٰهًا كَمَا لَهُمْ ءَالِهَةٌ﴾ [الأعراف ٧: ١٣٨] وإن أصحاب رسول الله صلى الله عليه وآله قالوا: يا [b٢٤] رسول الله لو جعلتَ لنا ذات أنواط كما لهم ذات أنواط، قال رسول الله صلى الله عليه وآله: الله أكبر، قلتم كما قالت بنو إسرائيل اجعل لنا إلهًا كما لهم آلهة، ثمّ قال: إنكم تستردّون سنّة من قبلكم، قال الله عزّ وجلّ مجيبًا عن نبيّه صلى الله عليه وآله يا محمّد ﴿وَسْـَٔلْ مَنْ أَرْسَلْنَا مِن قَبْلِكَ مِن رُّسُلِنَآ أَجَعَلْنَا مِن دُونِ ٱلرَّحْمَٰنِ ءَالِهَةً يُعْبَدُونَ﴾ [الزخرف ٤٣: ٤٥].

قال الله سبحانه وله الحمد لأصحاب نبيّه عليه السلام ﴿لَا تَكُونُواْ كَٱلَّذِينَ ءَاذَوْاْ مُوسَىٰ﴾ [الأحزاب ٣٣: ٦٩] [a٢٥] فقال بعض أصحابه: إنّ محمّدًا تفخّذ نساءنا، فوالله لو مات لأتزوّجنّ بعائشة، فأنزل الله عزّ وجلّ ﴿وَمَا كَانَ لَكُمْ أَن تُؤْذُواْ رَسُولَ ٱللَّهِ وَلَآ أَن تَنكِحُوٓاْ أَزْوَٰجَهُۥ مِن بَعْدِهِۦٓ أَبَدًا﴾ [الأحزاب ٣٣: ٥٣] وكان موسى عليه السلام يدعو على فرعون وقومه ويؤمّن هارون ﴿رَبَّنَا ٱطْمِسْ عَلَىٰٓ أَمْوَٰلِهِمْ وَٱشْدُدْ عَلَىٰ قُلُوبِهِمْ﴾ [يونس ١٠: ٨٨] قال الله عزّ وجلّ ﴿قَدْ أُجِيبَت دَّعْوَتُكُمَا فَٱسْتَقِيمَا﴾ [يونس ١٠: ٨٩] فجعل الله شكرهم حجازه، وكان رسول الله صلى الله عليه إذا غمّه وكربه شيء دعا عليًّا عليه السلام [b٢٥] فيدعو النبيّ صلى الله عليه وآله ويؤمّن علي عليه السلام كموسى وهارون صلوات الله عليهما.

وإن قوم فرعون قالوا لفرعون ﴿قَالُوٓاْ أَرْجِهْ وَأَخَاهُ وابعث[٢٧] فِي ٱلْمَدَآئِنِ حَٰشِرِينَ يَأْتُوكَ بِكُلِّ سحّار[٢٨] عَلِيمٍ وَجَآءَ ٱلسَّحَرَةُ فِرْعَوْنَ قَالُوٓاْ أئنّ[٢٩] لَنَا لَأَجْرًا إِن كُنَّا نَحْنُ ٱلْغَٰلِبِينَ قَالَ نَعَمْ وَإِنَّكُمْ لَمِنَ ٱلْمُقَرَّبِينَ قَالُواْ يَٰمُوسَىٰٓ إِمَّآ أَن تُلْقِيَ وَإِمَّآ أَن نَّكُونَ نَحْنُ ٱلْمُلْقِينَ قَالَ أَلْقُواْ فَلَمَّآ أَلْقَوْاْ

---

[٢٧] وأبعث: في المصحف العثماني: وأرسل.

[٢٨] سحار: في المصحف العثماني: ساحر.

[٢٩] أئن: في المصحف العثماني: إن.

سَحَرُوٓاْ أَعْيُنَ[٣٠] ٱلنَّاسِ وَٱسْتَرْهَبُوهُمْ وَجَآءُو بِسِحْرٍ عَظِيمٍ وَأَوْحَيْنَآ إِلَىٰ مُوسَىٰٓ أَنْ أَلْقِ عَصَاكَ فَإِذَا هِىَ تَلْقَفُ مَا يَأْفِكُونَ [a٢٦] فَوَقَعَ ٱلْحَقُّ وَبَطَلَ مَا كَانُواْ يَعْمَلُونَ فَغُلِبُواْ هُنَالِكَ وَٱنقَلَبُواْ صَٰغِرِينَ﴾ [الأعراف ٧: ١١١-١١٩] كذلك بعث الله بشياطين قريش يوم الأحزاب في أحيائهم حاشرين فجاءوا بأمر عظيم وبلغت القلوب الحناجر وظُنّ بالله ظنّ السوء، وقال ﴿ٱلَّذِينَ فِى قُلُوبِهِم مَّرَضٌ مَّا وَعَدَنَا ٱللَّهُ وَرَسُولُهُۥٓ إِلَّا غُرُورًا﴾ [الأحزاب ٣٣: ١٢] وعمرو يدعوهم إلى البراز ويقول: إما أن تقفوا وإما أن أقف لكم، فأخرج لهم رسول الله صلى الله عليه وآله أخاه عليًا عليه السلام، ﴿فَإِذَا هِىَ تَلْقَفُ مَا يَأْفِكُونَ فَوَقَعَ ٱلْحَقُّ وَبَطَلَ مَا كَانُواْ [b٢٦] يَعْمَلُونَ فَغُلِبُواْ هُنَالِكَ وَٱنقَلَبُواْ صَٰغِرِينَ﴾ [الأعراف ٧: ١١٨-١١٩] قال الله سبحانه ﴿وَرَدَّ ٱللَّهُ[٣١] ٱلَّذِينَ كَفَرُواْ بِغَيْظِهِمْ لَمْ يَنَالُواْ خَيْرًا وَكَفَى ٱللَّهُ ٱلْمُؤْمِنِينَ ٱلْقِتَالَ﴾ [الأحزاب ٣٣: ٢٥] بعليّ عليه السلام كما كفى بني إسرائيل بعصا موسى عليه السلام.

ولقد جمع الله عزّ وجلّ ليوسف في قميصه براهين[٣٢] ثلاثة، يوم ﴿جَآءُوٓ أَبَاهُمْ عِشَآءً يَبْكُونَ﴾ [يوسف ١٢: ١٦] ويوم ﴿جَآءُو عَلَىٰ

---

[٣٠] أعين: عين، الأصل.

[٣١] الله: سقط في الأصل.

[٣٢] براهين: تراهينًا، الأصل.

قَمِيْصِهِ بِدَمٍ كَذِبٍ﴾ [يوسف ١٢: ١٨] ويوم قذفته امرأة العزيز بالزور ﴿وَشَهِدَ شَاهِدٌ مِّنْ اَهْلِهَا اِنْ كَانَ قَمِيْصُهٗ قُدَّ مِنْ قُبُلٍ﴾ إلى آخر الآية [يوسف ١٢: ٢٦-٢٧] ويوم أرسل إخوته إلى أبيه، فقال [a٢٧] ﴿اِذْهَبُوْا بِقَمِيْصِيْ هٰذَا فَاَلْقُوْهُ عَلٰى وَجْهِ اَبِيْ يَأْتِ بَصِيْرًا﴾ [يوسف ١٢: ٩٣] كذلك جمع الله عزّ وجلّ لمحمد صلى الله عليه وآله في أخيه علي براهين[٣٣] كثيرة، أقامه الله عزّ وجلّ يوم الأحزاب مقام عصا موسى فتلقف ما كانوا يأفكون، وليلة الغار جعله الله تعالى مَكرهُ، قال الله سبحانه ﴿وَإِذْ يَمْكُرُ بِكَ الَّذِينَ كَفَرُوا لِيُثْبِتُوكَ أَوْ يَقْتُلُوكَ أَوْ يُخْرِجُوكَ وَيَمْكُرُونَ وَيَمْكُرُ اللَّهُ وَاللَّهُ خَيْرُ الْمَاكِرِينَ﴾ [الأنفال ٨: ٣٠] فكان عليّ عليه السلام مكْرَ الله على فراش رسول الله صلى الله عليه وآله، فشبّه لشياطين قريش حين همّوا بقتل رسول صلى الله عليه وآله كما شبه [b٢٧] أصطبانوس لليهود حين همّوا بصلب عيسى عليه السلام، وكان فداؤه لرسول الله صلى الله عليه وسلم كالكبش لإسمعيل عليه السلام، وكان في أمّته كسفينة نوح وكباب حِطّة في بني إسرائيل، ولقد كان في علي عليه السلام وقريش آيات للمؤمنين كما ﴿كَانَ فِي يُوسُفَ وَإِخْوَتِهِ آيَاتٌ لِّلسَّائِلِينَ﴾ [يوسف ١٢: ٧].

---

[٣٣] براهين: براهينًا، الأصل.

وإن نبيّ الله موسى عليه السلام لمّا عرض على قومه قتال الجبابرة الذين كانوا ببيت المقدس كان من جوابهم أن ﴿قَالُوا يَا مُوسَىٰ إِنَّ فِيهَا قَوْمًا [a٢٨] جَبَّارِينَ﴾ [المائدة ٥: ٢٢] و ﴿إِنَّا لَن نَّدْخُلَهَا أَبَدًا مَّا دَامُوا فِيهَا فَاذْهَبْ أَنتَ وَرَبُّكَ فَقَاتِلَا إِنَّا هَاهُنَا قَاعِدُونَ قَالَ رَبِّ[٣٤] إِنِّي لَا أَمْلِكُ إِلَّا نَفْسِي وَأَخِي﴾ [المائدة ٥: ٢٤-٢٥] ﴿قَالَ رَجُلَانِ مِنَ الَّذِينَ يَخَافُونَ أَنْعَمَ اللَّهُ عَلَيْهِمَا ادْخُلُوا عَلَيْهِمُ[٣٥] الْبَابَ فَإِذَا دَخَلْتُمُوهُ فَإِنَّكُمْ غَالِبُونَ وَعَلَى اللَّهِ فَتَوَكَّلُوا إِن كُنتُم مُّؤْمِنِينَ﴾ [المائدة ٥: ٢٣] كذلك كان رسول الله صلى الله عليه وآله ﴿يَوْمَ الْتَقَى الْجَمْعَانِ﴾ [آل عمران ٣: ١٥٥] لم يملك إلا نفسه وأخاه، وآخرون يصعدون ولا يلوون على أحد، والرسول يدعوهم في أخراهم، فقام [b٢٨] علي عليه السلام وأبو دُجانة مقام يوشع بن نون وكوكب بن يقني الرجلين اللذان يخافان،[٣٦] أنعم الله عليهما فتوكّلا على الله عزّ وجلّ، وقاتلا بين يدي رسول الله صلى الله عليه حتّى فتح الله على نبيّه صلى الله عليه وعلى آله، فعجبت الملائكة المقرّبون من مؤاساة علي عليه السلام للنبيّ صلى الله عليه وآله، فقال جبريل عليه السلام: لقد عجبت الملائكة من مواساة علي لك، قال صلى

---

[٣٤] رب: سقط في الأصل.

[٣٥] عليهم: عليهما، الأصل.

[٣٦] اللذان يخافان: الذين يخافون، الأصل.

الله عليه وآله: ما يمنعه من ذلك وهو منّي وأنا [a٢٩] منه؟ قال جبرئيل عليه السلام: وأنا منكما ما كان في حياة رسول الله صلى الله عليه من سُنن الأوّلين، حَذْوَ النعل بالنعل.

فلما أن فارق رسول الله صلى الله عليه وآله الدنيا انقلب أكثر أمّته على أعقابهم كما فعلت الأمم الماضية بعد أنبيائهم عليهم السلام، كما قال ابن عبّاس: ما بعث الله نبيًّا ثمّ قبضه إلا وكانت بعده موقفة تملأ منها جهنّم، قال الله عزّ وجلّ: ﴿وَمَا مُحَمَّدٌ إِلَّا رَسُولٌ قَدْ خَلَتْ مِن قَبْلِهِ الرُّسُلُ أَفَإِن مَّاتَ أَوْ قُتِلَ [b٢٩] انقَلَبْتُمْ عَلَىٰ أَعْقَابِكُمْ وَمَن يَنقَلِبْ عَلَىٰ عَقِبَيْهِ فَلَن يَضُرَّ اللَّهَ شَيْئًا وَسَيَجْزِي اللَّهُ الشَّاكِرِينَ﴾ [آل عمران ٣: ١٤٤] فنكصوا على أعقابهم وتركوا أخا نبيّهم صلى الله عليهما ووزيرهم ووليّ رسول الله صلى الله عليه ووصيّه في قومه وخليفته على أمّته كما فعلت بنو إسرائيل بهارون عليه السلام بعد ما غاب موسى عنهم واتّخذوا العجل في بني إسرئيل عشرة أيام، وواعد الله عزّ وجلّ موسى عليه السلام ثلاثين ليلة وأتمّها ﴿بِعَشْرٍ فَتَمَّ مِيقَاتُ رَبِّهِ أَرْبَعِينَ لَيْلَةً﴾ [الأعراف ٧: ١٤٢] فأضلّهم السامري وأغواهم [a٣٠] وأمرهم بعبادة العجل بعد الثلاثين، وقال ﴿هَٰذَا إِلَٰهُكُمْ وَإِلَٰهُ مُوسَىٰ﴾ [طه ٢٠: ٨٨]، ﴿فَرَجَعَ مُوسَىٰ إِلَىٰ قَوْمِهِ غَضْبَانَ أَسِفًا﴾ وقال ﴿أَلَمْ يَعِدْكُمْ رَبُّكُمْ وَعْدًا حَسَنًا أَفَطَالَ عَلَيْكُمُ الْعَهْدُ أَمْ أَرَدتُّمْ أَن يَحِلَّ عَلَيْكُمْ غَضَبٌ مِّن رَّبِّكُمْ﴾ [طه ٢٠: ٨٦]

فأصلحهم وكان توبتهم القتل، فقال الله تعالى لهم ﴿تُوبُوا إِلَىٰ بَارِئِكُمْ فَاقْتُلُوا أَنفُسَكُمْ ذَٰلِكُمْ خَيْرٌ لَّكُمْ عِندَ بَارِئِكُمْ﴾ [البقرة ٢: ٥٤] فجلس عبدة العجل مزمّلين بثيابهم بين يدي هارون وشيعته، من رفع منهم إليه الطرف أو حلّ حبوته لم [b٣٠] يقبل لهم توبة، فوضع هارون وشيعته فيهم السيف إلى أن أمر بالكفّ. فقُبض نبيّنا صلى الله عليه وآله ولم يغب كما غاب موسى عليه السلام، فبقي عبدة العجل من أمّتنا في غيّهم يتردّدون لا هم يتوبون ولا هم يذكرون لما أشرب في قلوبهم العجل بكفرهم إلى يوم خليفة الله المهدي، ويوم عجل أمّتنا مبسوطة لكرامة النبيّ صلى الله عليه وآله قبل خروج المهدي عليه السلام دون القتل، فإذا خرج خليفة المهدي غُلّقت [a٣١] أبواب التوبة عن عبدة العجل من أمّتنا كما تغلق عن جميع من لم يؤمن قبل طلوع الشمس من المغرب، قال الله عزّ وجلّ ﴿ يَوْمَ يَأْتِي بَعْضُ آيَاتِ رَبِّكَ لَا يَنفَعُ نَفْسًا إِيمَانُهَا لَمْ تَكُنْ آمَنَتْ مِن قَبْلُ أَوْ كَسَبَتْ فِي إِيمَانِهَا خَيْرًا﴾ [الأنعام ٦: ١٥٨] وهي طلوع الشمس من مغربها، فليس اليوم عند عبدة العجل إلا من آمن بالعجل وأطاع السامري ومن أطاع أخا نبيّهم عليه السلام وخليفته فهم[٣٧] استضعفوه كما فعلت بنو إسرئيل بهارون وشيعته ﴿قَالُوا [b٣١]

[٣٧] فهم: فيهم، الأصل.

اقْتُلُوا أَبْنَاءَ الَّذِينَ آمَنُوا مَعَهُ وَاسْتَحْيُوا نِسَاءَهُمْ﴾ [غافر ٤٠: ٢٥] تركيبًا لسنّة بني إسرائيل واحتذاءً بهم.

وإن نوحًا[٣٨] عليه السلام لما علم أن أمّته مغرقون بالماء اتّخذ سفينة قبل إطغاء الماء ودعا الناس إلي ركوبها، واستهزأوا به واستسخروه، وما ركب معه إلا قليل، وظنّ آخرون أن غير تلك السفينة تعصمهم من الماء، فتخلفوا عنه فأغرقوا وأدخلوا نارًا، وإن نبيّنا صلى الله عليه وآله لما علم أن أمّته مغرقون بالفتن كقوم نوح عليه السلام لما أنذر أمّته الفتن، فقال: [a٣٢] إنّي لأرى موقع الفتن خلال بيوتكم كموقع المطر، ثمّ دلّهم على سفينة النجاة فقال: إن مثل أهل بيتي كمثل سفينة نوح، مَن ركبها نجا ومن تخلّف عنها غرق، أي من سلك سبيلهم واستنّ بسنّتهم لا يغرق بالفتن كقوم نوح بالماء فيدخل النار مع الداخلين، قال الله عزّ وجلّ ﴿ثُمَّ أَغْرَقْنَا بَعْدُ[٣٩] الْبَاقِينَ﴾ [الشعراء ٢٦: ١٢٠] ﴿أُغْرِقُوا فَأُدْخِلُوا نَارًا﴾ [نوح ٧١: ٢٥]، فظنّوا أن سبيلهم كسبيل غيرهم، فلم يسلك من أمّته سبيلهم إلا قليل كما لم يركب مع نوح في سفينته من الناس [b٣٢] إلا قليل، فلم يركب مع نوح من قومه إلا ثلاثة بنين سام وحام ويافث، فمن قصد طريق علي عليه السلام نجا،

[٣٨] نوحًا: نوح، الأصل.

[٣٩] بعد: -، الأصل.

فلم يخالفه من أصحاب رسول الله صلى الله عليه وآله سلمان وأبو ذرّ والمقداد، تركيبًا لسنّة من قبلهم واحتذاءً بهم.

واختار موسى عليه السلام [من] قومه سبعين رجلًا ميقات ربّه يوم الطور، فسمعوا كلام ربّهم ورأوا العجائب، فلما رجعوا إلى بني إسرائيل حرّفوا ﴿الْكَلِمَ مِن بَعْدِ مَوَاضِعِهِ﴾ [المائدة ٥: ٤١] و﴿نَسُوا [a٣٣] حَظًّا مِّمَّا ذُكِّرُوا بِهِ﴾ [المائدة ٥: ١٣] وقد اختار[٤٠] رسول الله صلى الله عليه وآله [من قومه أصحاباً] منهم، فحرّفوا الكلم من بعد مواضعه وحرّفوا كتاب ربّهم، تركيبًا لسنّة بني إسرائيل واحتذاءًا بهم.

قال الله عزّ وجلّ ﴿وَهَلْ أَتَاكَ نَبَأُ الْخَصْمِ إِذْ تَسَوَّرُوا الْمِحْرَابَ إِذْ دَخَلُوا عَلَىٰ دَاوُودَ فَفَزِعَ مِنْهُمْ قَالُوا لَا تَخَفْ خَصْمَانِ بَغَىٰ بَعْضُنَا عَلَىٰ بَعْضٍ فَاحْكُم بَيْنَنَا بِالْحَقِّ وَلَا تُشْطِطْ وَاهْدِنَا إِلَىٰ سَوَاءِ الصِّرَاطِ إِنَّ هَٰذَا أَخِي لَهُ تِسْعٌ وَتِسْعُونَ [b٣٣] نَعْجَةً وَلِيَ نَعْجَةٌ وَاحِدَةٌ فَقَالَ أَكْفِلْنِيهَا وَعَزَّنِي فِي الْخِطَابِ قَالَ لَقَدْ ظَلَمَكَ بِسُؤَالِ نَعْجَتِكَ إِلَىٰ نِعَاجِهِ وَإِنَّ كَثِيرًا مِّنَ الْخُلَطَاءِ لَيَبْغِي بَعْضُهُمْ عَلَىٰ بَعْضٍ إِلَّا الَّذِينَ آمَنُوا وَعَمِلُوا الصَّالِحَاتِ وَقَلِيلٌ مَّا هُمْ وَظَنَّ دَاوُودُ أَنَّمَا فَتَنَّاهُ فَاسْتَغْفَرَ رَبَّهُ وَخَرَّ رَاكِعًا وَأَنَابَ﴾ [ص ٣٨: ٢١-٢٤] كذلك تحاكم علي والعبّاس عليهما السلام إلى أبي بكر في ميراث النبي صلى الله عليه وآله، فقال العباس: فبماذا أوجبتم

---

[٤٠] وقد اختار: ومن أخبار، الأصل.

إرث النبيّ صلى الله عليه وآله لعلي [a٣٤] وأنا عمّ النبي عليه السلام وهو ابن عمّه؟ فقال أبو بكر: على الخبير هجمتم، تذكر يا عباس يوم كنّا في شعب أبي طالب أربعين رجلًا لم يكن فيكم من غيركم غيري؟ فقال رسول الله صلى الله عليه وآله: إنه لم يكن نبيّ من قبلُ إلا وكان له وصيّ وخليفة، فمن يكن فيكم وصيّي وخليفتي ووارث أمري، يقضي ديوني وينجز وعدي ويبرئ ذمّتي؟ قال: فسكتّم فلم يجبه أحد، فقلتَ أنت يا عبّاس: ومن [b٣٤] يقدر على ذلك وأنت أسخى من الريح؟ ثمّ قام في الثالثة فقال: يا معشر بني هاشم كونوا في الإسلام رؤوسًا ولا تكونوا أذنابًا، إن كان فيكم وإلا كان في غيركم، فقام أحمشكم ساقًا وأعظمكم بطنًا وهو هذا، وأشار إلى عليّ عليه السلام، فقام علي فقال: أنا أكون وصيّك وخليفتك ووارث أمرك، أقضي ديونك وأنجز مواعيدك وأبرئ ذمّتك، أتعرف هذا له يا عبّاس من رسول الله صلى الله عليه وآله؟ قال: نعم يا أبا بكر، [a٣٥] قال: فلأيّ شيء تخاصمه وأنت تعرف هذا له من رسول الله صلى الله عليه وآله؟ فقال له العباس: وأنت يا أبا بكر لماذا توثبَتَ عليه في حقّه وتعرف هذا له من رسول الله صلى الله عليه وآله؟ فقال أبو بكر: أخرجوهما عنّي، فإنها مكيدة من بني هاشم. كان استفتياه كاستفتائه لم يكن [أحد] من المالكين[٤١] باغيًا لكنهما استفهماه، فعلم أنه

---

[٤١] المالكين: الملكين، الأَصل.

فُتن، فتاب وأناب، قال الله سبحانه وله الحمد[b٣٥] ﴿فَغَفَرْنَا لَهُ ذَٰلِكَ وَإِنَّ لَهُ عِندَنَا لَزُلْفَىٰ وَحُسْنَ مَآبٍ﴾ [ص ٣٨: ٢٥] وكذلك لم يكن أحد من هذين ظالمًا،[٤٢] أعنى عليًا والعباس، لكنّهما استفهماه، ولو تاب لوجد الله توابًا رحيمًا، حذو النعل بالنعل.

قال الله عز جل ﴿أَلَمْ تَرَ إِلَى الَّذِينَ أُوتُوا نَصِيبًا مِّنَ الْكِتَابِ يُؤْمِنُونَ بِالْجِبْتِ وَالطَّاغُوتِ وَيَقُولُونَ لِلَّذِينَ كَفَرُوا هَٰؤُلَاءِ أَهْدَىٰ مِنَ الَّذِينَ آمَنُوا سَبِيلًا أُولَٰئِكَ الَّذِينَ لَعَنَهُمُ اللَّهُ﴾ [النساء ٤: ٥١-٥٢] كذلك قالت ناصبة آل محمّد صلى الله [a٣٦] عليه وآله لشيعتهم: الكفّارُ واليهود والنصارى أهدى منهم سبيلًا، حَذْوَ النعل بالنعل.

وإن اليهود والنصارى اتخذوا أحبارهم ورهبانهم أربابًا من دون الله حين أحلّوا لهم حرامًا وحرّموا عليهم حلالًا، فأطاعوهم في ذلك، كذلك اتخذت أمّتنا فقهاءهم وعلماءهم أربابً من دون الله، فكلّما ذُكر لهم من مخالفتهم الكتاب والسنة قالوا: فلان عالم بكتاب الله وحديث رسول الله عليه السلام، فيعلمون الشيء بخلاف [b٣٦] السنة والكتاب، ويقول من اتخذوهم أربابًا من دون الله افتراءً على الله عزّ وجلّ، كما

---

[٤٢] ظالمًا: ظالم، الأصل.

فعل من كان قبلهم، يحلّون ويحرّمون ما لم يأذن به الله عزّ وجلّ افتراءً على الله، تركيبًا لسنة بني إسرائيل واحتذاءً بهم.

وإن اليهود والنصارى، حين طال عليهم الأمد وقست قلوبهم، نبذوا كتاب الله عزّ وجلّ وراء ظهورهم، أي لم يعملوا بما فيه من الأمر والنهي وإقامة الحدود والأحكام، كما قال حُذيفة بن اليمان: إن [a٣٧] الكتاب بين أيديهم والعمل وراء ظهورهم، فعيّرهم الله بذلك، قال الله عزّ وجلّ: نبذوا ﴿كِتَابَ اللَّهِ وَرَاءَ ظُهُورِهِمْ كَأَنَّهُمْ لَا يَعْلَمُونَ﴾ [البقرة ٢: ١٠١] فلما طال الأمد على أمّتنا وقست قلوبهم ضيّعوا الحدود والأحكام وما في القرآن من الحلال والحرام ونبذوه وراء ظهورهم كأنهم لا يعلمون، تركيبًا لسنّة بني إسرائيل واحتذاءً بهم.

وإن اليهود والنصارى، حين ضيّعوا ما في التوراة والإنجيل من الأمر والنهي والحلال والحرام، قوّموا الحروف [b٣٧] وحلّوا التوراة والإنجيل بالذهب والفضّة ولفّفوه بالديباج، ثمّ تلوا بالليل[٤٣] والنهار في بِيَعهم وكنائسهم من غير أن يعملوا بما فيه، فعيّرهم الله تعالى ذلك في قوله ﴿مَثَلُ الَّذِينَ حُمِّلُوا التَّوْرَاةَ ثُمَّ لَمْ يَحْمِلُوهَا كَمَثَلِ الْحِمَارِ يَحْمِلُ أَسْفَارًا بِئْسَ مَثَلُ الْقَوْمِ الَّذِينَ كَذَّبُوا بِآيَاتِ اللَّهِ﴾ [الجمعة ٦٢: ٥] وقال الله عزّ وجلّ ﴿يَا أَهْلَ الْكِتَابِ لَسْتُمْ عَلَىٰ شَيْءٍ حَتَّىٰ تُقِيمُوا التَّوْرَاةَ وَالْإِنجِيلَ﴾

---

[٤٣] تلوا بالليل: فلو انا الليل، الأصل.

[المائدة ٥: ٦٨] وقال تعالى ﴿وَلَوْ أَنَّهُمْ أَقَامُوا التَّوْرَاةَ وَالْإِنجِيلَ﴾ [المائدة ٥: ٦٦] [a٣٨] فإنكم لا تدرون معنى الكتاب والتفسير ما فسّرنا لكم، فصدّقوهم بذلك ولم يلتفتوا إلى قول من عنده علم الكتاب. فاحتذى علماء أمّتنا بهم، حرّفوا الكتاب والسنة، وفسّروا آياته[٤٤] على آرائهم وموافقة أهوائهم، وزعموا أن ما تحتاج إليه الأمّة فسّر لهم مفسّروهم، فضلّوا،[٤٥] وإنما تفسير الكتاب على قرينه الذي لا يفارقه، إلى الحقّ من عترة المصطفى الذين أنزلت في بيوتهم الحكمة والكتاب، وفيهم[٤٦] [b٣٨] كان مختلف الملائكة، وبلسانهم نزل الكتاب، فأنكرت الأمّة ما عبّرت الثقل الأصغر عن الثقل الأكبر، فليس عندهم تفسير الكتاب إلا ما فسّر مفسّروهم، وهم الذين اتّخذوهم أربابًا من دون الله، كما أن ليس عند اليهود إلا تفسير ما فسّر لهم أحبارهم ورهبانهم الذين اتّخذوهم أربابًا من دون الله عزّ وجلّ، تركيبًا لسنّة بني إسرائيل واحتذاء بهم.

وإن اليهود لما ضيّعوا مواقيت الصلاة واتّبعوا شهواتهم فقالوا: نشتهي [a٣٩] أن نرى أنبياءنا، فصوروا صور أنبيائهم في بيَعهم وكنائسهم، فزخرفوا البيَع والكنائس وضيّعوا المواقيت، قال الله عزّ وجلّ

[٤٤] وفسروا آياته: فسروا الامه، الأصل.

[٤٥] فضلوا: فيصلوا، الأصل.

[٤٦] وفيهم: وفيكم، الأصل.

﴿أَضَاعُوا الصَّلَاةَ وَاتَّبَعُوا الشَّهَوَاتِ فَسَوْفَ يَلْقَوْنَ غَيًّا﴾ [مريم ١٩: ٥٩] والغيّ وادٍ في جهنّم بعيد قعره منتن ريحه، وقد سألوا رسول الله صلى الله عليه وآله أن يزخرفوا المسجد، فقال عليه السلام: يعجب المنافقون إذا حلّيتم مصاحفكم وزخرفتم مساجدكم، فالدمار عليكم، وقيل: مساجدكم [b٣٩] عامرة وهي خراب من المدر،[٤٧] يجتمعون في المساجد ليس فيهم مؤمن، فلمّا أن خربوها من المدر[٤٨] وعمّروها بالطين والتزخرف اتّخذوا فيها محاريب[٤٩] كمذابيح النصارى، احتذاء بهم وتركيبًا لسنّتهم.

قال الله تعالى ﴿فَخَلَفَ مِن بَعْدِهِمْ خَلْفٌ وَرِثُوا الْكِتَابَ يَأْخُذُونَ عَرَضَ هَٰذَا الْأَدْنَىٰ وَيَقُولُونَ سَيُغْفَرُ لَنَا وَإِن يَأْتِهِمْ عَرَضٌ مِّثْلُهُ يَأْخُذُوهُ أَلَمْ يُؤْخَذْ عَلَيْهِم مِّيثَاقُ الْكِتَابِ أَن لَّا يَقُولُوا عَلَى اللَّهِ إِلَّا الْحَقَّ﴾ [الأعراف ٧: ١٦٩] كذلك قال من [a٤٠] احتذى بهم من امّتنا: سيغفر لنا، بعدما أخذوا عرضًا في هذا الأدنى، وقالوا: قال رسول الله صلى الله عليه وآله: لو لم تذنبوا، لجا الله بأقوام يذنبون فيغفر لهم، والله تبارك وتعالى يقول ﴿وَمَا خَلَقْتُ الْجِنَّ وَالْإِنسَ إِلَّا لِيَعْبُدُونِ﴾ [الذاريات ٥١:

---

[٤٧] المدر: الهدى، الأصل.

[٤٨] المدر: المهدي، الأصل.

[٤٩] محاريب: محاريبًا، الأصل.

٥٦] وهم[٥٠] يقولون: خلقهم ليعصوه، ألم[٥١] يؤخذ عليهم ميثاق الكتاب أن لا يقولوا على الله إلّا الحقّ، ولما أن رفع الله عزّ وجلّ على بني إسرائيل جبل [b٤٠] الطور رفعه في الهواء على رؤوسهم لمعصيتهم نبيّهم موسى عليه السلام، فخوّفهم الله عزّ وجلّ واسترهبهم، وأخبرهم موسى عليه السلام إن لم يعطوا العهد والميثاق في طاعته أنّ الجبل واقع بهم، فخافوا إن عصوا يقع عليهم فيشدَخهم، فأخذ موسى عليه السلام يأخذ عليهم العهد والأيمان، فكلّما شرط عليهم من الطاعة شرطًا حرّكوا رؤوسهم بالإنعام مذعورين[٥٢] فزعين، فأخبره أنّهم سيكونون سامعين مطيعين، فزعمت اليهود [a٤١] أنهم حين حرّكوا رؤرسهم يومئذ للخوف من الجبل والفزع جعلوا التحريك تذكرة ثانية عند القراءة للتوراة شرعةً عليهم من الشرع، وذلك، زعموا، أنه كان[٥٣] يقرأ التوراة عليهم وما عهد الله فيها عليهم، مع كلّ عهد عَهِدَه الله عزّ وجلّ إليهم أو فرض فرضه الله عزّ وجلّ في التوراة عليهم الأيمان بالسمع والطاعة يستجيبون[٥٤] مسرعين

[٥٠] وهم: لا يعبدوهم هم، الأصل.

[٥١] ألم: لم، الأصل.

[٥٢] مذعورين: مذعورون، الأصل.

[٥٣] أنه كان: وكان، الأصل.

[٥٤] يستجيبون: مستجيبون، الأصل.

محرّكين رؤوسهم خوفًا من الجبل في قلوبهم مذعورة مرتاعة، قالوا: فتحريك رؤوسهم ذلك اليوم مسرعين فزعين بطاعة موسى عليه السلام مقرّين مذعنين ألزموا تحريك الرؤوس عند القراءة، [b٤١] كلّما اقرّوا ليكونوا بذلك اليوم وتلك الآية التي نجوا منها بعد خوفها ذاكرين غير ناسين، فيعبدون الله عزّ وجلّ كل يوم [عهدًا] على أنفسهم وينكثونه[٥٥] على المكان لمخالفتهم التوراة، قال الله عزّ وجلّ ﴿فبما نقضهم ميثاقهم [لعنّاهم و] جعلنا قلوبهم قاسية يحرّفون الكلم عن مواضعه﴾ [المائدة ٥: ١٣] فهم يعرفون الحجّة على أنفسهم لله عزّ وجلّ كلّ يوم إذ يزعمون أنهم سامعون مطيعون لعهده ذاكرون غير ناسين وهم عن الحقّ لاهون، كذلك أخذ رسول الله صلى [a٤٢] الله عليه وآله [ميثاق] أصحابه واشترط عليهم ما كان اشترط على النساء، ألا يشركوا بالله شيئًا ولا يسرقوا ولا يزنوا ولا يأتوا ببهتان يفترونه بين أيديهم، ولا يعصونه في معروف، ففي كلّ ليلة يجدّدون لله عزّ وجلّ على أنفسهم عهدًا وينكثونه بالنهار، والله عزّ وجلّ يقول ﴿يَا أَيُّهَا الَّذِينَ آمَنُوا لِمَ تَقُولُونَ مَا لَا تَفْعَلُونَ كَبُرَ مَقْتًا عِندَ اللَّهِ أَن تَقُولُوا مَا لَا تَفْعَلُونَ﴾ [الصف ٦١: ٢-٣] فهم يعهدون الله عزّ وجلّ في وترهم فيقولون:[٥٦] نخلع ونترك [b٤٢] من

---

[٥٥] وينكثونه: ومكتوبة (؟)، الأصل.

[٥٦] فيقولون: فيقولوا، الأصل.

يفجرك اللهمّ، وينكثون بالنهار إذ[٥٧] يفجرون بأنفسهم ويوالون الفجّار كفعل اليهود سرًا، حَذْوَ النعل بالنعل.

قال الله تعالى ﴿لُعِنَ الَّذِينَ كَفَرُوا مِن بَنِي إِسْرَائِيلَ عَلَىٰ لِسَانِ دَاوُودَ وَعِيسَى ابْنِ مَرْيَمَ ذَٰلِكَ بِمَا عَصَوا وَكَانُوا يَعْتَدُونَ كَانُوا لَا يَتَنَاهَوْنَ عَن مُنكَرٍ فَعَلُوهُ لَبِئْسَ مَا كَانُوا يَفْعَلُونَ تَرَىٰ كَثِيرًا مِنْهُمْ يَتَوَلَّوْنَ الَّذِينَ كَفَرُوا لَبِئْسَ مَا قَدَّمَتْ لَهُمْ أَنفُسُهُمْ سَخِطَ اللَّهُ عَلَيْهِمْ وَفِي الْعَذَابِ هُمْ خَالِدُونَ﴾ [المائدة ٥: ٧٨-٨٠] وكذلك ترى كثيرًا من هذه الأمّة يتولّون الذين كفروا [a٤٣] بحكم الكتاب والسنّة، ويسمّونهم خلفاء الله في أرضه على عباده بعد ما سمعوا الله عزّ وجلّ ينهاهم عن مودّة من حادّ الله ورسوله ولو كان أباءهم أو أبناءهم أو إخوانهم أو عشيرتهم، فولّاهم الله عزّ وجلّ ما تولّوا وأملأهم جهنّم وسائت مصيرًا، سلكوا مسلك فجرة بني إسرائيل فلُعنوا كما لعنوا، حَذْوَ النعل بالنعل.

وإن اليهود والنصارى اتّخذوا أعيادهم لعبًا ولهوًا، قال الله عزّ وجلّ: يا محمّد ﴿وَذَرِ الَّذِينَ اتَّخَذُوا دِينَهُمْ﴾، [b٤٣] يعني عيدهم ﴿لَعِبًا وَلَهْوًا وَغَرَّتْهُمُ الْحَيَاةُ الدُّنْيَا﴾ [الأنعام ٦: ٧٠] فاتّخذت أمّتنا أعيادهم لعبًا

[٥٧] إذ: ان، الأصل.

ولهوًا، فيوم عيدهم يوم زينتهم، ويوم عيدهم يركب[٥٨] الملوك والأغنياء ويلبسون المشهرات، وفسّاقهم يشربون الخمر ويتغنّون، ويحلّون جواريهم ونساءهم، وفتيانهم يلعبون بالصوالج، وغلمانهم يلعبون بالجوز والكعاب، يخرجون فرحين بطرين إلى أن يعودوا،[٥٩] وإنما كان رسول الله صلى الله عليه وآله يخرج وأصحابه يوم العيد وجلين خائفين متضرّعين [a٤٤] مبتهلين إلى الله عزّ وجلّ بقلوب خاشعة، وأبدان متواضعة، وعيون باكية، لا يدرون قبل منهم ما عملوا أم لا، وتركت الأمّة تلك السنّة في الأعياد وضاهوا اليهود والنصارى تركيبًا لسنّتهم واحتذاء بهم.

قال رسول الله صلى الله عليه وآله: لُعن اليهود الذين اتّخذوا قبور أنبيائهم مساجدًا، فاتّخذت أمّتنا قبر نبيّنا صلى الله عليه وآله مسجدًا، تركيبًا لسنّة بني إسرائيل واحتذاءً [b٤٤] بهم.

قال الله عزّ وجلّ ﴿الَّذِينَ أُخْرِجُوا مِن دِيَارِهِم بِغَيْرِ حَقٍّ إِلَّا أَن يَقُولُوا رَبُّنَا اللَّهُ﴾ [الحج ٢٢: ٤٠] كذلك أخرج أمّتنا من ديارهم بغير حقّ مَن أصدقُ لهجة ممّن أصّلته الخضراء وأقلّته الغبراء، لم ينقموا منه إلا أن كان قوّالًا بمُرّ الحقّ، حذو النعل بالنعل.

---

٥٨ يركب: يركبون، الأصل.

٥٩ يعودوا: يعودون، الأصل.

قال الله عزّ وجلّ ﴿وَمِنَ الْبَقَرِ وَالْغَنَمِ حَرَّمْنَا عَلَيْهِمْ شُحُومَهُمَآ إِلَّا مَا حَمَلَتْ ظُهُورُهُمَآ أَوِ الْحَوَايَآ أَوْ مَا اخْتَلَطَ بِعَظْمٍ﴾ [الأنعام ٦: ١٤٦] فدكّوها وأذابوها وباعوها وأكلوا أثمانها، وقالوا:[٦٠] [a٤٥] إنما حرّم علينا جمادها، كذلك حُرّم الخمر على هذه الأمّة، قال رسول الله صلى الله عليه وآله: الخمر ما خامر العقل وما أسكر، فقليله وكثيره حرام، والمذقة منه حرام، فجاءت المرجئة بشراب يسكر، فقالوا: هذا حلال وليس بخمر، وسمّوه نبيذًا وقالوا: إذا تخلّل[٦١] رفع عنه اسم الخمر، وقال رسول الله صلى الله عليه وآله : سيشرب[٦٢] ناس من أمّتي الخمر يدعونها [b٤٥] بغير اسمها، فأحلّوا الخمر بالطبيخ وطبخوها كما ذابت اليهود الشحم ورفعوا اسم الشحم وسمّوه دهنًا، فطبخوا هؤلاء الخمر وسمّوه نبيذًا، وقالوا: إنما حرّم علينا الخمر، والخمر ما لم تطبخ، كما قالت اليهود: إنما حرّم علينا جمادها، تركيبًا لسنتهم واحتذاء بهم.

وإن النصارى يستحلّون لحم الميتة ولحم الخنزير ويتلون بذلك أنه من الزبور، كذا استحلّت المرجئة أكل السباع والثعلب [a٤٦]....

[٦٠] وقالوا: وقال، الأصل.

[٦١] تحلل: تخلى، الأصل.

[٦٢] سيشرب: شرب، الأصل.

...[﴿وقد أخذ الله جلّ و عزّ ميثاق بني إسرائيل] وَبَعَثْنَا مِنْهُمُ اثْنَيْ عَشَرَ نَقِيبًا﴾[٦٣] وقال الله تعالى ﴿وَلَقَدْ أَخَذَ اللَّهُ مِيثَاقَ بَنِي إِسْرَائِيلَ وَبَعَثْنَا مِنْهُمُ اثْنَيْ عَشَرَ نَقِيبًا وَقَالَ اللَّهُ إِنِّي مَعَكُمْ لَئِنْ أَقَمْتُمُ الصَّلَاةَ وَآتَيْتُمُ الزَّكَاةَ وَآمَنتُم بِرُسُلِي وَعَزَّرْتُمُوهُمْ وَأَقْرَضْتُمُ اللَّهَ قَرْضًا حَسَنًا لَّأُكَفِّرَنَّ عَنكُمْ سَيِّئَاتِكُمْ وَلَأُدْخِلَنَّكُمْ جَنَّاتٍ تَجْرِي مِن تَحْتِهَا الْأَنْهَارُ فَمَن كَفَرَ بَعْدَ ذَٰلِكَ مِنكُمْ فَقَدْ ضَلَّ سَوَاءَ السَّبِيلِ فَبِمَا نَقْضِهِم مِّيثَاقَهُمْ لَعَنَّاهُمْ وَجَعَلْنَا قُلُوبَهُمْ قَاسِيَةً﴾ [المائدة ٥: ١٢-١٣] كذلك أخذ الله الميثاق على هذه الأمّة، وأخذ رسول الله صلى الله عليه وآله يوم بايعوه [b٤٦] ليمنعنّ عن أولاده ما يمنعون عن[٦٤] أولادهم، فلمّا نقضوا ميثاقهم لعنهم الله وجعل قلوبهم قاسية، منعوا الحسين وأهل بيته عليهم السلام الفرات وحلفوا: لتذوقنّ الموت قبل أن تذوق الماء يا حسين، وزعموا أنهم لا يفرضون بينه وبين رسول الله صلى الله عليه وآله قرابة فيقتلوه عطشان،[٦٥] قال الله عزّ وجلّ ﴿وَقَدْ كَانَ فَرِيقٌ مِّنْهُمْ يَسْمَعُونَ كَلَامَ اللَّهِ ثُمَّ يُحَرِّفُونَهُ مِن بَعْدِ مَا عَقَلُوهُ وَهُمْ يَعْلَمُونَ﴾ [البقرة ٢: ٧٥] كذلك [a٤٧] قالت

---

[٦٣] وقد أخذ...تقيبًا: قارن سورة المائدة ٥/ ١٢.

[٦٤] عن: عنه، الأصل.

[٦٥] عطشان: عطشاناً، الأصل.

الناصبة: إن الحسن والحسين عليهما السلام ليسا ابني[٦٦] رسول الله صلى الله عليه وآله، وتأوّلوا قول الله عزّ وجلّ ﴿مَا كَانَ مُحَمَّدٌ[٦٧] أَبَا أَحَدٍ مِّن رِّجَالِكُمْ وَلَٰكِن رَّسُولَ اللَّهِ وَخَاتَمَ النَّبِيِّينَ﴾ [الأحزاب ٣٣: ٤٠] فزوّجه [تعالى] زينب كي لا يكون على المؤمنين حرج في أزواج أدعيائهم، ونهى المؤمنين بعد ذلك أن يقولوا: زيد بن محمّد، فقال ﴿ادْعُوهُمْ لِآبَائِهِمْ هُوَ أَقْسَطُ عِندَ اللَّهِ فَإِن لَّمْ تَعْلَمُوا آبَاءَهُمْ فَإِخْوَانُكُمْ فِي الدِّينِ وَمَوَالِيكُمْ﴾ [الأحزاب ٣٣: ٥]، فنفوا ابنيه الحسن والحسين عليهما السلام، ولم يصدّقوا الله عزّ وجلّ [b٤٧] ورسوله صلى الله عليه وآله أن سمّاهما ابنَي رسول الله صلى الله عليه وآله في غير موضع: قل يا محمّد ﴿تَعَالَوْا نَدْعُ أَبْنَاءَنَا وَأَبْنَاءَكُمْ وَنِسَاءَنَا وَنِسَاءَكُمْ وَأَنفُسَنَا وَأَنفُسَكُمْ ثُمَّ نَبْتَهِلْ فَنَجْعَل لَّعْنَتَ اللَّهِ عَلَى الْكَاذِبِينَ﴾ [آل عمران ٣: ٦١] ولم يكن الله عزّ وجلّ يأمر أن يدعوا أبناءه وليس له بنون، وكان ابناه يومئذٍ الحسن والحسين عليهما السلام، ولم يكن له عليه السلام ابن غيرهما، وقد سمّاهما رسول الله صلى الله عليه وآله ابنيه في غير موضع.

وكذلك [a٤٨] قالوا في آية التطهير، قالوا: إنّما نزلت في نساء النبيّ، ونسوا ما ذكر الله تعالى عن نبيّه موسى عليه السلام ﴿اجْعَل

[٦٦] ابني: ابنا، الأصل.

[٦٧] محمد: محمداً، الأصل.

لِّي وَزِيرًا مِّنْ أَهْلِي هَارُونَ أَخِي اشْدُدْ بِهِ أَزْرِي﴾ [طه ٢٠: ٢٩-٣١] ولما أنزل الله عزّ وجلّ على نبيّه عليه السلام ﴿وَأْمُرْ أَهْلَكَ بِالصَّلَاةِ﴾ [طه ٢٠: ١٣٢] كان يأتي ستة أشهر باب عليّ وفاطمة عليهما السلام فيناديهما: الصلاة يا أهل البيت ﴿إِنَّمَا يُرِيدُ اللَّهُ لِيُذْهِبَ عَنكُمُ الرِّجْسَ أَهْلَ الْبَيْتِ وَيُطَهِّرَكُمْ تَطْهِيرًا﴾ [الأحزاب ٣٣: ٣٣] ولو كانت المخاطبة للنساء [b٤٨] لذكرهنّ بالتأنيث كما ذكرهنّ ﴿وَقَرْنَ فِي بُيُوتِكُنَّ وَلَا تَبَرَّجْنَ تَبَرُّجَ الْجَاهِلِيَّةِ الْأُولَىٰ وَأَقِمْنَ الصَّلَاةَ وَآتِينَ الزَّكَاةَ﴾ [الأحزاب ٣٣: ٣٣] فلما بلغ موضع التطهير ذكّرهم وذهب عنهم التأنيث، فقال ﴿إِنَّمَا يُرِيدُ اللَّهُ لِيُذْهِبَ عَنكُمُ الرِّجْسَ أَهْلَ الْبَيْتِ وَيُطَهِّرَكُمْ تَطْهِيرًا﴾ ولم يقُل: ويطهّركن تطهيراً، وذهب عنهم التأنيث مع شهادة رسول الله صلى الله عليه وآله لهم أنه قال: نزلت هذه الآية في خمس نفر، فيّ وفي عليّ وفاطمة والحسن [a٤٩] والحسين صلوات الله عليهم ﴿إِنَّمَا يُرِيدُ اللَّهُ لِيُذْهِبَ عَنكُمُ الرِّجْسَ﴾ الآية، وروت عنه أمّ سلمة عليها السلام أنه جمعهم في بيتها تحت كساء خيبريّ، فقال: هؤلاء عترتي وأهل بيتي، فاذهب عنهم الرجس وطهّرهم تطهيرًا، فقلتُ: وأنا من أهل بيتك؟ قال لها: وأنتِ إلى خير، وهذا لهم خاصةً، وكذلك روت عائشة، وروى النواس بن سمعان كذلك، قال: ثمّ لفّ عليهم ثوبًا وأنا جالس في ناحية، [b٤٩] قال ﴿إِنَّمَا يُرِيدُ اللَّهُ لِيُذْهِبَ عَنكُمُ الرِّجْسَ أَهْلَ الْبَيْتِ وَيُطَهِّرَكُمْ تَطْهِيرًا﴾ اللهم هؤلاء أهل بيتي أحقّ، فقلتُ: وأنا من أهل بيتك؟ قال:

وأنتَ من أهلي، قال النواس: إنها لمن رجا[٦٨] ما أرجو، فحرّفوا عن موضعه، فقالوا: نزلت في نساء النبي صلى الله عليه وآله، حرّفوه من بعد ما عقلوه وهم يعلمون كاليهود، حذو النعل بالنعل.

وإن الله تعالى قال ﴿فَوَيْلٌ لِلَّذِينَ يَكْتُبُونَ الْكِتَابَ بِأَيْدِيهِمْ ثُمَّ يَقُولُونَ هَٰذَا مِنْ عِنْدِ اللَّهِ﴾ [البقرة ٢: ٧٩] كذلك [a٥٠] قال بعض الصحابة: كنّا نقرأ على عهد رسول الله صلى الله عليه وآله: لو أن لابن آدم واديين من مال لابتغى الثالث، ولا يملأ بطن ابن آدم إلا التراب ويتوب الله على من تاب، والشيخ والشيخة فارجموهما نكالًا لما زنيا، وأشباهه، قال الله عزّ وجلّ في أمثالهم ﴿فَإِذَا بَرَزُوا مِنْ عِنْدِكَ﴾ يا محمّد ﴿بَيَّتَ طَائِفَةٌ مِنْهُمْ غَيْرَ الَّذِي تَقُولُ وَاللَّهُ يَكْتُبُ مَا يُبَيِّتُونَ﴾ [النساء ٤: ٨١] أي يكتب ما يريدون، حذو النعل بالنعل.

قال الله [b٥٠] عزّ وجلّ ﴿وَإِذْ نَجَّيْنَاكُمْ مِنْ آلِ فِرْعَوْنَ يَسُومُونَكُمْ سُوءَ الْعَذَابِ يُذَبِّحُونَ أَبْنَاءَكُمْ وَيَسْتَحْيُونَ نِسَاءَكُمْ وَفِي ذَٰلِكُمْ بَلَاءٌ مِنْ رَبِّكُمْ عَظِيمٌ﴾ [البقرة ٢: ٤٩] ثمّ قال عزّ وجلّ ﴿وَأَوْرَثْنَا الْقَوْمَ الَّذِينَ كَانُوا يُسْتَضْعَفُونَ مَشَارِقَ الْأَرْضِ وَمَغَارِبَهَا الَّتِي بَارَكْنَا فِيهَا وَتَمَّتْ كَلِمَتُ رَبِّكَ الْحُسْنَىٰ عَلَىٰ بَنِي إِسْرَائِيلَ بِمَا صَبَرُوا وَدَمَّرْنَا مَا كَانَ يَصْنَعُ فِرْعَوْنُ وَقَوْمُهُ وَمَا كَانُوا يَعْرِشُونَ﴾ [الأعراف ٧: ١٣٧] كذلك فعلت ظلمة آل محمّد

[٦٨] رجا: ارجا، الأصل.

صلى الله عليه وآله يذبّحون أبناءهم ويستحيون نساءهم ووعدهم [a٥١] ليهلكنّ عدوّهم وليُنجينّهم من عدوّهم وليستخلفنّهم في الأرض كبني[٦٩] إسرائيل، فقال عزّ وجلّ ﴿وَعَدَ اللَّهُ الَّذِينَ آمَنُوا مِنكُمْ وَعَمِلُوا الصَّالِحَاتِ لَيَسْتَخْلِفَنَّهُمْ فِي الْأَرْضِ كَمَا اسْتَخْلَفَ الَّذِينَ مِن قَبْلِهِمْ وَلَيُمَكِّنَنَّ لَهُمْ دِينَهُمُ الَّذِي ارْتَضَىٰ لَهُمْ وَلَيُبَدِّلَنَّهُم مِّن بَعْدِ خَوْفِهِمْ أَمْنًا يَعْبُدُونَنِي لَا يُشْرِكُونَ بِي شَيْئًا﴾ [النور ٢٤: ٥٥] وقال ﴿وَعْدَ اللَّهِ لَا يُخْلِفُ اللَّهُ وَعْدَهُ﴾ [الروم ٣٠: ٦] وقال ﴿وَفِي السَّمَاءِ رِزْقُكُمْ وَمَا تُوعَدُونَ﴾ [الذاريات ٥١: ٢٢] المهدي قائم آل محمّد عليه السلام، حذو النعل بالنعل.

وقالت اليهود [b٥١] ﴿لَن تَمَسَّنَا النَّارُ إِلَّا أَيَّامًا مَّعْدُودَةً﴾ [البقرة ٢: ٨٠] لسوء أعمالهم قال الله عزّ وجلّ ﴿وَغَرَّهُمْ فِي دِينِهِم مَّا كَانُوا يَفْتَرُونَ﴾ [آل عمران ٣: ٢٤] ردًا عليهم، قال الله عزّ وجلّ ﴿بَلَىٰ مَن كَسَبَ سَيِّئَةً وَأَحَاطَتْ بِهِ خَطِيئَتُهُ فَأُولَٰئِكَ أَصْحَابُ النَّارِ هُمْ فِيهَا خَالِدُونَ﴾ [البقرة ٢: ٨١] وكذلك قالت طائفة من أمّتنا من ضارع قولهم قول اليهود: ﴿لَن تَمَسَّنَا النَّارُ إِلَّا أَيَّامًا مَّعْدُودَةً﴾، ولا يخلّد أحد منّا في النار، وكذبوا على نبيّنا محمّد صلى الله عليه وآله، ذكروا عنه أنه قال: لو كان هذا القرآن في إهابٍ ما مسّته النار أبدًا، [a٥٢] فادّعوا أنّ من قرأ القرآن لا يمسّه النار أبدًا ولو عمل بالموبقات، قال الله سبحانه لا

---

٦٩ كبني: لبني، الأصل.

شريك له ﴿وُجُوهٌ يَوْمَئِذٍ خَاشِعَةٌ عَامِلَةٌ نَّاصِبَةٌ تَصْلَىٰ نَارًا حَامِيَةً﴾ [الغاشية ٨٨: ٢-٤] وقال ﴿إِنَّ الَّذِينَ يَأْكُلُونَ أَمْوَالَ الْيَتَامَىٰ ظُلْمًا إِنَّمَا يَأْكُلُونَ فِي بُطُونِهِمْ نَارًا وَسَيَصْلَوْنَ سَعِيرًا﴾ [النساء ٤: ١٠] وقال تعالى ﴿وَمَن يَقْتُلْ مُؤْمِنًا مُّتَعَمِّدًا فَجَزَاؤُهُ جَهَنَّمُ خَالِدًا فِيهَا﴾ [النساء ٤: ٩٣] فزعمت المرجئة أن لا يخلّد أحد من أهل القبلة في النار وأنّ آخر من يخرج منها من هذه الأمّة رجل يبقى في [b٥٢] النار سبعين ألف عام وسبعين ألف عام معدودة كما قال اليهود، قال الله تعالى: يا محمّد ﴿قُلْ أَتَّخَذْتُمْ عِندَ اللَّهِ عَهْدًا فَلَن يُخْلِفَ اللَّهُ عَهْدَهُ أَمْ تَقُولُونَ عَلَى اللَّهِ مَا لَا تَعْلَمُونَ بَلَىٰ مَن كَسَبَ سَيِّئَةً وَأَحَاطَتْ بِهِ خَطِيئَتُهُ فَأُولَٰئِكَ أَصْحَابُ النَّارِ هُمْ فِيهَا خَالِدُونَ﴾ [البقرة ٢: ٨٠-٨١] وقال تعالى ﴿لَّيْسَ بِأَمَانِيِّكُمْ وَلَا أَمَانِيِّ أَهْلِ الْكِتَابِ مَن يَعْمَلْ سُوءًا يُجْزَ بِهِ﴾ [النساء ٤: ١٢٣] وقال تعالى ﴿لَا يَأْمَنُ مَكْرَ اللَّهِ إِلَّا الْقَوْمُ الْخَاسِرُونَ﴾ [الأعراف ٧: ٩٩] فأمنوا مكر الله وبهتوا رسول الله [a٥٣] صلى الله عليه وآله: لو كان هذا القرآن في إهاب ما مسّته النار أبدًا، وزعموا أن لا يبقى أحد[٧٠] في النار بعد سبعين ألف ألف عام، وأن الحجّاج بن يوسف وأبا العادية وعبيد الله بن زياد وعمر بن سعد ويزيد بن معاوية وابن ملجم وأشباههم من اللعناء يخرجون يومًا من النار فيدخلون الجنّة مكتوبًا على جباههم:

---

٧٠ أحد: -، الأصل.

هؤلاء الجهنّميون عتقاء الرحمن، وقد قال رسول الله صلى الله عليه وآله: أشقى الأوّلين والآخرين قدار بن سالف، وعبد [b٥٣] الرحمن بن ملجم قاتلك يا علي أشقى ولد آدم من الأوّلين والآخرين، أفيخرج من النار أشقى الخلق ويُترك فيها من هو أسعد منه؟

والله يقول ﴿فَأَمَّا الَّذِيْنَ شَقُوْا فَفِى النَّارِ لَهُمْ فِيْهَا زَفِيْرٌ وَّشَهِيْقٌ خٰلِدِيْنَ فِيْهَا مَا دَامَتِ السَّمٰوٰتُ وَالْاَرْضُ اِلَّا مَا شَآءَ رَبُّكَ﴾ [هود ١١: ١٠٦-١٠٧] ﴿وَاَمَّا الَّذِيْنَ سُعِدُوْا فَفِى الْجَنَّةِ خٰلِدِيْنَ فِيْهَا مَا دَامَتِ السَّمٰوٰتُ وَالْاَرْضُ﴾ [هود ١١: ١٠٨] كيف زالت عنهم اسم السعادة حين دخلوا النار ومرجعهم إلى الجنّة، أم كيف زال عنهم اسم الشقاء وكانوا في [a٥٤] النار لا يدخلها إلا شقيّ خزٍ[٧١] كافر؟ تعالى الله عن خُلف وعده ووعيده، قال الله تعالى ﴿يَوْمَ لَا يُخْزِي اللَّهُ النَّبِيَّ وَالَّذِينَ آمَنُوا مَعَهُ﴾ [التحريم ٦٦: ٨] وقال ﴿إِنَّ الْخِزْيَ الْيَوْمَ وَالسُّوءَ عَلَى الْكَافِرِينَ﴾ [النحل ١٦: ٢٧] وقال ﴿ رَبَّنَا إِنَّكَ مَن تُدْخِلِ النَّارَ فَقَدْ أَخْزَيْتَهُ وَمَا لِلظَّالِمِينَ مِنْ أَنصَارٍ﴾ [آل عمران ٣: ١٩٢] وقال ﴿وَإِنَّ جَهَنَّمَ لَمُحِيطَةٌ بِالْكَافِرِينَ﴾ [التوبة ٩: ٤٩] فمن أحاطته جهنم فهو كافر، إما كافر شرك وإما كافر نعمة، ومن لزمه اسم الكفر حرّم عليه نعيم الجنّة، قال [الله تعلى] يحكي عن مسألة أهل النار أهل الأعراف ﴿أَنْ أَفِيضُوا

---

[٧١] خز: خري، الأصل.

عَلَيْنَا مِنَ الْمَاءِ [b٥٤] أَوْ مِمَّا رَزَقَكُمُ اللَّهُ قَالُوا إِنَّ اللَّهَ حَرَّمَهُمَا عَلَى الْكَافِرِينَ﴾ [الأعراف ٧: ٥٠] ومن لم يلزمه هذا الاسم من الوجهين جميعًا فهم ﴿عَنْهَا مُبْعَدُونَ لَا يَسْمَعُونَ حَسِيسَهَا وَهُمْ فِي مَا اشْتَهَتْ أَنفُسُهُمْ خَالِدُونَ﴾ [الأنبياء ٢١: ١٠١-١٠٢].

وأما معنى الحديث الذي جاء في الشفاعة والخروج من النار، ما كان من لحق المواقف في الحساب وما يأخذهم النار على الصراط، منهم من أخذته النار إلى كعبيه ومنهم إلى ركبتيه وإلى حقويه وسُرّته وعنقه، وأما من حاطته جهنّم وأحاطت به خطيئته فهو مخلّد في النار أبدًا [a٥٥] سرمدًا خلودًا لا موت فيها ولا نهاية لعذابها، كما أنّ من أدخل الجنّة بقي فيها خالدًا مخلّدًا لا موت فيها ولا زوال لنعيمه، بل ﴿هُمْ فِي مَا اشْتَهَتْ أَنفُسُهُمْ خَالِدُونَ لَا يَحْزُنُهُمُ الْفَزَعُ الْأَكْبَرُ وَتَتَلَقَّاهُمُ الْمَلَائِكَةُ هَـٰذَا يَوْمُكُمُ الَّذِي كُنتُمْ تُوعَدُونَ﴾ [الأنبياء ٢١: ١٠٢-١٠٣] ويقولون ﴿سَلَامٌ عَلَيْكُمْ طِبْتُمْ فَادْخُلُوهَا خَالِدِينَ﴾ [الزمر ٣٩: ٧٣] ليس كمقالة من غرّهم في دينهم ما كانوا يقترفون حتّى عتت الأمّة على ربّها بقول علماء السوء، تركيبًا لسنّة بني إسرائيل واحتذاءً بهم.

وإن عُبّاد بني [b٥٥] إسرائيل لما ظهر لهم الفساد في أمّتهم اعتزلوهم واتّخذوا صوامع[٧٢] في رؤوس الجبال للعبادة، وتركوا الجهاد والأمر

---

[٧٢] صوامع: صوامعاً، الأصل.

بالمعروف والنهي عن المنكر، قال الله سبحانه ﴿وَرَهْبَانِيَّةً ابْتَدَعُوهَا مَا كَتَبْنَاهَا عَلَيْهِمْ إِلَّا ابْتِغَاءَ رِضْوَانِ اللَّهِ فَمَا رَعَوْهَا حَقَّ رِعَايَتِهَا﴾ [الحديد ٥٧: ٢٧] أي ما فرضنا عليهم ولا أمرنا بذلك. كذلك فعلت رهبانية أمّتنا، تركوا الأمر بالمعروف والنهي عن المنكر كما وُصفوا: يأتي على الناس يوم[٧٣] يتبع فيه قوم[٧٤] أحداثا سفهاءُ لا يرضون أمرًا [بالمعروف] ولا نهيًا عن منكر [a٥٦] إلا إذا أمنوا الضرّ، يتبعون زلّات العلماء وشاذّ علمهم، يُقبلون على الصلاة والصيام وما لا يكلّفهم[٧٥] في نفس ولا مال، ولو أضرّت الصلاة والصيام وسائر ما يعملونه بأموالهم وأبدانهم لرفضوهما كما رفضوا أمّ الفرائض واشرفها، الأمر بالمعروف والنهي عن المنكر، فهناك يتمّ غضب الله عليهم فيعمّهم بعذابه، فيهلك الأبرار في ذات الفجّار والضعفاء في ذات الكبار، كما روى مُعاذ بن جبل عن رسول الله صلى الله عليه وآله، [b٥٦] قال: يكون أقوام في آخر الزمان يحبسون أنفسهم في المساجد، يبتدعون كلامًا ليس من الكتاب ولا من السنّة، فإيّاكم وإيّاهم، وفي حديث آخر عن رسول الله صلى الله عليه وآله أنه قال: يلبسون جلود الضان، قلوبهم مثل قلوب الذئاب، ألسنتهم

---

٧٣ يوم: قوم، الأصل.

٧٤ قوم: قوماً، الأصل.

٧٥ يكلفهم: يكلمهم، الأصل.

أحلى من السكر، كما غلب الأمّة المتمزقة ببدعٍ كلامُهم الذي ليس من الكتاب ولا من السنّة. وقد وعظ عباده على لسان نبيّه صلى الله عليه وآله وسلّم ما يغنيهم عن مواعظ [a٥٧] شقيق وحاتم ومُعاذ وابن كرام وسائر رهابن الأمّة، لم يكتفوا بمواعظ الله حتّى اخترعوا من ذات أنفسهم، وقال الله عزّ وجلّ ﴿وَلَقَدْ جَاءَهُم مِّنَ الْأَنبَاءِ مَا فِيهِ مُزْدَجَرٌ﴾ [القمر ٥٤: ٤] فمن لم يُزجر[٧٦] بما زجره الله لم يُغنينّه[٧٧] ما قالت الرهابنة الذين ابتدعوا ما لم يفرض الله عليهم، تركيبًا لسنّة بني إسرائيل واحتذاءً بهم.

ثمّ إن الله امتحن بني إسرائيل في يوم سبتهم، قال الله جلّ جلاله ﴿وَقُلْنَا لَهُمْ لَا تَعْدُوا فِي السَّبْتِ وَأَخَذْنَا مِنْهُم مِّيثَاقًا غَلِيظًا﴾ [النساء ٤: ١٥٤] فلمّا طال عليهم الأمد اعتدت [b٥٧] عُصبة منهم في السبت، فصاروا ثلاث فرق، فرقة اصطادوا فرقة خرجوا من بين أظهرهم حين رأوا عداوتهم ولم يقدروا التغيير عليهم، وفرقة لم يتناهوا عنه، فمسخ الفرقتين قردة وأنجى الثالثة،[٧٨] قال الله سبحانه وله المثل الأعلى ﴿أَنجَيْنَا الَّذِينَ يَنْهَوْنَ عَنِ السُّوءِ وَأَخَذْنَا الَّذِينَ ظَلَمُوا بِعَذَابٍ بَئِيسٍ﴾ [الأعراف

---

[٧٦] يزجر: يزجره، الأصل.

[٧٧] يغنينه: يغينه، الأصل.

[٧٨] الثالثة: الثالث، الأصل.

٧: ١٦٥] ثمّ إن الله جلّ جلاله امتنحن أمّتنا بطاعتهم وليّهم واعتدت عليهم فرقة من الأمّة عدوان اليهود في السبت، وهم [a٥٨] القاسطون، وفرقة اعتزلوهم، لم ينهوهم عن بغيهم وهم المعتزلة الأول فلم يقتلوا الباغي من الطائفتين، قال الله سبحانه ﴿وَإِن طَائِفَتَانِ مِنَ الْمُؤْمِنِينَ اقْتَتَلُوا فَأَصْلِحُوا بَيْنَهُمَا فَإِن بَغَتْ إِحْدَاهُمَا عَلَى الْأُخْرَىٰ فَقَاتِلُوا الَّتِي تَبْغِي حَتَّىٰ تَفِيءَ إِلَىٰ أَمْرِ اللَّهِ﴾ [الحجرات ٤٩: ٩] فزعموا أن الأمر اشتبه عليهم، ولم يدروا من الباغي منهما، وقد سمعوا جميعًا من رسول الله صلى الله عليه وآله يقول: ويحًا لعمّار، تقتله الفئة الباغية، وسمعوا من رسول الله صلى الله عليه وآله، يقول: تقتتل[٧٩] فئتان عظيمتان[٨٠] [b٥٨] دعواهما واحدة، يخرج من بينهما فئة مارقة تقتل أولاهما بالحقّ، سوى ما سمعوا من رسول الله صلى الله عليه وآله يقول: عليّ مع الحقّ والحقّ مع علي، لن يفترقا حتّى يردا على الحوض، وإن عمّارًا قُتل مع علي عليه السلام ويمرق الجاحدون من عسكره، وهم لقوله[٨١] مستمعون،[٨٢] ونحوه[٨٣] من

---

[٧٩] تقتتل: تقتل، الأصل.

[٨٠] فئتان عظيمتان: عئين عظيمتين، الأصل.

[٨١] لقوله: بياض في الأصل.

[٨٢] مستمعون: مستمع، الأصل.

[٨٣] ونحوه: ونحو، الأصل.

الدلالات ما أخبرهم الصدوق، والقاسطة والمعتزلة كالذين اعتدوا في السبت، والمعتزلة وصف الله تعالى طائفة من المنافقين ﴿قَالُوا لَوْ نَعْلَمُ قِتَالًا[٨٤] لَّاتَّبَعْنَاكُمْ هُمْ لِلْكُفْرِ [a٥٩] يَوْمَئِذٍ أَقْرَبُ مِنْهُمْ لِلْإِيمَانِ﴾ [آل عمران ٣: ١٦٧] وهم متردّدون بين ذلك، لا إلى هؤلاء ولا إلى هؤلاء، لا هم عرفوا حقًّا فاتّبعوه، ولا أنكروا[٨٥] باطلًا فاجتنبوه، وهم بمنزلة من لم يتناه[٨٦] عن منكر من بني إسرائيل، والذين نصروا الولي هم بمنزلة من فارق فجّار بني إسرائيل لعدوانهم، إنّما كان أمران من الله واجبان، قال الله عزّ وجلّ لهم ﴿لَا تَعْدُوا فِي السَّبْتِ﴾ [النساء ٤: ١٥٤] وقال لنا ﴿أَطِيعُوا الرَّسُولَ وَأُولِي الْأَمْرِ مِنكُمْ﴾ [النساء ٤: ٥٩] فلم يُطع الله الفريقان في وليّ أمرهم، [b٥٩] تركيبًا لسنّة بني إسرائيل واحتذاءً بهم.

قال الله عزّ وجلّ ﴿أَلَمْ تَرَ إِلَى الْمَلَإِ مِن بَنِي إِسْرَائِيلَ مِن بَعْدِ مُوسَىٰ إِذْ قَالُوا لِنَبِيٍّ لَّهُمُ ابْعَثْ لَنَا مَلِكًا نُّقَاتِلْ فِي سَبِيلِ اللَّهِ قَالَ هَلْ عَسَيْتُمْ إِن كُتِبَ عَلَيْكُمُ الْقِتَالُ أَلَّا تُقَاتِلُوا قَالُوا وَمَا لَنَا أَلَّا نُقَاتِلَ فِي سَبِيلِ اللَّهِ وَقَدْ أُخْرِجْنَا مِن دِيَارِنَا وَأَبْنَائِنَا فَلَمَّا كُتِبَ عَلَيْهِمُ الْقِتَالُ تَوَلَّوْا إِلَّا قَلِيلًا مِّنْهُمْ وَاللَّهُ عَلِيمٌ بِالظَّالِمِينَ﴾ [البقرة ٢: ٢٤٦] كذلك قيل لرسول الله

---

[٨٤] قتالًا: قتال، الأصل.

[٨٥] أنكروا: نكروا، الأصل.

[٨٦] يتناه: يتناها، الأصل.

صلى الله عليه وآله يوم صلح [a٦٠] الحُدَيبية: ألسنا على الحقّ وهم على الباطل؟ قال: بلى، قالوا: فعلامَ نعطى الدنيّة في وليّنا ومن لم يحكم بيننا وبينهم؟ سألوه القتال وأعرضوا عن الصلح، فلما كُتب عليهم[٨٧] قتال أهل البغي ﴿تَوَلَّوْا إِلَّا قَلِيلًا مِّنْهُمْ وَاللَّهُ عَلِيمٌ بِالظَّالِمِينَ﴾ [البقرة ٢: ٢٤٦] وذكر الله عزّ وجلّ عن بني إسرائيل إذ ﴿قَالَ لَهُمْ نَبِيُّهُمْ إِنَّ اللَّهَ قَدْ بَعَثَ لَكُمْ طَالُوتَ مَلِكًا قَالُوا أَنَّىٰ يَكُونُ لَهُ الْمُلْكُ عَلَيْنَا وَنَحْنُ أَحَقُّ بِالْمُلْكِ مِنْهُ وَلَمْ يُؤْتَ سَعَةً مِّنَ الْمَالِ قَالَ إِنَّ اللَّهَ اصْطَفَاهُ [b٦٠] عَلَيْكُمْ وَزَادَهُ بَسْطَةً فِي الْعِلْمِ وَالْجِسْمِ وَاللَّهُ يُؤْتِي مُلْكَهُ مَن يَشَاءُ وَاللَّهُ وَاسِعٌ عَلِيمٌ﴾ [البقرة ٢: ٢٤٧] ﴿وَقَالَ لَهُمْ نَبِيُّهُمْ إِنَّ آيَةَ مُلْكِهِ أَن يَأْتِيَكُمُ التَّابُوتُ فِيهِ سَكِينَةٌ مِّن رَّبِّكُمْ وَبَقِيَّةٌ مِّمَّا تَرَكَ آلُ مُوسَىٰ﴾ [البقرة ٢: ٢٤٨] وكذلك قال للنبيّ صلى الله عليه وآله بعض أصحابه: واللهِ ما ندري ما يصحبنا، أفلا[٨٨] تُعلمنا بخليفتك فينا فيكون مفزعنا إليه؟ فقال النبي صلى الله عليه وآله: أما إني أعلمه وأرى مكانه، ولو فعلتُ ذلك لتفرّقتم عنه كما تفرّق بنو إسرائيل عن هارون ...

[ففال موسى كما أخبر الله] [a٦١] عزّ وجلّ للسامري ﴿إِنَّ لَكَ فِي الْحَيَاةِ أَن تَقُولَ لَا مِسَاسَ وَإِنَّ لَكَ مَوْعِدًا لَّن تُخْلَفَهُ﴾ [طه ٢٠:

---

[٨٧] عليهم: -، الأصل.

[٨٨] أفلا: فلا، الأصل.

٩٧]، كذلك قالت سامرة الأمّة: لا قتال، وسئل رسول الله صلى الله عليه وآله يوم ذكر أنهم على ملّة السامري، قالوا: يا رسول الله يقولون لا مساس؟ قال: لا، لكن لا قتال، حذو النعل وبالنعل.

قال الله جلّ جلاله ﴿وَإِذْ أَخَذْنَا مِيثَاقَكُمْ لَا تَسْفِكُونَ دِمَاءَكُمْ وَلَا تُخْرِجُونَ أَنفُسَكُم مِّن دِيَارِكُمْ ثُمَّ أَقْرَرْتُمْ وَأَنتُمْ تَشْهَدُونَ﴾ إلى قوله ﴿وَمَا اللَّهُ بِغَافِلٍ﴾ [البقرة ٢: ٨٤-٨٥] كذلك أخذ الله الميثاق على هذه الأمّة بلسان نبيّه عليه السلام يوم بايعوه [b٦١] أن يمنعوا أولاد رسول الله صلى الله عليه وآله عما يمنعون أولادهم، ثمّ خذلوهم وسلّموهم إلى الدعيّ بن الدعيّ، فقتلهم وسباهم، فلمّا أرسلهم[٨٩] يزيد لعنه الله إلى المدينة فأمر أهلها على أن لا يدخلوا إلى المدينة، وقد أوجب الله عليهم إن يأتوهم أسارى يفدوهم وهو محرّم عليهم إخراجهم، فجزاهم الله تعالى الخزي في الحياة الدنيا، جريان العذل وذهاب نصيبهم من الفيء وتسليط من يسوءهم سوء العذاب ﴿وَيَوْمَ [a٦٢] الْقِيَامَةِ يُرَدُّونَ إِلَىٰ أَشَدِّ الْعَذَابِ وَمَا اللَّهُ بِغَافِلٍ عَمَّا تَعْمَلُونَ﴾ [البقرة ٢: ٨٥]، حذو النعل بالنعل.

---

[٨٩] أرسلهم: راسلهم، الأصل.

وأمر الله تعالى بني إسرائيل أن يدخلوا الباب سُجّدًا ويقولوا ﴿حِطَّةٌ نَّغْفِرْ لَكُمْ خَطَايَاكُمْ وَسَنَزِيدُ الْمُحْسِنِينَ﴾ [البقرة ٢: ٥٨]،[٩٠] فدخلوا الباب رافعي رؤوسهم وقالوا حنطة، قال الله تعالى ﴿فَبَدَّلَ الَّذِينَ ظَلَمُوا قَوْلًا غَيْرَ الَّذِي قِيلَ لَهُمْ فَأَنزَلْنَا عَلَى الَّذِينَ ظَلَمُوا رِجْزًا مِنَ السَّمَاءِ بِمَا كَانُوا يَفْسُقُونَ﴾ [البقرة ٢: ٥٩] والرجز العذاب الذي غرقوا به. وأمر الله عزّ [b٦٢] وجلّ أمّتنا بمودّة نبيّهم صلى الله عليه وآله، قال الله عزّ وجلّ ﴿قُل لَّا أَسْأَلُكُمْ عَلَيْهِ أَجْرًا إِلَّا الْمَوَدَّةَ فِي الْقُرْبَىٰ وَمَن يَقْتَرِفْ حَسَنَةً نَّزِدْ لَهُ فِيهَا حُسْنًا﴾ [الشورى ٤٢: ٢٣] فقد[٩١] جحدوا أهل بيته من بعد مودّتهم، فبخسوا أجره، وصغّروا قدره، وخالفوا أمره واستضعفوه "بدّل الذين ظلموا قولًا غير الذي قيل لهم[٩٢] فأنزل الله من السماء رجزًا بما كانوا يفسقون" عمّتهم فتنة بقي الحليم فيها حيران،[٩٣] قال الله سبحانه ﴿فَلْيَحْذَرِ [a٦٣] الَّذِينَ يُخَالِفُونَ عَنْ أَمْرِهِ أَن تُصِيبَهُمْ فِتْنَةٌ أَوْ يُصِيبَهُمْ عَذَابٌ أَلِيمٌ﴾ [النور ٢٤: ٦٣] قال الله سبحانه ﴿وَاتْلُ عَلَيْهِمْ نَبَأَ الَّذِي آتَيْنَاهُ آيَاتِنَا فَانسَلَخَ مِنْهَا فَأَتْبَعَهُ الشَّيْطَانُ فَكَانَ مِنَ الْغَاوِينَ وَلَوْ

---

[٩٠] أن يدخلوا...المحسنين: قارن البقرة ٢/ ٥٨ و الأعراف ٧/ ١٦١.

[٩١] فقد: أي، الأصل.

[٩٢] لهم: سقط في الأصل.

[٩٣] حيران: حيرانًا، الأصل.

شِئْنَا لَرَفَعْنَاهُ بِهَا وَلَٰكِنَّهُ أَخْلَدَ إِلَى الْأَرْضِ وَاتَّبَعَ هَوَاهُ فَمَثَلُهُ كَمَثَلِ الْكَلْبِ إِن تَحْمِلْ عَلَيْهِ يَلْهَثْ أَوْ تَتْرُكْهُ يَلْهَث﴾ [الأعراف ٧: ١٧٥-١٧٦] لم ينتفع بما أتاه الله من الآيات أن خسف الله بحماره الذي يشطنه، كذلك الزبير منّ الله عليه أن عرف حقّ من أوجب عليه حقّه [b٦٣] فكان يقاتل دون بيعته، ثمّ استغواه ابنه وطلحة، فانسلخ منها، فأتبعه الشيطان، فكان من الغاوين ولو شاء الله لرفعه بولائه من أوجب الله ولايته، لكنّه أخلد إلى الأرض، فطلب الأثرة ولم يرض الأسوة، ﴿فَمَثَلُهُ كَمَثَلِ الْكَلْبِ إِن تَحْمِلْ عَلَيْهِ يَلْهَثْ أَوْ تَتْرُكْهُ يَلْهَث﴾، ذُكر له ما حذّره رسول الله صلى الله عليه وآله: لتقاتلنّه وأنت له ظالم، كان كما كان ناسيًا[٩٤] قولًا من الصغر،[٩٥] لم ينصر من أوجب الله نصره.

وإن صفراء بنت شعيب خرجت [a٦٤] على يوشع بن نون بعد لاوي عليه السلام وقتل فيما بينهم سبعون ألفًا، قال الله سبحانه للحميراء ﴿يَا نِسَاءَ النَّبِيِّ لَسْتُنَّ كَأَحَدٍ مِّنَ النِّسَاءِ إِنِ اتَّقَيْتُنَّ فَلَا تَخْضَعْنَ بِالْقَوْلِ فَيَطْمَعَ الَّذِي فِي قَلْبِهِ مَرَضٌ وَقُلْنَ قَوْلًا مَّعْرُوفًا وَقَرْنَ فِي بُيُوتِكُنَّ وَلَا تَبَرَّجْنَ تَبَرُّجَ الْجَاهِلِيَّةِ الْأُولَىٰ﴾ [الأحزاب ٣٣: ٣٢-٣٣] يعني

---

[٩٤] ناسياً: ناسي، الأصل.

[٩٥] الصغر: الصغير، الأصل.

صفراء بنت شُعيب المخاطبة على التسعة،[٩٦] والمعنيّ[٩٧] منهنّ واحد لسابق علم الله فيها أنها صاحبة كلاب حوئب[٩٨] والمحرّضة على قتال المؤمنين [b٦٤] وهاتكة ستر رسول الله صلى الله عليه وآله، كقوله ﴿وَأَنذِرْ عَشِيرَتَكَ الْأَقْرَبِينَ﴾ [الشعراء ٢٦: ٢١٤] كانت المخاطبة على أربعين رجلًا من بني عبد المطّلب دون الأمّة القاطبة ليكون لهم المسبقة إلى دين الله عزّ وجلّ دون غيرهم، والمعنيّ[٩٩] فيهم علي بن أبي طالب عليه السلام إذ علم الله تعالى أنه لا يجيبه[١٠٠] أحد في ذلك اليوم غيره.

قال الله سبحانه ﴿إِنَّ آيَةَ مُلْكِهِ أَن يَأْتِيَكُمُ التَّابُوتُ فِيهِ سَكِينَةٌ مِّن رَّبِّكُمْ وَبَقِيَّةٌ مِّمَّا تَرَكَ آلُ مُوسَىٰ وَآلُ هَارُونَ تَحْمِلُهُ ...﴾ [البقرة ٢: ٢٤٨] ...

---

[٩٦] التسعة: السبعة، الأصل.

[٩٧] والمعني: والمعنا، الأصل.

[٩٨] حوئب: الحوب، الأصل.

[٩٩] والمعني: والمُعنا، الأصل.

[١٠٠] يجيبه: يجبه، الأصل.

... [a٦٥] وقال رسول الله صلى الله عليه وآله: ليلة أُسري بي إلى السماء رأيت أقوامًا تُقرَض شفاههم بمقاريض من نار، فقلتُ: يا جبريل من هؤلاء؟ قال: هؤلاء خطباء أمّتك الذين يأمرون بالقسط وينسون أنفسهم، وهم يتلون الكتاب، أفلا يعقلون؟ وإنّ بني إسرائيل لما عصوا رسول الله غضب الله عليهم، فتاهوا أربعين سنة في الأرض، كلّما ارتحلوا دارت بهم الأرض إلى دورهم عقوبة لهم حيث قالوا لنبيّهم عليه السلام ﴿اذْهَبْ [b٦٥] أَنتَ وَرَبُّكَ فَقَاتِلَا إِنَّا هَاهُنَا قَاعِدُونَ﴾ [المائدة ٥: ٢٤] وإن أمّتنا لما عصوا وصيّ رسول الله صلى الله عليهما غضب الله تعالى عليهم فكانوا يتيهون في الأرض ثمانين سنة متحيّرين في الدين عقوبة لهم بمخالفة أمر وليّهم، فكان زمن بني أميّة على هذه الأمّة كتيه بني إسرائيل، حذو النعل بالنعل.

﴿وَقَالَتِ الْيَهُودُ يَدُ اللَّهِ مَغْلُولَةٌ غُلَّتْ أَيْدِيهِمْ وَلُعِنُوا بِمَا قَالُوا﴾ [المائدة ٥: ٦٤] كذلك قالت إخوانهم من المرجئة: يُملأ جهنّم من قدم الرحمن تبارك وتعالى حين تقول النار: قط [a٦٦] قط، يعني حسبي حسبي سبحان الله عمّا يصفون إلا عباد الله المخلصين، فوصفوا الله كما وصفت اليهود، حَذْو النعل بالنعل.

وإن اليهود والنصارى، لما رأوا ضلالة أهل الأديان وكان في أنبيائهم الكتاب، أعجبهم أنفسهم، قالوا ﴿لَن يَدْخُلَ الْجَنَّةَ إِلَّا مَن كَانَ هُودًا أَوْ

نَصَارَىٰ﴾ [البقرة ٢: ١١١] قال الله سبحانه ﴿تِلْكَ أَمَانِيُّهُمْ قُلْ هَاتُوا بُرْهَانَكُمْ إِن كُنتُمْ صَادِقِينَ﴾ [البقرة ٢: ١١١] وقد كانوا من قبل يشهد بعضهم على بعض بالضلالة، ﴿قَالَتِ[١٠١] الْيَهُودُ لَيْسَتِ النَّصَارَىٰ عَلَىٰ شَيْءٍ وَقَالَتِ النَّصَارَىٰ [b٦٦] لَيْسَتِ الْيَهُودُ عَلَىٰ شَيْءٍ﴾ [البقرة ٢: ١١٣] فلما افترق أمّتنا صاروا فرقًا يلعن بعضهم بعضًا، فسلخ الله تعالى الحروريّة بمروقهم من الدين والمعتزلة بخذلهم والجهمية بضلالتهم وسائر الأهواء بأهوائهم وبدعتهم، بقيت فرقتان متناسبتان،[١٠٢] أحدهما زعم أنه جماعي، والآخر زعم أنه سنّي، وقد ظهر لهم فحش مقالة سائر الأهواء وضلالتهم، أعجبهم أنفسهم، قالوا: لن يدخل الجنة إلا من كان [a٦٧] اختار أن يقتل الحسين، فقاتل الحسين حتّى قتل الحسين ووُجّه برأسه إلى اللعين بن اللعين، فوضعه في طست من ذهب، حَذْوَ النعل بالنعل.

وقد أحرق فجرة بني إسرائيل في زمنهم خير أهل زمانهم، أمرهم بالقسط ودعاهم إلى الرحمن، لم ينقموا منهم إلا أن آمنوا ﴿بِاللَّهِ الْعَزِيزِ الْحَمِيدِ الَّذِي لَهُ مُلْكُ السَّمَاوَاتِ وَالْأَرْضِ﴾ [البروج ٨٥: ٨-٩] قال الله سبحانه ﴿قُتِلَ أَصْحَابُ الْأُخْدُودِ النَّارِ ذَاتِ الْوَقُودِ إِذْ هُمْ عَلَيْهَا قُعُودٌ وَهُمْ عَلَىٰ مَا يَفْعَلُونَ بِالْمُؤْمِنِينَ شُهُودٌ وَمَا نَقَمُوا مِنْهُمْ إِلَّا [b٦٧] أَن يُؤْمِنُوا

---

١٠١ قالت: في المصحف العثماني: وقالت.

١٠٢ فرقتان متناسبتان: فرقتين متناسبتين، الأصل.

بِاللَّهِ الْعَزِيزِ الْحَمِيدِ﴾ [البروج ٨٥: ٤-٨] كذلك أحرق فجرة بني أميّة خير أهل زمانهم، لم ينقموا منهم إلا أنهم آمنوا بالله العزيز الحميد وولادة نبيّهم في الأمّة وإقامة الكتاب وإحياء السنّة مثل زيد بن علي صلوات الله عليهما، أحرقوه بالنار صليًّا كما فُعل بأصحاب الأخدود من المؤمنين، قال لهم زيد بن علي: لا تعبدوا فراعنة بني أميّة، أي لا تطيعوهم في معصية الخالق، فغضبت فراعنتهم وقالوا: أحرقوه وانصروا آلهتكم، كما غضب كفّار قوم إبراهيم صلى الله عليه لأوثانهم، قالوا: حرّقوه [a٦٨] وانصروا آلهتكم، حَذْوَ النعل بالنعل.

قال الله عزّ وجلّ ﴿وَمِن قَوْمِ مُوسَىٰ أُمَّةٌ يَهْدُونَ بِالْحَقِّ وَبِهِ يَعْدِلُونَ﴾ [الأعراف ٧: ١٥٩] وهم قِبَل المشرق وراء الصين عند المطلع، قال الله سبحانه ﴿وَقَطَّعْنَاهُمْ فِي الْأَرْضِ أُمَمًا مِّنْهُمُ الصَّالِحُونَ﴾ [الأعراف ٧: ١٦٨]، وهم وراء نهر الدهل (كذا) ﴿وَمِنْهُمْ دُونَ ذَٰلِكَ﴾ [الأعراف ٧: ١٦٨] يعني ما ههنا من اليهود الذين ترون، فكذلك من أمّة محمّد صلى الله عليه وآله ﴿أُمَّةٌ يَهْدُونَ بِالْحَقِّ وَبِهِ يَعْدِلُونَ﴾ وهم قبل المغرب كما أن قوم موسى قبل المشرق في حدّ ولد إدريس بن إدريس، حكمُ الكتاب [b٦٨] فيهم[١٠٣] ظاهر والقسم بالسوية، والعدل

---

١٠٣ فيهم: فهم، الأصل.

في الرعية، خلاف ما ههنا من المرجئة في عدل أئمتهم وسيرتهم، حَذْوَ النعل بالنعل.

وإن فرعون، حيث علم أن ولادة موسى بن عمران كائن في ملكه، يُذهب ملكه ويسفّه رأيه ويغيّر دينه على يديه، ذبح أبناء بني إسرائيل واستحيي نساءهم ووكّل على الحابلات[١٠٤] من نسائهم ليردّ أمر الله، ﴿وَظَهَرَ أَمْرُ اللَّهِ وَهُمْ كَارِهُونَ﴾ [التوبة ٩:٤٨] صاغرون، وإن الجبابرة من أمّتنا، حين علموا ولادة العبد الصالح كائن فيهم، [a٦٩] يذهب عنهم ملكهم ويسفّه رأيهم ويحيي الله تعالى به الكتاب والسنّة على يديه، قتلوا أبناء آل محمّد صلى الله عليه وآله واستحيوا نساءهم ووكّلوا على نساء آل محمّد كما فعل فرعون في أيّام مولد موسى على نساء بني إسرائيل، حتّى قال:اقتلوا أبناء الذين آمنوا معه واستحيوا ﴿نِسَاءَهُمْ وَإِنَّا فَوْقَهُمْ قَاهِرُونَ﴾ [الأعراف ٧: ١٢٧] وسيظهر الله دينه على يدي خليفته المهدي صلوات الله عليه وهم كارهون، قال الله عزّ وجلّ ﴿وَعَدَ اللَّهُ الَّذِينَ آمَنُوا مِنكُمْ وَعَمِلُوا الصَّالِحَاتِ [b٦٩] لَيَسْتَخْلِفَنَّهُمْ فِي الْأَرْضِ كَمَا اسْتَخْلَفَ الَّذِينَ مِن قَبْلِهِمْ وَلَيُمَكِّنَنَّ لَهُمْ دِينَهُمُ الَّذِي ارْتَضَىٰ لَهُمْ وَلَيُبَدِّلَنَّهُم مِّن بَعْدِ خَوْفِهِمْ أَمْنًا يَعْبُدُونَنِي لَا يُشْرِكُونَ بِي شَيْئًا﴾ [النور ٢٤: ٥٥] وقال الله تعالى ﴿وَيَوْمَئِذٍ يَفْرَحُ الْمُؤْمِنُونَب بِنَصْرِ اللَّهِ يَنصُرُ

[١٠٤] الحابلات: الحلافات، الأصل.

مَن يَشَاءُ﴾ [الروم ٣٠: ٤-٥] وقال تعالى ﴿وَعْدَ اللَّهِ لَا يُخْلِفُ اللَّهُ الْمِيعَادَ﴾ [الزمر ٣٩: ٢٠] وقال ﴿يَا أَيُّهَا الَّذِينَ آمَنُوا مَن يَرْتَدَّ مِنكُمْ عَن دِينِهِ فَسَوْفَ يَأْتِي اللَّهُ بِقَوْمٍ يُحِبُّهُمْ وَيُحِبُّونَهُ أَذِلَّةٍ عَلَى الْمُؤْمِنِينَ أَعِزَّةٍ عَلَى الْكَافِرِينَ يُجَاهِدُونَ فِي سَبِيلِ اللَّهِ وَلَا يَخَافُونَ لَوْمَةَ لَائِمٍ﴾ [المائدة ٥: ٥٤] [a٧٠] وإن فرعون موسى في كفره وطغيانه خدع قومه بعظة الدين، فقال لأوليائه ﴿مَا أُرِيكُمْ إِلَّا مَا أَرَىٰ وَمَا أَهْدِيكُمْ إِلَّا سَبِيلَ الرَّشَادِ﴾ [غافر ٤٠: ٢٩] وقال ﴿إِنِّي أَخَافُ أَن يُبَدِّلَ دِينَكُمْ أَوْ أَن يُظْهِرَ فِي الْأَرْضِ الْفَسَادَ﴾ [غافر ٤٠: ٢٦] فاستخفّ قومه، فأطاعوه، فحارب موسى عليه السلام مخافة أن يبدّل دينهم الذي ارتضوا لأنفسهم، وكذلك خوّف فراعنة أمّتنا بإظهار آل محمّد صلى الله عليه وعليهم بلسان أوليائهم: إنّا نخاف أن يظهر آل محمّد عليكم، فيبدّل دينكم [B٧٠] الذي أنتم عليه ظاهرين لما جعلهم الله سلفًا ومثلًا للآخرين، فرأت الأمّة جهاد آل محمّد صلوات الله عليهم فريضة مخافة أن يبدّل دينهم المبدّلة المنحرفة عن الصحيح كدأب آل فرعون، تركيبًا لسنّتهم واحتذاءً بهم.

وإن سبعين رجلًا من آل فرعون آمنوا بموسى وهارون ورفضوا فرعون، فسمّا هم فرعون الرافضة، فأوحى الله تعالى إلى موسى أن أثبتْ أسماءهم في التوراة الرافضة لرفضهم الشرّ واتّباعهم الخير، ثمّ جلّل الله تعالى إخوانهم على لسان محمد [a٧١] صلى الله عليه وآله في

القرآن، فقال ﴿رِجَالٌ صَدَقُوا مَا عَاهَدُوا اللَّهَ عَلَيْهِ فَمِنْهُم مَّن قَضَىٰ نَحْبَهُ وَمِنْهُم مَّن يَنتَظِرُ﴾ [الأحزاب ٣٣: ٢٣] والنحب القتل، قضوا نحبهم على حبّ آل محمّد صلى الله عليه وآله، ومنهم أحياء ينتظرون دولة الحقّ، وما بدّلوا بآل محمّد صلى الله عليه وآله تبديلًا. فكان شرّ الناس عند فرعون وأتباعه شيعة موسى وهارون، وعند اليهود شيعة عيسى وشمعون الذين لقبوهم الرافضة وحواريًّا، وإنما سمّوا الحواريون لبيض [b٧١] ثيابهم، كذلك شرّ الأمّة عند من احتذى بهم شيعة محمّد صلى الله عليه وآله الذين لقبوهم رافضة ومبيّضة كما لُقبت قرناؤهم في الأمم الماضية والأسلاف الخالية، وهم حواريّ الأمّة الذين رفضوا الشر واتّبعوا الخير وأهله كما فعل الشيع من قوم فرعون أيّام موسى بموسى عليه السلام والحواريّون أيام عيسى عليه السلام، وكانوا أقلّ القليل، وقليل من الأمّة احتذى بهم، ولقد ذمّ الله تعالى أكثر بني إسرائيل، [a٧٢] فقال لنبيّه صلى الله عليه وآله ﴿قُلْ يَا أَهْلَ الْكِتَابِ هَلْ تَنقِمُونَ مِنَّا إِلَّا أَنْ آمَنَّا بِاللَّهِ وَمَا أُنزِلَ إِلَيْنَا وَمَا أُنزِلَ مِن قَبْلُ وَأَنَّ أَكْثَرَكُمْ فَاسِقُونَ﴾ [المائدة ٥: ٥٩] وقال تعالى ﴿مِنْهُمْ أُمَّةٌ مُّقْتَصِدَةٌ وَكَثِيرٌ مِّنْهُمْ سَاءَ مَا يَعْمَلُونَ﴾ [المائدة ٥: ٦٦] وقال تعالى ﴿وَلَقَدْ ضَلَّ قَبْلَهُمْ أَكْثَرُ الْأَوَّلِينَ﴾ [الصافات ٣٧: ٧١] وقال تعالى ﴿وَلَقَدْ جَاءَتْهُمْ رُسُلُنَا بِالْبَيِّنَاتِ ثُمَّ إِنَّ كَثِيرًا مِّنْهُم بَعْدَ ذَٰلِكَ فِي الْأَرْضِ لَمُسْرِفُونَ﴾ [المائدة ٥: ٣٢] وقال تعالى ﴿فَقَسَتْ قُلُوبُهُمْ وَكَثِيرٌ مِّنْهُمْ فَاسِقُونَ﴾ [الحديد ٥٧: ١٦] وقال ﴿تَرَىٰ

كَثِيرًا مِنْهُمْ [b٧٢] يُسَارِعُونَ فِي الْإِثْمِ وَالْعُدْوَانِ وَأَكْلِهِمُ السُّحْتَ لَبِئْسَ مَا كَانُوا يَعْمَلُونَ﴾[١٠٥] [المائدة ٥: ٦٢] وقال ﴿وَمَا وَجَدْنَا لِأَكْثَرِهِم مِّنْ عَهْدٍ وَإِن وَجَدْنَا أَكْثَرَهُمْ لَفَاسِقِينَ﴾ [الأعراف ٧: ١٠٢] وقال ﴿كُلَّمَا عَاهَدُوا عَهْدًا نَّبَذَهُ فَرِيقٌ مِّنْهُم بَلْ أَكْثَرُهُمْ لَا يُؤْمِنُونَ﴾ [البقرة ٢: ١٠٠] ولم يمدح إلا القليل منهم، فقال: ﴿وَلَا تَزَالُ تَطَّلِعُ عَلَىٰ خَائِنَةٍ مِّنْهُمْ إِلَّا قَلِيلًا مِّنْهُمْ﴾ [المائدة ٥: ١٣] وقال ﴿وَلَٰكِن لَّعَنَهُمُ اللَّهُ بِكُفْرِهِمْ فَلَا يُؤْمِنُونَ إِلَّا قَلِيلًا﴾ [النساء ٤: ٤٦] وقال ﴿وَمَنْ آمَنَ وَمَا آمَنَ مَعَهُ إِلَّا قَلِيلٌ﴾ [هود ١١: ٤٠] وقال تعالى "وَإِذْ[١٠٦] أَخَذْنَا مِيثَاقَ بَنِي إِسْرَائِيلَ لَا تَعْبُدُونَ...﴾ [البقرة ٢: ٨٣].

... [a٧٣] أجزا(؟)، فينقل به تولّجه إلى قالب آخر من أجناس الخبائث فيها أو ليذيقه وبال أمره مقالةُ اليهود، قال الله جلّ جلاله ﴿ وَحَرَامٌ عَلَىٰ قَرْيَةٍ أَهْلَكْنَاهَا أَنَّهُمْ لَا يَرْجِعُونَ﴾ [الأنبياء ٢١: ٩٥] وقال سبحانه ﴿أَمَتَّنَا اثْنَتَيْنِ وَأَحْيَيْتَنَا اثْنَتَيْنِ﴾ [غافر ٤٠: ١١] تفسيرها آية اخرى ﴿كُنتُمْ أَمْوَاتًا فَأَحْيَاكُمْ ثُمَّ يُمِيتُكُمْ ثُمَّ يُحْيِيكُمْ﴾ [البقرة ٢: ٢٨] وقال

---

[١٠٥] يعملون: ما يعملون، الأصل.

[١٠٦] وإذ: وإذا، الأصل.

أمير المؤمنين عليه السلام: وجدنا الله جلّ جلاله إنما صرف خلقه في تسع تارات ذكرها في كتابه إذ يقول ﴿لَقَدْ خَلَقْنَا الْإِنسَانَ مِن سُلَالَةٍ مِّن طِينٍ ثُمَّ جَعَلْنَاهُ نُطْفَةً فِي قَرَارٍ مَكِينٍ [b٧٣] ثُمَّ خَلَقْنَا النُّطْفَةَ عَلَقَةً فَخَلَقْنَا الْعَلَقَةَ مُضْغَةً فَخَلَقْنَا الْمُضْغَةَ عِظَامًا فَكَسَوْنَا الْعِظَامَ لَحْمًا ثُمَّ أَنشَأْنَاهُ خَلْقًا آخَرَ فَتَبَارَكَ اللَّهُ أَحْسَنُ الْخَالِقِينَ ثُمَّ إِنَّكُم بَعْدَ ذَٰلِكَ لَمَيِّتُونَ ثُمَّ إِنَّكُمْ يَوْمَ الْقِيَامَةِ تُبْعَثُونَ﴾ [المؤمنين ٢٣: ١٢-١٦] وإن التارة[١٠٧] العاشرة لم يذكرها الله تعالى في هذه التارات من خلق الإنسان من سلالة من طين إلى يوم البعث الذي[١٠٨] زعموا أنه ينقلهم من قالب آخر إلى قالب آخر، لكن الله عزّ ذكره قال فيمن ابتغى الهدى في غير كتابه ﴿وَمَن يَعْشُ عَن ذِكْرِ الرَّحْمَٰنِ نُقَيِّضْ لَهُ شَيْطَانًا [a٧٤] فَهُوَ لَهُ قَرِينٌ﴾ [الزخرف ٤٣: ٣٦] إلى آخر الآية، وإن اليهود كانوا يقتلون النبيّين بغير حقّ ويقتلون الذين يأمرون بالقسط من الناس، فلمّا أن ختم الله النبوّة بمحمّد صلى الله عليه وآله وكان لا محالة كائن في هذه الأمّة كما كان في بني إسرائيل، قتلت يهود أمّتنا من كان يعدل دمّه مثل[١٠٩] دم الأنبياء الذين هم حجج الله في زمانهم كالأنبياء في زمنهم وهم عترة المصطفى أولاد الأنبياء ونسل

---

[١٠٧] التارة: تارة، الأصل.

[١٠٨] الذي: الذين، الأصل.

[١٠٩] مثل: عند، الأصل.

الأصفياء، أخّرهم مأخوذين[١١٠] بدماء العترة الذين قتلوا قبلهم من لدن الحسين بن علي عليهما السلام إلى يومنا كاليهود [b٧٤] الذين[١١١] كانوا في زمان النبي صلى الله عليه وآله ألزمهم[١١٢] الله دماء الأنبياء الذين سفكت في زمنهم قبلهم كمن نضخ سيفه بدمائهم، مصوّبون رأي آبائهم، قال الله تعالى ﴿قُلْ﴾ يا محمّد ﴿فَلِمَ تَقْتُلُونَ أَنبِيَاءَ اللَّهِ مِن قَبْلُ إِن كُنتُم مُّؤْمِنِينَ﴾ [البقرة ٢: ٩١] فاحتذت المرجئة سنّة بني إسرائيل من قتل أولاد الأنبياء والآمرين بالقسط من الناس وإيجاب ولاية قاتليهم فريضةً عليهم، حَذْوَ النعل بالنعل.

ولقد كثرت دماء الأنبياء في الأمم ما انتقم الله بدم نبيّ عليه السلام في دار الدنيا مثل....

﴿[وَيَقُولُونَ عَلَى اللَّهِ] [a٧٥] الْكَذِبَ وَهُمْ يَعْلَمُونَ﴾ [آل عمران ٣: ٧٥ و ٧٨] وكذلك استحلت أموال غيرهم بعضُ من يقول بالأمامة رأوا موازرة سلطان الجور وأخذ الرشى، وقالوا: الدار دار كفر لا علينا

---

١١٠ مأخوذين: بمأخوذين، الأصل.

١١١ الذين: والذين، الأصل.

١١٢ ألزمهم: لزمهم، الأصل.

أن نأخذ أموال الجاحد بحق الإمام ﴿وَيَقُولُونَ عَلَى اللَّهِ الْكَذِبَ وَهُمْ يَعْلَمُونَ﴾ [آل عمران ٣: ٧٥ و ٧٨] تركيبًا لسنّة بني إسرائيل واحتذاءً بهم.

وقالت اليعقوبية من النصارى[١١٣] أن عيسى بن مريم هو الله، ظهر ما أراد، فلمّا أوذي اجتنّ وبطن ، قال الله عزّ وجلّ فيهم ﴿لَقَدْ كَفَرَ الَّذِينَ [b٧٥] قَالُوا إِنَّ اللَّهَ هُوَ الْمَسِيحُ ابْنُ مَرْيَمَ﴾ [المائدة ٥: ١٧] وقالت فرقة من الزنادقة منتحلي الشيعة في علي مثل مقالة اليعقوبية من النصارى، تركيبًا لسنّة بني إسرائيل واحتذاءً بهم.

وقالت الملكانية من النصارى: إن السراج لا يضيء إلا بالدهن والفتيلة والنار، والآلهة ثلاثة[١١٤] بطن اثنان وظهر واحد، قال الله عزّ وجلّ فيهم ﴿لَا تَقُولُوا ثَلَاثَةٌ انتَهُوا خَيْرًا لَّكُمْ﴾ [النساء ٤: ١٧١] و﴿لَقَدْ كَفَرَ الَّذِينَ قَالُوا إِنَّ اللَّهَ ثَالِثُ ثَلَاثَةٍ﴾ [المائدة ٥: ٧٣] وزعمت البَشيرية من الزنادقة منتحلي الشيعة أن عليًا هو الله، لأن الأوصياء هو اللهب واللهب بالعبرانية [a٧٦] عشراء بالألوهية وزعموا أنه لا نعبد إلهًا لم نره، وزعموا أن الله عزّ وجلّ لما أن أراد أن يُري خلقه قدرته فلم يدرك العباد

---

[١١٣] من النصارى: والنصارى، الأصل.

[١١٤] ثلاثة: ثلاث، الأصل.

إلا بالقلب، وقالوا: إن عليًا حفر الأنهار وغرس الأشجار وبنى الجبال، واحتجّوا بالقرآن، قالوا: نحن وإنّا وأرسلنا وأوحينا وأشباهه، قالوا: لو كان هذا واحدًا[١١٥] كان كما تقولون، ولكن هذا جماعة، والدليل على ما قلنا الآيات، فلُعنوا بما قال منهم[١١٦] الذين احتذوا حذو الملكانية، وقال أمير [b٧٦] المؤمنين صلوات الله عليه: يهلك فيّ اثنان محبّ مفرط ومبغض مفترٍ، وقال: إنما مثلي في هذه الأمّة كمثل عيسى في النصارى، أحبّه قوم أفرطوا فهلكوا وأبغضه قوم حتّى هلكوا، فكما أن اليعقوبية والملكانية من النصارى أفرطوا في عيسى أفرط هاذان في علي عليه السلام.

وقالت اليهود: قد رأينا السحرة والكهنة تفعل مثل ما فعل عيس عليه السلام، وزعموا أن مريم عليها السلام بغيّ[١١٧] وأن عيس لغير رشده فتعلّم السحر [a٧٩] والكهانة وكان ساحرًا، قال الله عزّ وجلّ فيهم ﴿وَقَوْلِهِمْ عَلَىٰ مَرْيَمَ بُهْتَانًا عَظِيمًا وَقَوْلِهِمْ إِنَّا قَتَلْنَا الْمَسِيحَ عِيسَى ابْنَ مَرْيَمَ رَسُولَ اللَّهِ وَمَا قَتَلُوهُ وَمَا صَلَبُوهُ وَلَـٰكِن شُبِّهَ لَهُمْ﴾ [النساء ٤: ١٥٦-١٥٧] فأنكر اليهود حقّه ودعواه أنه عبد الله ورسوله وأنكروا

---

١١٥ واحدًا: واتحد، الأصل.

١١٦ قال منهم: قالوا فيهم، الأصل.

١١٧ بغي: بغيًا، الأصل.

نبوّته، وقالت يهود أمّتنا: إن النبيّ صلى الله عليه وآله لم يؤمّر عليًا، وليس هو أولى بالمؤمنين بعد رسول الله صلى الله عليه وآله، فكذّبوا أنه أخو رسول الله صلى الله عليه وآله وأنه وزيره ووصيّه في أهله وخليفته [b٧٩] في أمّته، كما أنكرت اليهود نبوّة عيسى، تركيبًا لسنّة بني إسرائيل واحتذاء بهم.

وزعمت اليهود أن إيمانهم بالله وبموسى والنبيّين من قبله يغنيهم عن إيمانهم بمحمّد صلى الله عليه وآله، وهم يعرفونه كما يعرفون أبناءهم، وكفروا به حسدًا من عند أنفسهم، وزعمت يهود أمّتنا أن إيمانهم بمحمّد صلى الله عليه وآله يغنيهم عن معرفة إمام[١١٨] المتّقين وقائد الغرّ المحجّلين، وأمير المؤمنين، وأخي[١١٩] سيّد المرسلين، وطاعته، وكفروا بالوليّ حسدًا من عند أنفسهم وقالوا هذا الذي...

... [a٧٧] وأصبح مجيبًا للنبي صلى الله عليه وآله، وسمّوا عثمان ذا النورين، وكان الحسن والحسين نورَي رسول الله صلى الله عليه وآله، وكان أبوهما علي عليه السلام وأمّهما فاطمة ابنة رسول الله صلى

١١٨ إمام: إيمان بإمام، الأصل.

١١٩ أخيك أخو، الأصل.

الله عليه وآله، وسمّوا خالد بن الوليد سيف الله، سلّه على المشركين والمنافقين، وسيف الله لا يخطئ، وقد عمل خالد بن الوليد في بني جَذيمة ما لم يرض الله ورسوله صلى الله عليه وآله حتّى خرج نبيّ الله صلى الله عليه وآله وهو يجرّ ثوبه، وهو يقول: اللهمّ إني أبرأ [b٧٧] إليك ممّا فعل خالد بن الوليد، ثمّ وجّه عليًا إليهم، فأصلحه، فردّ قتلاهم حتى ردّ تبلغة[١٢٠] الكلب، وفضل عنده سبعمائة أو خمسمائة، فقال: هذا لكم بروعات النساء والصبيان، فأجلّوا رسول الله صلى الله عليه وآله، وعليّ سيف الله الذي سلّه على المشركين والمنافقين واستأصل به صناديدهم ومبارزيهم، وإنّما سمّي أمير المؤمنين لأن المؤمنين كانوا يمتارون منه العلم كما يمتار ممتار الطعام، وقال له رسول الله صلى الله عليه وآله: يا علي إنّ [a٧٨] أهل السموات يسمّونك أمير المؤمنين، قالت أمّ سلمة: قال لي رسول الله صلى الله عليه وآله: إذا صعد أمير المؤمنين منبري فنزل فيسألكِ[١٢١] هذا الكتاب فادفعيه إليه، قالت: لما صعد أبو بكر انتظرته يسألنيه فلم يفعل، ثمّ صعد عمر فانتظرته يسألنيه فلم يفعل، ثمّ صعد عثمان فانتظرته يسألنيه فلم يفعل، ثمّ صعد علي، فنزل فقال: يا أمّ سلمة أين الكتاب الذي دفعه إليكِ رسول الله صلى الله عليه وآله؟

---

[١٢٠] تبلغة: مبلغة، الأصل.

[١٢١] فيسألك: فيالك، الأصل

قالت: فدفعتُه إليه، فهو أمير المؤمنين [b٧٨] حقًا، قيل: يا أمير المؤمنين ما كان في الكتاب؟ قال: علم ما يحتاج إليه الأمّة إلى يوم القيامة، وقيل لأبي ذرّ: لو أوصيتَ إلى أمير المؤمنين، يعنون عثمان بن عفّان، قال: لقد أوصيتُ إلى أمير المؤمنين حقًا، يعني عليًا، فضاهوه بهذه الأسماء، ولقد جعل الله تعالى دم عيسى عليه السلام أعظم دم سُفك، وقال رسول الله صلى الله عليه وسلم وآله: أشقى الأوّلين والآخرين عاقر الناقة وأشقى الآخرين والأوّلين قاتلك يا علي، فحوّلوا هذه الحرمة العظيمة إلى دم [a٨٠] كلّ من منّ الله عليه من بيننا، أليس الله بأعلم بالشاكرين؟ قال الله تبارك وتعالى ذكره ﴿أَمْ يَحْسُدُونَ النَّاسَ عَلَىٰ مَا آتَاهُمُ اللَّهُ[١٢٢] مِن فَضْلِهِ فَقَدْ آتَيْنَا آلَ إِبْرَاهِيمَ الْكِتَابَ وَالْحِكْمَةَ وَآتَيْنَاهُم مُّلْكًا عَظِيمًا﴾ [النساء ٤: ٥٤] وقال محمّد صلى الله عليه وآله: علي أسد المحسودين الذين آتاهم الله تعالى ما آتى آل إبراهيم، الكتاب والحكمة، فكفرت بهم المرجئة، قال الله تعالى ﴿تُؤْمِنُونَ بِبَعْضِ الْكِتَابِ وَتَكْفُرُونَ بِبَعْضٍ﴾ [البقرة ٢: ٨٥] معناه يؤمنون بالنبيّ ويكفرون بالوليّ الوصيّ، فآمنوا بزعمهم بالرسول [b٨٠] وكفروا بالولي، قال رسول الله صلى الله عليه وآله: أنا مدينة الإيمان وعلي بابها، فمن أراد أن يتورّد الإيمان فليأتِ الباب، وقال الله عزّ وجلّ: ﴿وَأْتُوا الْبُيُوتَ مِنْ أَبْوَابِهَا﴾ [البقرة ٢: ١٨٩] معناه: اتوا

---

١٢٢ الله: -، الأصل

الأنبياء بأبواب الأوصياء، فكفروا به وهم يعرفونه كما يعرفون أبناءهم، تركيبًا لسنّة بني إسرائيل واحتذاء بهم.

وزعمت اليهود أن الله تبارك وتعالى عذّب روح بخت نصّر في أجناس كثيرة من أخابث الحيوان والهوام نحو القردة والخنازير

كتاب مفاتيح النّعمة

منسوب إلى أبي العبّاس محمّد

[كتاب مفاتيح النعمة]

بسم الله الرحمن الرحيم

الحمد لله وليّ[1] التوفيق، وصلى الله على سيّدنا محمّد وآله أهل الحقّ والتحقيق.

أعانك الله يا أخي على طاعته وتولّاك[2] بحفظه وأسعدك برضوانه، ووفّقك لإرشاده[3] وبصّرك معالم دينه ولا حجب بينك وبين أوليائه، وجعلك ممن يسعى في أرض[4] قدسه فيكونَ له قلبٌ يعقل به أمثالَه وأُذُن يسمع بها[5] أمره ونهيَه، فإنّه لا حول ولا قوّة إلّا به. ونسأله أن يصلّي[6] على المصطفى من خلقه الأمين على وحْيه،[7] محمّدٍ نبيّه، وعلى

---

[1] ولي: ذي، ب.

[2] تولاك: توالاك، ب.

[3] لإرشاده: لإرشاد، ب.

[4] أرض: أرضه، ب.

[5] بها: به، ب أ.

[6] يصلي: تصلي، ب.

[7] على وحيه: وعلى وصي، ب.

عترته أعلام الهدى وكهوف الورى، حُججِ الله على عباده وأرباب دينه ومتولّيي[٨] كتابه، سُفُن النجاة التي من ركبها نجا ومن تخلّف عنها غرق وهوى

وبعد: فقد كان أخونا أبو الحسن البغدادي أعزّه الله يؤدّي إلينا[١] ما ركّبه الله تعالى فيك ووهبه لك من الذكاء اللطيف،[٢] والفهم الثاقب المنيف، والطلب للعلوم[٣] الشريفة والآداب الجليلة، ما شوّقنا إلى معرفتك والاتّصال بحبلك والخلطة بك والمودّة لله، وحقّق ذلك عندنا انزعاجُك إلى ناحيتنا المعروفة بسِليانة[٤] لتتصل بنا، لكن وافيتَنا أكرمك الله ونحن على حال لم نتمكن[٥] معها من مرادنا منك وما نأمله لك، إذ كنتُ في الغيبة عن مستقرّي، فكتبتُ إلى أخي أبي عبد الله بخبرك

---

[٨] متوليي: متأول، أ.

[١] إليها: -، ب.

[٢] اللطيف: -، أ.

[٣] والطلب للعلوم: والطالب للعلوم، ب؛ والعلوم، أ.

[٤] بسليانة: بثلبانة، ب.

[٥] نتمكن: يتمكن، أ و ب.

وعرّفتُه بموضعك[٦] ووصَيتُه بالكشف لك عن[٧] بعض ما قصدتَ له إلى أن يسهّل الله لنا الاجتماع معك والالتقاء بك، فنتفاوض فيما تحتاج إليه إن شاء الله تعالى، وقد كان ظني بك حسُنَ لما بلغني من اتّساع علمك، ورجحان فهمك، وأنك عارف بالقصد الذي تطلبه والغرض الذي تريده سيما، وقد اتّصلت بالمعدن ووقفتَ على طرف من الأمر[٨] وقرأتَ من الكتب، وإن كنتَ لم تقف منها على الأمر الكلي ولا قرأتَ من الكتب المصونة إلّا عن أهلها البالغين، فإن المقدار الذي وصلتَ إليه وعرفته[٩] وقرأته قد كان يجب عليك أن تتأمّله وتستشهد ببعضه على بعض في ظاهره وباطنه، فإن[١٠] وجدتَ هناك اختلافًا سألت عنه، مع ما أنه ليس هنالك اختلاف، وما كان أشكل عليك وتعذّر واستعجم عليك عند وقوفك عليه واستُنكر كان الواجب عليك أن تردَّه إلى من نُصب لبيانه، ولم يكن يجب أن تُشنّع به ولا أن تردّ ما أشكل. وقد قال الصادق عليه السلام: ما أشكل عليك من علومنا فردّوه إلينا ولا تردّوه

---

[٦] بموضعك: بمرجعك، ب.

[٧] عن: -، أ.

[٨] الأمر: الأمور، ا.

[٩] وعرفته: وشرفته، ب.

[١٠] فإن: ما ان، أ.

علينا بأن تكذّبوا به، يعني رُدّوه إلينا لنبرهن لكم برهانه ونُعرّفكم تأويله ولا تردّوه علينا بأن تكذّبوا به وترجعوا عنه.[١١] ولعمري مَن فتح تجارته ونشر بضعته على من لم يكن من أهلها ولا ممّن يعرف قيمتها ولا ربحها من خسارتها كان هو المستخفّ بنفسه والمنسوبُ إلى التهوّر في أمره.

وقد أقرأني أبو عبد الله كتابك تطلب ما كنتُ أخرجته لوليّ[١٢] الله صلوات الله عليه وإن كان الله عزّ وجلّ قد أغناه[١٣] من أعراض هذه الدنيا الفانية، لكن أخْذه لها لتطهير الأنفس وتزكية الأموال، وقد كنتَ أنت الذي ابتدأت بذلك من غير إجبار ولا إكراه[١٤] لكن لما عرّفك به أخي أبو عبد الله ممّا يجب لوليّ الله عليكم، فمن أخرج ذلك عن طيبة من نفسه طهّر الله عزّ وجلّ بذلك روحه وزكّى ماله، وحلّ لداعيه ومُربّيه مفاتحتُه بالعلوم التأويلية وتعريفُه الحقائق المستورة عن أعداء دين الله. فإنّ الله تعالى امتحن الخلق بالمحن الشديدة، فصبر على ذلك من صبر وتردّى من تردّى، وليس في العالم أحبُّ إلى الإنسان من نفسه

---

[١١] عنه: منه، ب.

[١٢] لولي: بولي، ب.

[١٣] أغناه: + الله تعالى، أ.

[١٤] إجبار ولا إكراه: اختبار ولا أكره، ب.

وماله، فامتحن[١٥] الله الخلق فيهما جميعًا، فقال: ﴿إِنَّ اللَّهَ اشْتَرَىٰ مِنَ الْمُؤْمِنِينَ أَنفُسَهُمْ وَأَمْوَالَهُم بِأَنَّ لَهُمُ الْجَنَّةَ يُقَاتِلُونَ فِي سَبِيلِ اللَّهِ فَيَقْتُلُونَ وَيُقْتَلُونَ وَعْدًا عَلَيْهِ حَقًّا فِي التَّوْرَاةِ وَالْإِنجِيلِ وَالْقُرْآنِ﴾ [التوبة ٩: ١١١] فأمرهم بالاجتهاد بالأنفس وأمرهم بإخراج الأموال في وجوه شتّى وحدود محدودة، وسأُعرّفك[١٦] بعض ما أوجب الله عزّ وجلّ على المؤمنين في إخراج أموالهم إلى وليّ الله ليصرفه في مصالح الأمور،[١٧] لأن الله تعالى ذكره حرّم عليه[١٨] الصدقات تنزيهًا له[١٩] عن أوساخ الأمّة، فلا يسبقْ إلى وهمك أن هذه حيلة عملها داعيك لأخذ مالك أو مال غيرك، نعوذ بالله من ذلك، لكنّ دين الله تعالى ظاهر وباطن لتكون الفردانية له تعالى[٢٠] ظاهرًا وباطنًا، يؤدي إلى ثلاثة أحوال وثلاث منافع، إحداها[٢١]

---

[١٥] فامتحن: وامتحن، ب أ.

[١٦] وسأُعرفك: وما عرفك، ب.

[١٧] الأمور: الأمر، ب.

[١٨] عليه: عليكم، ب.

[١٩] له: لهم، ب.

[٢٠] ظاهر وباطن لتكون الفردانية له تعالى: -، ب.

[٢١] إحداها: احدها، أ و ب.

تعبّد الله عزّ وجلّ، والثانية أنّ به عمران الدنيا، أعني بأحكامه[٢٢] وقضاياه،[٢٣] والثالثة أنه إشارة إلى باطن الشريعة وتأويل التنزيل وإلى الحدود الروحانية والجسمانية، وظاهر الشريعة محكم[٢٤] مجمل معمول به يؤدي إلى الذين هم أسباب النجاة، وبهم الارتقاء إلى دار المعاد.

يقول الله جلّ ثناءه: ﴿وَاللَّيْلِ إِذَا يَغْشَىٰ وَالنَّهَارِ إِذَا تَجَلَّىٰ وَمَا خَلَقَ الذَّكَرَ وَالْأُنثَىٰ إِنَّ سَعْيَكُمْ لَشَتَّىٰ﴾ [الليل ٩٢: ١-٤] يعني في دين الله وطلبكم لمرضاة أوليائه، ولولا كراهية التطويل لتأوّلتُ لك في معنى الليل والنهار والذكر والأنثى، لكن أوردتُ لك المعاني الدالّة على ما أوجب الله عزّ وجلّ على خلقه. وأيضًا، فإن التأويل المحض إنما يُخرج به إلى من كان طالبًا راغبًا غير رادّ ولا معاند. ثمّ قال تعالى: ﴿فَأَمَّا مَنْ أَعْطَىٰ وَاتَّقَىٰ وَصَدَّقَ بِالْحُسْنَىٰ﴾ [٩٢: ٥-٦] يعني من أعطى ما يجب عليه بحسب ما يؤمر به في ماله واتّقى ما فيه الحيرة والضلال، وصدّق بالحسنى فيما يسمع من البيان والبرهان ﴿فَسَنُيَسِّرُهُ لِلْيُسْرَىٰ﴾ [الليل ٩٢: ٧] وهو تيسير الأيسار، ومعنى ذلك أن المالٌ مالان، فمال جعله الله تعالى قوامًا

---

[٢٢] بأحكامه: أحكامه، ب.

[٢٣] وقضاياه: ووصاياه، ب.

[٢٤] محكم: متحكم، أ.

للأجساد ومصالح الأمور الدنياوية، ومال جعله الله تعالى قوامًا للأرواح ومصالح الأمور الأخروية،[٢٥] وهو العلم جعله الله قوامًا للأنفس في دار المعاد، وقوله: ﴿فَسَنُيَسِّرُهُ لِلْيُسْرَىٰ﴾، إذا أعطى ما يأمر به داعيه وأتّقى ما فيه أهل الحيرة والاختلاف الذين لا يعرفون تأويل كتب الله عزّ وجلّ، إذا فعل ذلك أيسر وكثر علمُه وارتفع عند المؤمنين وعند وليّ الله قدرُه، وارتفعت درجته وعلت منزلته ﴿وَأَمَّا مَن بَخِلَ وَاسْتَغْنَىٰ وَكَذَّبَ بِالْحُسْنَىٰ﴾ [الليل ٩٢: ٨-٩] أي من بخل بما[٢٦] يؤمر به من الواجب عليه فلم يُخرجه، واستغنى عن طلب[٢٧] الذي به حياته، وكذب بالتأويل الذي شرح الله به صدور المؤمنين، ﴿فَسَنُيَسِّرُهُ لِلْعُسْرَىٰ﴾ [الليل٩٢: ١٠] والمسكنة[٢٨] وانقطاع مادّة العلم عنه الذي به نجاته، فتخلّف عن اليسرى واللحوق بأدلّاء الزمان وأولياء الناطق والبرهان. ثمّ ذمّه فقال: ﴿وَمَا يُغْنِي عَنْهُ مَالُهُ إِذَا تَرَدَّىٰ إِنَّ عَلَيْنَا لَلْهُدَىٰ وَإِنَّ لَنَا لَلْآخِرَةَ وَالْأُولَىٰ﴾ [الليل٩٢: ١١-١٣]، ثمّ حذّر ﴿فَأَنذَرْتُكُمْ نَارًا تَلَظَّىٰ لَا يَصْلَاهَا إِلَّا الْأَشْقَى الَّذِي كَذَّبَ وَتَوَلَّىٰ﴾ [٩٢: ١٤-١٦] ثمّ مدح مَن

---

٢٥ الأخروية: الآخرة، أ و ب.

٢٦ بما: مما، ب.

٢٧ طلب: الطلب، أ.

٢٨ والمسكنة: والمسكنة والذلة، أ (الهامش).

سارع إلى ذلك ﴿وَسَيُجَنَّبُهَا الْأَتْقَى الَّذِي يُؤْتِي مَالَهُ يَتَزَكَّىٰ وَمَا لِأَحَدٍ عِندَهُ مِن نِّعْمَةٍ تُجْزَىٰ إِلَّا ابْتِغَاءَ وَجْهِ رَبِّهِ الْأَعْلَىٰ وَلَسَوْفَ يَرْضَىٰ﴾ [الليل٩٢: ١٨-٢١] فتأمّل السورة إلى آخرها، هل تجد فيها معنى غير ذلك؟

وقوله جلّ من قائل ﴿أَلَمْ نَجْعَل لَّهُ عَيْنَيْنِ وَلِسَانًا وَشَفَتَيْنِ وَهَدَيْنَاهُ النَّجْدَيْنِ﴾ [البلد ٩٠: ٨-١٠] عنى بالعينين الناطق والأساس، إذ هما عينا الله في أرضه، واللسان الحجّة لأنّه يبرهن للمؤمنين علمَ التأويل والتنزيل، وبالشفتين الداعي والمأذون إذ هما بابا الحجة وجاهدان في دين الله عزّ وجلّ، وهديناه النجدين: أي[٢٩] الطريقين الظاهر والباطن، ﴿فَلَا اقْتَحَمَ الْعَقَبَةَ﴾ [البلد٩٠: ١١] ثمّ فسّرها فقال: ﴿وَمَا أَدْرَاكَ مَا الْعَقَبَةُ فَكُّ رَقَبَةٍ﴾ [البلد٩٠: ١٢-١٣] ومعنى الفكاك أن يُخرج المستجيب ما يأمره به داعيه، إذ جعل ذلك محنة له، فالصبر على تلك المحنة هو اقتحام العقبة ليميّز الله الخبيث من الطيّب، ﴿يَهْلِكَ مَنْ هَلَكَ عَن بَيِّنَةٍ وَيَحْيَىٰ مَنْ حَيَّ عَن بَيِّنَةٍ﴾[٣٠] [الأنفال ٨: ٤٢].

وفي هذا المعنى قال الله عزّ وجلّ: ﴿وَالَّذِينَ يَبْتَغُونَ الْكِتَابَ مِمَّا مَلَكَتْ أَيْمَانُكُمْ فَكَاتِبُوهُمْ إِنْ عَلِمْتُمْ فِيهِمْ خَيْرًا وَآتُوهُم مِّن مَّالِ اللَّهِ الَّذِي

---

[٢٩] أي: إلى، أ.

[٣٠] ويهلك، ب؛ وليهلك، أ.

أتاك﴾[31] [النور ٢٤: ٣٣] يعني فكّوهم من الوثاق وأطلقوهم للكسر والاحتجاج، وأفيدوهم من العلم الذي أفادكم الله، وذلك بعد فكّهم رقابَهم وإخراجهم ما يجب عليهم. وسأكشف لك معنى الفكاك لئلّا تقول: ومتى كنتُ مأسورًا فأحتاجَ إلى الفكاك؟ اعلم أن الله تعالى أمر بجهاد الكفّار في جميع الأقطار، فمن ابتُزّ منهم عنها كان[32] عبدًا مأسورًا في حال الإسلام[33] إلى أن يُعتَق أو يفكّ هو رقبته بنفسه، وكذلك في باطن الشريعة مَن كسر عليه الداعي الظاهرَ الذي هو عليه، إذ لا يعرف تأويله ومعانيه، كان بمنزلة المأسور من أرض الجهل إلى أرض المعرفة، وإذا أراد الداعي أن يرفع درجته ويكشف له سرائر الشريعة أمره بإخراج ما يجب عليه ليمتحنه بذلك ويُظهر ما في قلبه، ولا يُخرج إليه من العلم شيئًا إلا على قدر درجته ويقينه، لقول الله تعالى: ﴿إِذَا جَاءَكُمُ الْمُؤْمِنَاتُ مُهَاجِرَاتٍ فَامْتَحِنُوهُنَّ اللَّهُ أَعْلَمُ بِإِيمَانِهِنَّ﴾ [الممتحنة ٦٠: ١٠] ففي ظاهر الشريعة هو مجيئ الامرأة من دار الشرك إلى دار الإسلام، فتُستحلف أنها ما جاءت إلا محبّة للإسلام، فهذا تفسيرها في الظاهر. وأمّا التأويل في هذه

[31] أتاكم:أتيكم، أ و ب.

[32] عنها كان:كان عنها، ب؛ كان، أ.

[33] عبدًا مأسورًا في حال الإسلام:عبدًا في دار الإسلام، ب؛ عبدًا مأسورًا في حال الإسلام، أ.

الآية فهو أن المؤمنات في دين الله هم المتعلّمون، لأن الذّكر كالمفيد والمستفيد كالأنثى، ومعنى المهاجرة خروج المتعلّم من حدّ الجهل إلى حدّ الطلْبة ومعرفة النور والبيان، وقوله: ﴿فَامْتَحِنُوهُنَّ اللَّهُ أَعْلَمُ بِإِيمَانِهِنَّ﴾، فذلك[٣٤] أن القلوب بيد الله لا يطّلع على ما فيها غيره، وليس للداعي من الإنسان إلا ما ظهر، فأمره الله تعالى بامتحان المؤمنين الطالبين لفوائد الدين ليبلو سرائرهم، فإن صبروا على المحنة حلّ للمفيد مفاتحتهم وتربيتهم بالعلوم التأويلية، ومن انكسر وتردّى[٣٥] ولم يصبر على الامتحان والبلوى كان حرام عليه مفاتحته، ﴿اللَّهُ أَعْلَمُ بِإِيمَانِهِنَّ﴾، يعني أنه المطّلع على ضمائرهم، ﴿فَإِنْ عَلِمْتُمُوهُنَّ مُؤْمِنَاتٍ﴾ [الممتحنة ٦٠: ١٠] يعني إن صبروا على الامتحان والاختبار ﴿فَلَا تَرْجِعُوهُنَّ إِلَى الْكُفَّارِ﴾ [الممتحنة ٦٠: ١٠] يعني إلى أهل الظاهر الذي كانوا عليه ولا تقطعوا عنهم مراد العلم.

وتأمّلْ قوله جلّ من قائل: ﴿حُرِّمَتْ عَلَيْكُمُ الْمَيْتَةُ وَالدَّمُ وَلَحْمُ الْخِنزِيرِ وَمَا أُهِلَّ لِغَيْرِ اللَّهِ بِهِ وَالْمُنْخَنِقَةُ وَالْمَوْقُوذَةُ وَالْمُتَرَدِّيَةُ وَالنَّطِيحَةُ وَمَا أَكَلَ السَّبُعُ إِلَّا مَا ذَكَّيْتُمْ وَمَا ذُبِحَ عَلَى النُّصُبِ﴾ الآية [المائدة ٥: ٣]

---

[٣٤] فذلك: وذلك، أ و ب.

[٣٥] تردى: تؤدي، ب.

لتعلم[٣٦] أن المراد بذلك هو منع المفاتحة لمن لا يحلّ مفاتحته، فمعنى الميتة الظاهري الذي لا حركة فيه لطلب الحكمة والتأويل وفوائد البرهان، ومعنى الدم الرجل الذي كان في الدعوة، فأظهر البيان والتأويل من غير إذن داعيه، ومعنى الخنزير الذي يُقرّ بجميع الحدود وبما يسمعه من البيان والحكمة ويُنكر منزلة الإمام، وذلك أن الخنزير ظلفه مقسوم شبه ظلف الشاة ما خلا رأسه، فإنه ممسوخ، وذلك مثل جحده إمام الزمان الذي هو رأس المؤمنين، وما أُهلّ لغير الله به، يعني من في رقبته عهدٌ لغير الإمام الحقيقيّ، لأن العهد إنما افترضه الله للإمام الحقيقي، فمن أُخذ عليه عهد لغيره لم تحلّ مفاتحته، والمنخنقة الذي يقطع العهد في وقت الأخذ عليه، فيقول: أمهلني واصبر عليّ، والموقوذة التي يضربها الراعي، والراعي مثل الداعي، وضربه بالعصا مثل امتحانه، والشاة مثل المستجيب، فإذا امتحن الداعي المستجيب فصبر على الامتحان كان له أن يفاتحه، فإن هرب ولم يصبر على الامتحان حُرّمت عليه مفاتحته، والمتردّية الذي لا يُطيق حمل التأويل ولا يحيط به معرفته، وقد يكون بلغ إلى حد من حدوده، فيرجع[٣٧] إلى الظاهر وأهله، والنطيحة الذي يحاجج الداعي ويجادله من غير معرفة ولا بصيرة، ثمّ لا ينتهي عن ذلك إذا نُهي عنه،

[٣٦] لتعلم: ليعلم، أ و ب.

[٣٧] فيرجع: فرجع، أ.

وما أكل السبع إلا ما ذكّيتم، يعني من أفسده أحد من أهل الظاهر وصرف وجهه عن دعوة الحقّ، فلا يفاتح، إلا ما ذكّيتم، يعني من جُدّد عليه العهد، وما ذُبح على النصب، فهو[٣٨] الذي قد أُخذ عليه عهد إمام نصب نفسه بغير اختيار من الله له، وقام مقام وليّ الله ودعا الناس إلى نفسه، فكلّ هؤلاء حرام مفاتحتهم بالبيان والتأويل.

وقال تعالى ﴿خُذْ مِنْ أَمْوَالِهِمْ صَدَقَةً تُطَهِّرُهُمْ وَتُزَكِّيهِم بِهَا﴾ [التوبة ٩: ١٠٣] وإنما سُمّيت صدقة لأنها مصداق المؤمنين بما يُسمع من البيان والتأويل، فجعلها الله في باطن الشريعة محنةً يمتحن بها المؤمنين ليستدلّ بها الداعي على صحّة يقينهم،[٣٩] ثمّ قال عزّ وجلّ ﴿وَصَلِّ عَلَيْهِمْ إِنَّ صَلَاتَكَ سَكَنٌ لَهُمْ﴾ [التوبة ٩: ١٠٣] يعني إذا قبضتَ منهم ذلك فادعُ لهم، فإنّ بركة دعائك وصلة لهم وسكنة[٤٠] لاضطرابهم وفزعهم، وقال جلّ ذكره ﴿يَا أَيُّهَا الَّذِينَ آمَنُوا إِذَا نَاجَيْتُمُ الرَّسُولَ فَقَدِّمُوا بَيْنَ يَدَيْ نَجْوَاكُمْ صَدَقَةً ذَٰلِكَ خَيْرٌ لَّكُمْ وَأَطْهَرُ﴾ [المجادلة ٥٨: ١٢] وقد رُوي أنه لما أُنزلت هذه الآية بادر أمير المؤمنين علي بن أبي طالب صلوات الله عليه فباع

---

[٣٨] فهو: وهو، أ؛ وامر، ب.

[٣٩] يقينهم: يقينه، أ.

[٤٠] سكنة: سكينة، أ.

درعه بأربعين دينارًا وجلس بين يدي رسول الله صلى الله عليه، وكان يسأله عن مسألة مسألة ويُخرج دينارًا دينارًا، وتوقّف الناس عن ذلك، فأنزل الله عزّ وجلّ: ﴿أَأَشْفَقْتُمْ أَن تُقَدِّمُوا بَيْنَ يَدَيْ نَجْوَاكُمْ صَدَقَاتٍ فَإِذْ لَمْ تَفْعَلُوا وَتَابَ اللَّهُ عَلَيْكُمْ فَأَقِيمُوا الصَّلَاةَ وَآتُوا الزَّكَاةَ﴾ [المجادلة ٥٨: ١٣] يعني إنّكم أشفقتم على إخراج أموالكم عند كلّ مسألة، فتاب عليكم ورفع عنكم ثقل ذلك، فأقيموا الصلاة وآتوا الزكاة، يعني الطهارة والتزكية، ولولا قوله: ﴿أَأَشْفَقْتُمْ أَن تُقَدِّمُوا بَيْنَ يَدَيْ نَجْوَاكُمْ صَدَقَاتٍ فَإِذْ لَمْ تَفْعَلُوا وَتَابَ اللَّهُ عَلَيْكُمْ﴾، لكان يجب على كلّ مؤمن عند كلّ مسألة إخراجُ صدقة[٤١] النجوى، ولكن بتفضّله[٤٢] ومنّه رضي منهم مرة واحدة في الحين والوقت.

وذكرتَ أكرمك الله في كتابك أن الله عزّ وجلّ يقول ﴿وَلَا يَسْأَلْكُمْ أَمْوَالَكُمْ﴾ [محمّد ٤٧: ٣٦] فتأمّل الآية أكرمك الله فإنّ الحجّة فيها عليك لا لك، فمعنى قوله: فلا يسألكم أموالكم، أي جميعَ ما تملكون ﴿إِن يَسْأَلْكُمُوهَا فَيُحْفِكُمْ تَبْخَلُوا﴾ [محمّد ٤٧: ٣٧] يعني لو سألكم وألحّ عليكم المسألة ظهر نفاقكم وبخلتم، فعفا عن ذلك بفضله، وأمر تعالى[٤٣]

---

[٤١] صدقة: صدقات، أ.

[٤٢] بتفضله: بتفضيله، ب.

[٤٣] تعالى: -، ب.

بإخراج بعض أموالكم[٤٤] لتكون نفقة في سبيل الله على يدَي وليّ الله وفي مصالح المؤمنين. فقال تعالى ﴿هَٰٓأَنتُمۡ هَٰٓؤُلَآءِ تُدۡعَوۡنَ لِتُنفِقُواْ فِي سَبِيلِ ٱللَّهِ فَمِنكُم مَّن يَبۡخَلُۖ وَمَن يَبۡخَلۡ فَإِنَّمَا يَبۡخَلُ عَن نَّفۡسِهِۦ﴾ [محمّد ٤٨: ٣٧] وهذه الآية نظير الآية في النجوى وهي[٤٥] قوله: إذا ناجيتم الرسول فقدموا بين يدي نجواكم صدقات،[٤٦] يعني عند كلّ مسألة، ثمّ رحم عباده وعفا من ذلك، وأمر بإخراج بعض الأموال. ثمّ أخبر أنه غنيّ عن أموالكم لكن للامتحان والاختبار أمركم، فمنكم من يصبر على الامتحان ومنكم من يتولّى، فقال عزّ وجلّ: ﴿وَٱللَّهُ ٱلۡغَنِيُّ وَأَنتُمُ ٱلۡفُقَرَآءُۚ وَإِن تَتَوَلَّوۡاْ يَسۡتَبۡدِلۡ قَوۡمًا غَيۡرَكُمۡ ثُمَّ لَا يَكُونُوٓاْ أَمۡثَٰلَكُم﴾ [محمّد ٤٧: ٣٨] ثمّ حكم على إخراج ذلك والمسارعة فيه، فقال عزّ وجلّ: ﴿وَأَنفِقُواْ مِن مَّا رَزَقۡنَٰكُم مِّن قَبۡلِ أَن يَأۡتِيَ أَحَدَكُمُ ٱلۡمَوۡتُ فَيَقُولَ رَبِّ لَوۡلَآ أَخَّرۡتَنِيٓ إِلَىٰٓ أَجَلٖ قَرِيبٖ فَأَصَّدَّقَ وَأَكُن مِّنَ ٱلصَّٰلِحِينَ﴾ [المنافقون ٦٣: ١٠].

وقال تعالى ﴿أَنفِقُواْ مِمَّا رَزَقۡنَٰكُم مِّن قَبۡلِ أَن يَأۡتِيَ يَوۡمٞ لَّا بَيۡعٞ فِيهِ وَلَا خُلَّةٞ وَلَا شَفَٰعَةٞۗ وَٱلۡكَٰفِرُونَ هُمُ ٱلظَّٰلِمُونَ﴾ [البقرة ٢: ٢٥٤] ثمّ أمر

---

[٤٤] أموالكم: أموالنا، ب.

[٤٥] وهي: -، ب.

[٤٦] صدقات: صدقة، أ و ب.

بإخراج الطيّب من المال فقال ﴿اَنْفِقُوْا مِنْ طَيِّبٰتِ مَا كَسَبْتُمْ وَمِمَّآ اَخْرَجْنَا لَكُمْ مِنَ الْاَرْضِ وَلَا تَيَمَّمُوا الْخَبِيْثَ مِنْهُ تُنْفِقُوْنَ﴾ [البقرة ٢: ٢٦٧] وأمر بأن تُخرجوا ذلك من طيبة نفوسكم، فقال ﴿لَا تُبْطِلُوْا صَدَقٰتِكُمْ بِالْمَنِّ وَالْاَذٰىۙ﴾ [البقرة ٢: ٢٦٤] ثمّ ضمن البركة والتزكية لمن أنفق في ذاته، فقال ﴿مَثَلُ الَّذِيْنَ يُنْفِقُوْنَ اَمْوَالَهُمْ فِىْ سَبِيْلِ اللّٰهِ كَمَثَلِ حَبَّةٍ اَنْۢبَتَتْ سَبْعَ سَنَابِلَ فِىْ كُلِّ سُنْۢبُلَةٍ مِائَةُ حَبَّةٍ وَاللّٰهُ يُضٰعِفُ لِمَنْ يَشَآءُ﴾ [البقرة ٢/٢٦١] وقال ﴿مَثَلُ الَّذِيْنَ يُنْفِقُوْنَ اَمْوَالَهُمُ ابْتِغَآءَ مَرْضَاتِ اللّٰهِ وَ تَثْبِيْتًا مِنْ اَنْفُسِهِمْ كَمَثَلِ جَنَّةٍ بِرَبْوَةٍ اَصَابَهَا وَابِلٌ فَاٰتَتْ اُكُلَهَا ضِعْفَيْنِ﴾ [البقرة ٢: ٢٦٥] وقال ﴿اَلَّذِيْنَ يُنْفِقُوْنَ اَمْوَالَهُمْ بِالَّيْلِ وَالنَّهَارِ سِرًّا وَّعَلَانِيَةً فَلَهُمْ اَجْرُهُمْ عِنْدَ رَبِّهِمْ وَلَا خَوْفٌ عَلَيْهِمْ وَلَا هُمْ يَحْزَنُوْنَ﴾ [البقرة ٢: ٢٧٤] وجعل إخراج ذلك تزكية وطهارة للأنفس والأموال، فقال ﴿قَدْ اَفْلَحَ مَنْ تَزَكّٰىۙ وَذَكَرَ اسْمَ رَبِّهٖ فَصَلّٰى﴾ [الأعلى ٨٧: ١٤-١٥] ثمّ قال ﴿قَدْ اَفْلَحَ مَنْ زَكّٰىهَا وَقَدْ خَابَ مَنْ دَسّٰىهَا﴾ [الشمس ٩١: ٩-١٠].

ثمّ أدّب نبيّه صلوات الله عليه وزجره عن طلب مَن هرب من الامتحان ولم يُطهّر نفسه ورجع عن استماع البيان، فقال ﴿اَمَّا مَنِ اسْتَغْنٰى فَاَنْتَ لَهٗ تَصَدّٰى وَمَا عَلَيْكَ اَلَّا يَزَّكّٰى وَاَمَّا مَنْ جَآءَكَ يَسْعٰى وَهُوَ يَخْشٰى فَأَنت عَنْهُ تَلَهّٰى كَلَّآ اِنَّهَا تَذْكِرَةٌ فَمَنْ شَآءَ ذَكَرَهٗ﴾ [عبس ٨٠: ٥-١٢] ثمّ أشار إلى أوليائه وأئمّة دينه، فقال ﴿فِىْ صُحُفٍ مُكَرَّمَةٍ مَرْفُوْعَةٍ

مُطَهَّرَةٍۭ﴾ [عبس ٨٠: ١٣-١٤] ثمّ أشار إلى الحجج الذين هم أبواب الأئمّة صلوات الله عليهم، فقال ﴿بِأَيۡدِي سَفَرَةٖ كِرَامِۭ بَرَرَةٖ﴾ [عبس ٨٠: ١٥-١٦] لأنّ الحجج تُسفر عن سرائر التأويل والتنزيل ويبرهنون للأمّة معاني كلّ شيء.

ثمّ أمر بإخراج الصدقات إلى أهل دعوة التأويل، فقال تعالى ﴿إِنَّمَا ٱلصَّدَقَٰتُ لِلۡفُقَرَآءِ﴾ [التوبة ٩: ٦٠] يعني النطقاء إذ[٤٧] ليس في العالم من يُفيدهم، فهم مفتقرون إلى ما يأتيهم من الموادّ الروحانيّة، ﴿وَٱلۡمَسَٰكِينِ﴾، يعني الأسس لأن الخلق يسكنون إلى تأويلهم وبراهينهم ﴿وَٱلۡعَٰمِلِينَ عَلَيۡهَا﴾ يعني الأئمّة، لأنّهم قد ورثوا علوم التنزيل والتأويل، فهم عاملون عليها ويحثّون الأمّة على التمسّك بها، ﴿وَٱلۡمُؤَلَّفَةِ قُلُوبُهُمۡ﴾ يعني الحجج لأنّ الله عزّ وجلّ ألّف قلوبهم، فهم كنفس واحدة لا اختلاف[٤٨] بينهم، ﴿وَفِي ٱلرِّقَابِ﴾ يعني الدعاة، لأنّ خدمة الدعوة عليهم[٤٩] وهم يكسرون على أهل الظاهر ويجعلون العهد في رقاب[٥٠] من

[٤٧] إذ:إن، ب.

[٤٨] لا اختلاف:للاختلاف، ب.

[٤٩] عليهم:-، ب.

[٥٠] رقاب:الرقاب، ب.

استجاب لدعوة الحقّ من المؤمنين ﴿وَالْغَٰرِمِينَ﴾ يعني المأذونين، لأنّ التربية بالعلوم التأويلية إليهم من غير أن يأخذوا على أحد منهم عهدًا، فهم دايات[٥١] اللاتي يربّين من لم يلدن ﴿وَفِي سَبِيلِ اللَّهِ﴾ يعني المأذونين المحدودين[٥٢] الذين بلغوا من العلم حاجتهم، وقد أُذن لهم في تربية المستجيبين وإفادتهم،[٥٣] ولا يكسرون على أحد من أهل الظاهر، وأما المأذونون الأوّلون فهم يكسرون ويفيدون، وهؤلاء يفيدون ولا يكسرون على أحد من أهل الظاهر،[٥٤] ﴿وَابْنِ السَّبِيلِ﴾، يعني المؤمنين الطالبين المستفيدين لفوائد الدين. فهؤلاء ثمانية أجناس جعلهم الله تعالى ذكره قوّام دينه وخزّان علمه، وفرض على الخلق معرفتهم وأوجب عليهم طاعتهم، وأمر بإخراج الصدقات والزكاة إليهم ووضْعِها مواضعها عندهم ليصرفها من كان منهم ليس بإمام إلى الإمام ليصرفها في مصالح الدين.

وقد رُوي عن رسول الله صلى الله عليه وعلى آله أنّه كان يقسم الصدقات، فقال له رجل: أعطِني منها، فقال له: إن كنت من الثمانية،

---

[٥١] دايات: الرايات، ب.

[٥٢] المحدودين: -، ب.

[٥٣] وإفادتهم: لإفادتهم، أ.

[٥٤] من أهل الظاهر: -، ب.

وإلا فهي داء في الجوف وصداع في الرأس، فأعلم الأمّة أنه لا يجب وضع ذلك إلا في هؤلاء الثمانية الذين هم أرباب الدين،[٥٥] ولذلك قال الصادق عليه السلام: ضعوا الزكاة في أهلها وأنا الضّامن لكم ما ذهب من أموالكم. ولو سئل أهل الظاهر ما الفرق[٥٦] بين الفقراء والمساكين ومن قد ذكرهم الله في كتابه في هذه الآية لوجدتَهم مختلفين، فبعض يقول: الفقير الذي لا شيء له، وأما المسكين الذي له شيء يرجع إليه، وإذا كان الأمر كذلك كان الوصول إلى معرفة هؤلاء الأجناس الثمانية معدومًا[٥٧] إلا بالبحث والتفتيش، فهذا ما لا يقدر عليه أحدٌ في ظاهر الأمر ولا في باطنه إلا من جهة أولياء الله صلوات الله عليهم.

واعلم أن السنّة في دين الله عزّ وجلّ أن يُخرج الناطق عليه السلام من جميع ما يملكه ويتجرّد إلى الله من قليله وكثيره كلّما حال عليه الحول، لا يسعُه غير ذلك، وأما الأساس عليه السلام فإنه لا يُخرج من نصف ما يملكه في كلّ سنتين لأنه شطرُ الناطق وله حدّ واحد من حدَّي الناطق، وأما الإمام عليه السلام فإنه يُخرج من ثلث ما يملكه في

---

[٥٥] الدين: دين الله، ب.

[٥٦] الفرق: لفرق، أ و ب.

[٥٧] معدومًا: معدومة، ب.

كل ثلاث سنين، وأما الحجة فإنه يُخرج من ربع ما يملكه في كلّ أربع سنين، وأمّا الداعي فإنه يُخرج من خُمس ما يملكه في كلّ خمس سنين، وأمّا المؤمن فإنه يُخرج ما يخرجه على قدر يقينه وبحسب ما يفرض عليه داعيه يريد بذلك محنته، فإن أخرج ذلك مرة واحدة فقد أدّى الدين اللازم وأدّى الفرض الواجب الذي بأدائه إيّاه تميّز من أهل الظاهر وخرج من حدّهم، فإن أخرج ثاني مرة عرف داعيه حسن نيّته وثباتَ يقينه وكشف له سرائر التأويل، وإن أخرج ثالث مرة ارتفعت عند ولي الله منزلته، وعند المؤمنين درجته، وقد بيّن رسول الله صلى الله عليه هذا المعنى في الوضوء والصلاة، وذلك أنه توضّأ وغسل جوارحه مرّة مرّة، فقال: هذا وضوء من لا يقبل الله صلاته إلا به،[٥٨] والصلاة هي الطاعة، والوضوء هي الطهارة والتزكية التي أوجب الله إخراجها على كلّ مؤمن، فقال: لا يقبل طاعة المرء إلا بإخراج ما يجب عليه لأن تطهّره بذلك، ثمّ غسل جوارحه مرّتين مرّتين، فقال: هذا وضوء من يُضاعف الله له الأجر مرّتين، عنى بذلك أن المؤمن إذا أخرج ما يجب عليه مرّة واحدة فقد تطهّر لأن أداء ذلك طهارته، وإن أخرجه ثاني مرة ضاعف الله له أجره مرّتين وعرف داعيه حسن نيّته وثبات يقينه، ثمّ غسل جوارحه ثلاثًا ثلاثًا، وقال: هذا وضوئي ووضوء الأنبياء قبلي، عنى أن

[٥٨] به: بصلاة به؟، ب.

المؤمن إذا أخرج واجبه ثلاث مرّات ارتفعت عند ولي الله درجته وعند داعيه منزلته، وصار حدًا من حدود الدين.

وقد بيّن رسول الله صلى الله عليه هذا المعنى في مراتب الصلاة، وذلك أنه جعل الصلاة ثلاث مراتب، فريضة وسنّة ونافلة، فالفريضة لا رخصة فيها ولا يجوز تركها، فإن أدّاها العبد وإلا كان كافرًا، عنى بذلك أن إخراج الواجب مرّة واحدة واجب على المستجيب، لا يسعه في ذلك تقصير، فإذا أدّاه كان مؤمنًا، وإن لم يؤدّه كان ظاهريًّا لا يُفاتح بالبيان.[٥٩] وأما المرتبة الثانية، وهي السنّة، فإن أدّاها بعد الفريضة كان تقيًّا، وإن رخص لنفسه فيها كان مقصّرًا لا كافرًا، عنى بذلك أن المستجيب إن أخرج واجبه ثاني مرّة طهرت نفسه، وعرف وليُّه صحّة نيّته وثبات يقينه، وإن قصّر في ذلك ولم يُخرجه لم يكن ظاهريًا ولكنّ مقصّرًا عن طلب العلوّ والرفعة والشرف عند الله وعند وليّه. وأما المرتبة الثالثة فهي النافلة، فإن أتى بها العبد بعد السنة والفريضة كمل إيمانه، عنى بذلك أن المستجيب إذا أخرج واجبه ثلاث مرّات ارتفعت[٦٠] عند وليّ الله منزلته وفي المؤمنين درجته. فصار، أكرمك الله، طهارةُ النفس

---

٥٩ بالبيان: البيان، ب.

٦٠ عنى بذلك...ارتفعت: وارتفعت، ب.

وتزكيةُ المال بإخراج ما قد شرحتُه في هذه الثلاث المراتب، فأمّا الأولى فإنها محنة يُمتحن بها المستجيب، فيجب عليه إخراج ذلك بحسب ما يفرضه عليه داعيه، فربّما أمره بمشاطرة ماله نصفين، وربما أمره بإخراج الثلث أو الربع أو غير ذلك، وربّما يقنع منه بأن يقول له: أخرِج كذا وكذا، وربّما نظر الداعي إلى ما مضى من عمر المستجيب، أعني مبلغ سنّه، فيُسقط من ذلك سنّ[٦١] الصبيّ ويأمره لما بقي بعد ذلك إخراجَ شيء يراه في كلّ سنة، وربّما افترض عليه أن يُخرج بعدد النطقاء والأسُس والأئمّة من لدن آدم إلى قائم القيامة[٦٢] عينًا أو ورقًا، وذلك أنها سبعة أدوار، في كل دور ناطق وأساس وإمام ولاحق وجناح واثنا عشر حجة، جملة ذلك سبعة عشر، ولأجل ذلك جُعل في الفرض في الصلاة سبعة عشر ركعة، فإذا ضُربت سبعة عشر في سبعة كان من ذلك مائة وتسعة عشر، فيأمر الداعي أن يُخرج لكلّ حدّ من هذه الحدود شيئًا معلومًا محنةً له، لا يسعه أن يتخلّف عن ذلك، وأما إخراج المؤمن واجبَه ثاني مرّة وثالث مرّة فإنه ابتداء من نفسه حسب ما تطيب به نفسه، قلّ ذلك أو كثر، مقبول منه ذلك.

---

[٦١] سن: معنى، ب.

[٦٢] قائم القيامة: القائم، ب.

وقد بيّن رسول الله صلى الله عليه هذا المعنى في أعمال الصلاة بأمره الرجال عند الركوع أن يعدلوا ظهورهم حتّى لو صُبّ على ظهر أحدهم ماء لا تقسّم نصفين لاعتدال ظهره، فأما المرأة فيُقنع منها أن توفي ركوعها برأسها وتميل بترائبها، عنى[٦٣] بالرجال، أكرمك الله، المفيدين وعنى بالنساء المستفيدين وعنى بالركوع إقامة الطاعة لله ووليّه، وذلك أن الطاعة إنّما كان مثلها في مبتدأ الأمر السجود، لقول الله عزّ وجلّ ﴿وَإِذْ قُلْنَا لِلْمَلَائِكَةِ اسْجُدُوا لِآدَمَ فَسَجَدُوا إِلَّا إِبْلِيسَ﴾[٦٤] [البقرة ٢: ٣٤ وغيرها]، ثمّ صار الركوع طاعة لقوله جلّ وعزّ ﴿يَا أَيُّهَا الَّذِينَ آمَنُوا ارْكَعُوا وَاسْجُدُوا﴾ [الحج ٢٢: ٧٧] فالسجود حدّ الإمام عليه السلام، دلّ بذلك أن الإمام كان يفاتح المؤمنين بالبيان، فلمّا أقام لنفسه بابًا، وهو الحجّة، أمر الله عزّ وجلّ بالركوع ثمّ بالسجود، أي أقيموا الطاعة للحجّة، ثمّ ادخلوا منه إلى علم الإمام إذ هو بابه، ولذلك قال جلّ ذكره ﴿وَأْتُوا الْبُيُوتَ مِنْ أَبْوَابِهَا وَاتَّقُوا اللَّهَ﴾[٦٥] [البقرة ٢: ١٨٩] والاعتدال في الركوع للرجال، عنى به أن العلماء المفيدين لا يُقنّع منهم بالتقصير ولا بأن يدخل في أعمالهم خلل ولا زللٌ، فأمّا المستفيد فيُقنّع منه ببعض العمل ولو كان

---

٦٣ فأعني :عنى، أ.

٦٤ إلا إبليس:-، ب.

٦٥ أبوابها واتقو الله:أبواب، ب.

مقصّرًا لقلّة علمه وضعف يقينه، وكان الفضل في أداء الواجب أن يحمل المؤمن قدر طاقته، ولذلك يقول الله عزّ وجلّ ﴿ وَيَسْأَلُونَكَ مَاذَا يُنفِقُونَ قُلِ الْعَفْوَ﴾ [٢: ٢١٩] يعني الطاعة وحسن الاحتمال.

ومن الناس من يُخرج ذلك بخبث من نفسه وضعف يقين، ولذلك يقول الله جل ذكره ﴿وَمِنَ الْأَعْرَابِ مَن يَتَّخِذُ مَا يُنفِقُ مَغْرَمًا وَيَتَرَبَّصُ بِكُمُ الدَّوَائِرَ عَلَيْهِمْ السَّوْءِ﴾ [التوبة ٩: ٩٨] ومنهم من يُخرج بطيبة من نفسه وقوّة يقين وتصديق، ولذلك يقول الله تعالى ذكره فيهم ﴿وَمِنَ الْأَعْرَابِ مَن ... وَيَتَّخِذُ مَا يُنفِقُ قُرُبَاتٍ عِندَ اللَّهِ وَصَلَوَاتِ الرَّسُولِ أَلَا إِنَّهَا قُرْبَةٌ لَهُمْ﴾ [التوبة ٩: ٩٩] والأعرابيّ الظاهريّ الذي يطلب فوائد الدين، والدليل على ذلك قول رسول الله صلى الله عليه: لا يؤمّ الأعرابي مهاجرًا، عنى بالأعرابي الظاهريّ وبالمهاجر المؤمن، لأنه قد هاجر من حدّ الجهل والحيرة والاختلاف إلى حدّ التأويل المحض والبرهان بالبيان،[٦٦] يقول: لا يحلّ[٦٧] للمؤمن أن يتّخذ أحدًا من أهل الظاهر إمامًا يقتدي به ويتمسّك بهداه[٦٨] للنجاة.

---

[٦٦] بالبيان: والبيان، ب.

[٦٧] يحل: يحمل، ب.

[٦٨] بهداه: بهدية، ب.

وقد بيّن رسول الله صلى الله عليه معنى الواجب الذي هو الفكاك في الحجّ ومناسكه وسأشرح لك هذا باختصار إذ[٦٩] بلغت إلى ذكر[٧٠] الشرائع وما فيها من الإشارات إلى القرابين لا لحاجة من الله عزّ وجلّ إلى ذلك، لكن لتطهير الأنفس وتزكية الأموال ليكون قوت المؤمن أيّام حياته طيّبًا لا خبيثًا ويكون في معاده ناجيًا لا هالكًا، يقول الله تعالى ذكره ﴿لَن يَنَالَ اللَّهَ لُحُومُهَا وَلَا دِمَاؤُهَا وَلَـٰكِن يَنَالُهُ التَّقْوَىٰ مِنكُمْ﴾ [الحج ٢٢: ٣٧] ونظير هذا القول في التوراة: بالفعل تسرون لا بالذبيحة،[٧١] وقال تعالى: ﴿وَمَا تُنفِقُوا مِنْ خَيْرٍ يُوَفَّ إِلَيْكُمْ وَأَنتُمْ لَا تُظْلَمُونَ﴾ [البقرة ٢: ٢٧٢] وقال الله تعالى ذكره ﴿وَمَا تُنفِقُوا مِنْ خَيْرٍ فَلِأَنفُسِكُمْ وَمَا تُنفِقُونَ إِلَّا ابْتِغَاءَ وَجْهِ اللَّهِ﴾ [البقرة ٢: ٢٧٢] وقال عزّ وجلّ ﴿وَمَا تُقَدِّمُوا لِأَنفُسِكُم مِّنْ خَيْرٍ تَجِدُوهُ عِندَ اللَّهِ﴾ [البقرة ٢: ١١٠] ... ﴿إِنَّ اللَّهَ غَفُورٌ رَّحِيمٌ﴾ [المزمل ٧٣: ٢٠] ونظير هذا في الإنجيل: اجعلوا

---

[٦٩] إذ: إذا، أ و ب.

[٧٠] ذكر: ذكره، أ.

[٧١] قابل بصموئيل ١٥/٢٢.

ذبائحكم وكنوزكم بحيث لا يأكلها آكلة ولا لص يقدر عليها،[٧٢] يعني عند الله.

واعلم أن الله تعالى ذكره وهب هذه الدنيا بجميع ما فيها لرسوله صلى الله عليه وآله الطاهرين، فهو لوليّ الزمان، وإذا كان ذلك كذلك، وكان أولى بهم من أنفسهم بأمر الله تعالى، فجميع ما في أيدي المؤمنين وغيرهم فهو له، عرف ذلك من عرفه وجهله من جهله، يقول الله عزّ وجلّ "النبي أولى بالمؤمنين من أنفسهم" وإذا كان ذلك كذلك وكان أولى بهم من أنفسهم بأمر الله تعالى فهو بأموالهم أحقّ وأولى منهم، والإمام عليه السلام في كلّ عصر وزمان هو خليفة رسول الله صلى الله عليه، فهو أولى بالمؤمنين، بأموالهم وبأنفسهم، ولولا إشفاق من الإطالة لبيّنتُ من جهة تراكيب العالم أن الإمام صاحب الزمان لبّ العالم ومحصوله، وجميع ما في العالم من حيوان ونبات آلة له ووقاية كالقشور حول كلّ ذي قشر، ولبّه بمنزلة القلب من الجسم، وجميع الجوارح والتراكيب آلة له ووقاية، يستعملهم ويأمرهم وينهاهم إذ لا فرق بين الإنسان الذي هو العالم الصغير وبين العالم الكبير، وإذا كان في هذا العالم بهذه المنزلة فهو صلوات الله عليه أولى بالمؤمنين وغير المؤمنين منهم بأموالهم وبأنفسهم.

---

[٧٢] قابل بمتى ١٩/٦.

فأما المؤمن فهو يعلم أن ماله ونفسه لوليّ الله، فهو على يقين وبصيرة من ذلك،[٧٣] لا يختلجه فيما يُخرجه لوليّ الله شكٌّ لعلمه بذلك لقول الله تعالى ذكره ﴿اِنَّ اللّٰهَ اشْتَرٰى مِنَ الْمُؤْمِنِيْنَ اَنْفُسَهُمْ وَاَمْوَالَهُمْ بِاَنَّ لَهُمُ الْجَنَّةَ يُقَاتِلُوْنَ فِيْ سَبِيْلِ اللّٰهِ فَيَقْتُلُوْنَ وَ يُقْتَلُوْنَ وَعْدًا عَلَيْهِ حَقًّا فِي التَّوْرٰىةِ وَالْاِنْجِيْلِ وَالْقُرْاٰنِ وَمَنْ اَوْفٰى بِعَهْدِهٖ مِنَ اللّٰهِ فَاسْتَبْشِرُوْا بِبَيْعِكُمُ الَّذِيْ بَايَعْتُمْ بِهٖ وَذٰلِكَ هُوَ الْفَوْزُ الْعَظِيْمُ﴾ [التوبة ٩: ١١١] فجميع ما في أيدي المؤمنين لله عزّ وجلّ، وما كان لله فهو لوليّه صلوات الله عليه، لكن بفضل الله ورحمته أمرهم بإخراج بعض ما يملكون إلى الله عزّ وجلّ وإلى رسوله صلى الله عليه وإلى ولي الزمان عليه السلام من بعده، فقال الله تعالى ذكره ﴿وَاعْلَمُوْٓا اَنَّمَا غَنِمْتُمْ مِنْ شَيْءٍ فَاَنَّ لِلّٰهِ خُمُسَهٗ وَ لِلرَّسُوْلِ﴾ [الأنفال ٨: ٤١] وقال الصادق صلوات الله عليه: الله عزّ وجلّ وهب لرسوله صلى الله عليه خُمس الدنيا، فما كان لله فهو لرسوله، وما كان لرسوله فهو لنا، فكلّ من اكتسب درهمًا واحدًا فما فوقه فهو غنيمة، فمن تخلّص إلينا من حقّنا فقد[٧٤] تخلّص مما يجب عليه، ومَن بخل به طوّقه الله

[٧٣] وبصيرة من ذلك: ورهنوه من ذلك، ب؛ بصيرة وذلك، أ.

[٧٤] فقد: فهو، ب.

بطوق من نار، وإن شيعتنا من ذلك في حلّ[٧٥] إذ[٧٦] عفونا، ثمّ قال صلوات الله عليه: وقد وهب الله لنا الأنفال، قيل له: وما الأنفال؟[٧٧] قال معادن الذهب والفضّة والجوهر والجبال والأودية وكلّ أرض لا ربّ لها.

وقد دخل سُدير الصيرفي الكوفي رضوان[؟][٧٨] يومًا على الصادق صلوات الله عليه ومعه زكاة المؤمنين وصدقاتهم وصِلاتهم فتركها بين يديه، فقال له: ما هذا؟ فقال: زكاة عبيدك وصلاتهم، فقال: إنّا لنقبل ذلك منهم، وما بنا إليه من حاجة ولكن لنطهّرهم لقول الله عز وجل: ﴿خُذْ مِنْ اَمْوَالِهِمْ صَدَقَةً تُطَهِّرُهُمْ وَتُزَكِّيهِمْ بِهَا﴾ [التوبة ٩: ١٠٣] والتزكية الطهارة من المعاصي والخطايا، وقال الله عزّ وجلّ لموسى عليه السلام ﴿اِذْهَبْ اِلَى فِرْعَوْنَ اِنَّهُ طَغٰى فَقُلْ هَلْ لَكَ اِلٰى اَنْ تَزَكّٰى وَاَهْدِيَكَ اِلٰى رَبِّكَ فَتَخْشٰى﴾ [النازعات ٧٩: ١٧-١٩] ولا تكون الطهارة إلا بالصبر

---

٧٥ حلّ: حال، أ و ب.

٧٦ إذ: إن، أ.

٧٧ قيل له: وما الأنفال: -، ب.

٧٨ الكوفي: + رحمورة (كذا) الله عليه، ب.

على المحنة والبلوى، قال الله جلّ ذكره ﴿وَلَنَبۡلُوَنَّكُمۡ حَتَّىٰ نَعۡلَمَ ٱلۡمُجَٰهِدِينَ مِنكُمۡ وَٱلصَّٰبِرِينَ وَنَبۡلُوَاْ[٧٩] أَخۡبَارَكُمۡ﴾ [محمّد ٤٧: ٣١].

فانظر إلى ما امتحن الله به ابنَي آدم عليه السلام ﴿إِذۡ قَرَّبَا قُرۡبَانٗا فَتُقُبِّلَ مِنۡ أَحَدِهِمَا وَلَمۡ يُتَقَبَّلۡ مِنَ ٱلۡأٓخَرِ﴾ [المائدة ٥: ٢٧]، فحسده ﴿قَالَ لَأَقۡتُلَنَّكَۖ قَالَ إِنَّمَا يَتَقَبَّلُ ٱللَّهُ مِنَ ٱلۡمُتَّقِينَ﴾ [المائدة ٥: ٢٧] وذلك أن هابيل عليه السلام بحسن نيّته وثابت يقينه أخرج من جميع ما يملكه أفضله وأحسنه وأطيبه، وأخرج قابيل بسوء نيّته واستهزائه بأمر ربّه من كلّ ما يملكه أشرّه وأدونه وأخبثه، فكان من أمرهما ما قد سمعتَه، وانظر إلى إبراهيم عليه السلام إذ[٨٠] امتحنه الله عزّ وجلّ بذبح ابنه أن يقرّبه إلى الله عزّ وجلّ قربانًا، ألا ترى أنه إنّما[٨١] أراد بذلك محنته لا لحاجة[٨٢] منه أن يذبح إبراهيم ولده، وانظر إلى ما أمر الله به بني إسرائيل من القرابين والذبائح في الكنائس من أفضل ما يقدرون عليه وأجلّه وأطيبه وأن يجعلوا شحوم الذبائح على المذبح ويلطّخ بالدم المذبح وبين

---

[٧٩] ونبلو: ونبلوكم، أ.

[٨٠] إذ: إذا، أ و ب.

[٨١] إنّما: لما، أ؛ ما، ب.

[٨٢] لحاجة: حاجة، ب.

يدي الكاهن وستور الكنيسة، فإن القربان مقبول إن نزلت النار فأكلت الشحوم ولحست الدم بين يدي الكاهن من ستور الكنيسة، وإن لم تنزل النار ولم تفعل ما ذكرناه علموا أنه قربان غير متقبّل وأن سريرة الذي قرّبه خبيثة[٨٣] وأن نيّة[٨٤] غيره الذي تنزل النار فتفعل ما ذكرناه جميلة، فيأمرونه[٨٥] لذلك بالتوبة إلى الله، فانظر إلى هذا الأمر، كيف هو محنة لعبد،[٨٦] فالقربان هو محنة يُمتحن بها العبد ليُعلم سريرته ويقينه ونيّته.

وانظر إلى سنّة رسول الله صلى الله عليه في فطرة الصوم إذ أوجبها على الصغير والكبير، والذَّكَر والأنثى، والحرّ والعبد، والحاضر والغائب، أشار بذلك إلى إخراج الواجب والفكاك ودعوة التأويل، ثمّ أمر بالحركة فيها والمسارعة بها قبل طلوع الشمس إلى مسجد الجماعات، فإن أُخرجت قبل طلوع الشمس كانت فطرة، وإن أُخرجت بعد طلوع الشمس كانت صدقة، فمعنى الصوم الستر والكتمان والسكوت، ومعنى

---

[٨٣] خبيثة: خشية، ب.

[٨٤] نية: بنية، ب.

[٨٥] فيأمرونه: فيأمروا، ب.

[٨٦] محنة لعبد: محبة للعبد، ب.

الفطرة إخراج الواجب لله ولوليّه من الفكاك والقربان، ومعنى طلوع الشمس ظهور الإمام وكشفه عن الدعوة، وإخراج المرء الفطرة قبل طلوع الشمس بمعنى التصديق بالإمام قبل ظهوره، فيُخرج من الواجب تصديقًا وبرًّا وانفكاكًا، وإخراج الفطرة بعد طلوع الشمس بمعنى التصديق بالإمام[٨٧] بعد ظهوره، فيُخرج الفكاك بلا برّ، ومعنى إخراج ذلك إلى مسجد الجماعات، أي إخراجه إلى الداعي الذي هو موضع طاعتك وسجودك، وفي المسارعة وطلب العلوّ في الدرجات بالعمل يقول الله تعالى ﴿فَمَنْ يَعْمَلْ مِثْقَالَ ذَرَّةٍ خَيْرًا يَرَهُ وَمَنْ يَعْمَلْ مِثْقَالَ ذَرَّةٍ شَرًّا ي يَرَهُ﴾ [الزلزال ٩٩: ٧-٨] ويقول جلّ اسمُه ﴿وَلِكُلٍّ دَرَجٰتٌ مِمَّا عَمِلُوا﴾ [الأنعام ٦: ١٣٢] ويقول تعالى ذكره ﴿وَسَارِعُوٓا اِلٰى مَغْفِرَةٍ مِنْ رَبِّكُمْ﴾ [آل عمران ٣: ١٣٣] وانظر إلى السنّة في المولود، إذا خرج من بطن أمّه أُخرج عنه دينار، ويُدهن ويُقمط ويُحنّك بالعسل والصبر، ثمّ يُسقى اللبن بعد ذلك، ويسمّى في اليوم السابع ويُحلق وسط رأسه، ويُتصدّق عنه ويوزن شَعر رأسه فضّةً، ويُذبح عنه، فمعنى المولود المستجيب، ومعنى إخراج الدينار عنه ما يلزم المستجيب من أداء[٨٨] النجوى، ومعنى القِماط العهد الذي يوثق به، ومعنى العسل والصبِر ما يُكشف له

[٨٧] بالإمام: بلا إمام، ب.

[٨٨] أداء: تأدية، أ.

من البيان والتأويل، وما يلزمه من الصبر على كتمان ذلك، ومعنى تسميته في اليوم السابع إظهار إمام العصر له، إذ الإمام صاحب العصر هو واحد من الأئمّة السبعة، ومعنى حلق وسط رأسه كشف أمر رئيسه الذي هو إمام زمانه،[٨٩] والصدقة عنه بوزن شعر رأسه بمعنى الفكاك، والذبيحة عنه بمعنى كسره، أعني المستجيب بمستجيب آخر وأخذه عليه العهد، وذلك إذا بلغ مبلغًا يقدر فيه على تربية غيره، ولذلك يقول الله جلّ ذكره ﴿وَابْتَلُوا الْيَتٰمٰى حَتّٰىٓ اِذَا بَلَغُوا النِّكَاحَ فَاِنْ اٰنَسْتُمْ مِنْهُمْ رُشْدًا فَادْفَعُوْٓا اِلَيْهِمْ اَمْوَالَهُمْ وَلَا تَاْكُلُوْهَآ﴾ [النساء ٤:٦] وفي هذا المعنى يقول الله تعالى ﴿وَمَا عَلَّمْتُمْ مِنَ الْجَوَارِحِ مُكَلِّبِيْنَ تُعَلِّمُوْنَهُنَّ مِمَّا عَلَّمَكُمُ اللّٰهُ فَكُلُوْا مِمَّآ اَمْسَكْنَ عَلَيْكُمْ﴾ [المائدة ٥:٤] أي خذوا من كسروا عليه وأضبطوه ﴿وَاذْكُرُوا اسْمَ اللّٰهِ﴾ [المائدة ٥:٤] أي ادعوه إلى إقامة[٩٠] طاعة الإمام والحجّة عند أخذ العهد عليه، ويُقال عند الذبح: بسم الله، فبسم ثلاثة أحرف، دليل على الحجّة، الله أربعة أحرف، إشارة إلى الإمام، ولهذا المعنى يقول الله تعالى ﴿وَاِذَا بَلَغَ الْاَطْفَالُ مِنْكُمُ الْحُلُمَ فَلْيَسْتَاْذِنُوْا كَمَا اسْتَاْذَنَ الَّذِيْنَ مِنْ قَبْلِهِمْ﴾ [النور ٢٤: ٥٩].

---

[٨٩] زمانه: الزمان، ب.

[٩٠] إقامة: مافاته، ب.

فجميعُ ما ذكرتُه من كتاب الله عزّ وجلّ ظاهرهُ مُحكم معمول به، يؤدي ثلاثة أحوال وثلاثة معانٍ كما ذكرتُ لك في أول هذا الكتاب، أحدها أنه تعبّد لله عزّ وجلّ، والثاني تأديب وأحكام وقضايا لعمران الدنيا، والثالث أنه إشارة إلى حدود دين الله والأسباب المذكورة في كتاب الله عزّ وجلّ، فهم الارتفاء إلى دار المعاد، عرفهم من عرفهم وجهلهم من جهلهم، ﴿وَمَا يَذَّكَّرُ إِلَّا أُولُو الْأَلْبَابِ﴾ [آل عمران ٣: ٧].

وانظر إلى أعمال الحجّ والمناسك والإشارة إلى ما أوجب الله عزّ وجلّ على كلّ مؤمنٍ من إخراج قربانه الذي يتقرّب به إلى الله عزّ وجلّ، يقول الله تعالى ذكره ﴿وَلِلَّهِ عَلَى النَّاسِ حِجُّ الْبَيْتِ مَنِ اسْتَطَاعَ إِلَيْهِ سَبِيلًا﴾ [آل عمران ٣: ٩٧] فالاستطاعة الزاد[٩١] والراحلة[٩٢] وأمن السبيل والنفقة للعيال، فمن وجد ذلك وجب عليه الحجّ لا رخصة في ذلك لمسلم بإجماع، فمعنى الزاد العلم الذي هو غذاء الأنفس، ومعنى الراحلة الداعي الذي يسير بك في دين الله من حدٍّ إلى حدٍّ حتى يُبلغك مأمنك ويُعرّفك ما يجب لك وعليك، فمن وجد داعيًا وجب عليه طلب الإمام حتى يصل إليه ويُقيم طاعته، ويعرف حدود

---

[٩١] الزاد: الزادة، ب.

[٩٢] الراحلة: الرحلة، ب.

دين الله من لدن آدم إلى القيامة، ومعنى طرح الثياب المخيطة التي كانت عليك طرحكَ لعلم كلّ إمام ظاهريّ كنتَ تتعلق به، ولبسكَ مئزرًا ورداء[٩٣] دخولُك تحت طاعة الإمام والحُجّة، وتطهيرك بالماء قبولك للعلم الذي به تطهّرك،[٩٤] وقولك: لبّيك اللهمّ لبّيك إجابتك لإمام زمانك إذ بعث إليك الداعي ليدعوك إلى الله وإلى معرفة دينه، فأجبتَه بالتلبية، أي بالتصديق، واستلامكَ الحجة قبولك العلم وإقرارك بأنه باب الإمام عليه السلام وطوافك سبع مرّات إقرارك بالسبعة الأئمّة، ووقوفك على الصفا والمروة معرفتكَ الناطق والأساس، وسعيك بينهما طلبك علومك منهما،[٩٥] ومجيئكَ إلى منى مجيئك إلى من منّ عليك بالمعرفة، وهو داعيك، وصلاتك بمنى إقامتك طاعة داعيك والخضوع له، ووقوفك بعَرَفة والجمع بين صلاتي الظهر والعصر بها إقامتك طاعة الناطق والقائم وإقرارك بهما، وصعودك بعد ذلك إلى الموقف ارتقاؤك إلى معرفة الحدود الروحانية السماوية، وصلاتك بالمزدلفة المغرب والعشاء[٩٦] إقرارك بالأساس والإمام والمستورين من الأئمّة، وجمعك الحصى سبعين عددًا

---

[٩٣] ميزرًا ورداء: ميزرًا أو إزارًا ورداء، ب.

[٩٤] تطهرك: تطهيرك، ب.

[٩٥] علومك منهما: علومهما، ب.

[٩٦] والعشاء: + الأخرة، أ.

إقرارك سبعين حدًا الذين[٩٧] هم خيرة الله المجتمعون[٩٨] مع كلّ إمام، ورميكَ بإحدى وعشرين حصاة براءتك من أضداد النطقاء السبعة والأوصياء السبعة والأئمّة السبعة، ودفنك لباقي ذلك الحصى سترك على حدود دين الله، وهم سبعة أسابيع، وسياقتك لهديك مسارعتك إلى إخراج ما أوجب الله عليك وعلى كلّ مؤمن من الفكاك وهو قربانك الذي يُتقرّب إلى الله عزّ وجلّ لتطهير نفسك، وحلقك لرأسك كشفك عن رئيسك الذي هو إمام زمانك ومعرفتك به، وإفطارك ثلاثة أيّام نطقك بالبيان وإظهار ما كنت تستره من علم الناطق والأساس والإمام، ورجوعك إلى مكّة رجوعك إلى داعيك لطلب الاستفادة منه ما بقي عليك وأن لا تلبث مع أهل الظاهر ولا تجعل علومهم ذخيرتك وكنزك إذ كان ذلك[٩٩] قشورًا لا نجاة فيه.

فهذا أكرمك الله، معنى الحجّ والمناسك، قد اختصرتُه لك، أردتُ بذلك إظهار ما أوجبه الله عليك وعلى كلّ مؤمن من القرابين التي تتقرب بها إلى الله عزّ وجلّ، وأما قولك عند ذبحك لما يُتقرّب به: اللهمّ

[٩٧] سبعين حدًا: بالسبعين حد، ب.

[٩٨] المجتمعون: المجتمعين، أ و ب.

[٩٩] إذ كان ذلك: إذا كان تلك، أ و ب.

تقبّل مني كما تقبّلتَ من إبراهيم الخليل، فهو ظاهر، يشير إلى ما يأمرك به داعيك من إخراج ما أوجبه الله عليك رحمةً من الله لك وامتنانًا عليك وعلى المؤمنين لتطهير الأنفس، كما أعلمتُك ذلك بقول الله تعالى ﴿وَلَوْلَا فَضْلُ اللَّهِ عَلَيْكُمْ وَرَحْمَتُهُ مَا زَكَىٰ مِنكُم مِنْ أَحَدٍ أَبَدًا وَلَٰكِنَّ اللَّهَ يُزَكِّي مَن يَشَاءُ﴾ [النور ٢٤: ٢١] ولو استقصيتُ لك الشرح فيما أوجب الله عزّ وجلّ عليك وعلى المؤمنين في هذا المعنى من كتاب الله عزّ وجلّ وسنّة رسوله صلى الله عليه وآله، وما في الشرائع لذلك من الدلائل لطال الكتاب بذلك، وفيما ذكرتُه من ذلك كفاية لمن كان له قلب يعقل به وأُذن يسمع بها، فإنها لا تعمي الأبصار، ولكن تعمى القلوب التي في الصدور، ولو تأمّلتَ بعض ما ذكرتُه لك من الإشارات ووقفتَ عليه بالبحث والتفتيش أو بالسؤال والاستدلال لما نسبتَ إلى داعيك ومن فرض[١٠٠] الله عزّ وجلّ عليك طاعته في أخذ ما لك وما لغيرك حيلةً، نعوذ بالله من ذلك، أوتظنّ أنه يصل إليه من ذلك حبّة واحدة؟ كلّا أن يكون ذلك أبدًا، وقد تقدّمتُ بردّ ما أخذه منك إليك إذا كانت الكتب وقرائتها لا تنجح فيك، وهذا لمثلك إشفاق عليك، فأقلع إن أردتَ ذلك وإن استغنيتَ عنه فبالله وبأوليائه الغنى عنك، والسلام

[١٠٠] فرض: فوض، أ و ب.

عليك ورحمة الله وبركاته وصلّى الله على رسوله سيّدنا محمّد وآله وسلّم تسليمًا.

فهرس الآيات القرآنية

البقرة ٢: ٢٨ .... ٦٤
البقرة ٢: ٣٤ .... ٩٦
البقرة ٢: ٤٩ .... ٤٤
البقرة ٢: ٥٤ .... ٢٧
البقرة ٢: ٥٨ .... ٥٤
البقرة ٢: ٥٩ .... ٤١
البقرة ٢: ٦٠ .... ٥٤
البقرة ٢: ٧٥ .... ٧
البقرة ٢: ٧٩ .... ٤٣
البقرة ٢: ٨٠-٨١ .... ٤٥
البقرة ٢: ٨٠ .... ٤٤
البقرة ٢: ٨١ .... ٤٤
البقرة ٢: ٨٣ .... ٦٣
البقرة ٢: ٨٥ .... ٥٤, ٨٥
البقرة ٢: ٨٤-٨٥ .... ٥٣
البقرة ٢: ٩١ .... ٦٥
البقرة ٢: ١٠٠ .... ٦٣
البقرة ٢: ١٠١ .... ٣٢
البقرة ٢: ١٠٨ .... ٢١
البقرة ٢: ١١٠ .... ٩٩
البقرة ٢: ١١١ .... ٥٨
البقرة ٢: ١١٣ .... ٥٨
البقرة ٢: ١١٨ .... ٣
البقرة ٢: ١٢٤ .... ١٧
البقرة ٢: ١٨٩ .... ٧١, ٩٧
البقرة ٢: ٢٠٧ .... ١٨
البقرة ٢: ٢١٩ .... ٩٧
البقرة ٢: ٢٤٦ .... ٥٢
البقرة ٢: ٢٤٧ .... ٥٢
البقرة ٢: ٢٤٨ .... ٥٢, ٥٧
البقرة ٢: ٢٥٤ .... ٨٩
البقرة ٢: ٢٦١ .... ٨٩
البقرة ٢: ٢٦٤ .... ٨٩
البقرة ٢: ٢٦٥ .... ٨٩
البقرة ٢: ٢٦٧ .... ٨٩
البقرة ٢: ٢٧٢ .... ٩٨

فهرس الآيات القرآنية

البقرة ٢: ٢٧٤ .... ٨٩
آل عمران ٣: ٧ .... ١٠٦
آل عمران ٣: ٢٤ .... ٤٤
آل عمران ٣: ٣٧ .... ١٦
آل عمران ٣: ٦١ .... ٤١
آل عمران ٣: ٧٥ .... ٦٦
آل عمران ٣: ٧٨ .... ٦٦
آل عمران ٣: ٩٧ .... ١٠٦
آل عمران ٣: ١٣٣ .... ١٠٤
آل عمران ٣: ١٤٤ .... ٢٦
آل عمران ٣: ١٥٥ .... ٢٥
آل عمران ٣: ١٦٧ .... ٥١
آل عمران ٣: ١٩٢ .... ٤٧
النساء ٤: ٦ .... ١٠٥
النساء ٤: ١٠ .... ٤٥
النساء ٤: ٢٦ .... ١
النساء ٤: ٥١-٥٢ .... ٣١
النساء ٤: ٥٤ .... ٧١
النساء ٤: ٥٩ .... ٥٢
النساء ٤: ٤٦ .... ٦٣
النساء ٤: ٨١ .... ٤٣
النساء ٤: ٩٣ .... ٤٥
النساء ٤:١٢٣ .... ٤٥
النساء ٤:١٥٤ .... ٥٠, ٥١
النساء ٤:١٥٦-١٥٧ .... ٦٨
النساء ٤:١٧١ .... ٦٧
المائدة ٥:٣ .... ٢٠, ٨٤
المائدة ٥:٤ .... ١٠٥
المائدة ٥:١٢-١٣ .... ٤٠
المائدة ٥:١٣ .... ٢٩, ٣٧, ٦٣
المائدة ٥:١٧ .... ٦٦
المائدة ٥:١٩ .... ١
المائدة ٥:٢٢ .... ٢٥
المائدة ٥:٢٣ .... ٢٥
المائدة ٥:٢٤ .... ٥٧
المائدة ٥:٢٤-٢٥ .... ٢٥
المائدة ٥:٢٧ .... ١٠٢
المائدة ٥:٣٢ .... ٦٣
المائدة ٥:٤١ .... ٢٩
المائدة ٥:٥٤ .... ٦١
المائدة ٥:٥٩ .... ٦٢
المائدة ٥:٦٢ .... ٦٣
المائدة ٥:٦٤ .... ٥٧
المائدة ٥:٦٦ .... ٣٣, ٦٢

فهرس الآيات القرآنية

المائدة ٥:٦٧ .... ١٨, ١٩
المائدة ٥:٦٨ .... ٣٣
المائدة ٥:٧٣ .... ٦٧
المائدة ٥:٧٨-٨٠ .... ٣٧
المائدة ٥:١٠١-١٠٢ .... ٢١
المائدة ٥:١١٢ .... ٦
الأنعام ٦:٧ .... ٥
الأنعام ٦:٣٤ .... ٥
الأنعام ٦:٥٢ .... ١١
الأنعام ٦:٥٤ .... ١١
الأنعام ٦:٦٦ .... ٩
الأنعام ٦:٧٠ .... ٣٨
الأنعام ٦:١٣٢ .... ١٠٤
الأنعام ٦:١٤٦ .... ٣٩
الأنعام ٦:١٥٨ .... ٢٧
الأعراف ٧:٥٠ .... ٤٧
الأعراف ٧:٩٩ .... ٤٥
الأعراف ٧:١٠٢ .... ٦٣
الأعراف ٧:١٠٦-١٠٨ .... ٤
الأعراف ٧:١٠٩ .... ٥
الأعراف ٧:١١١-١١٩ .... ٢٣
الأعراف ٧:١١٨-١١٩ .... ٢٣
الأعراف ٧:١٢٧ .... ٦٠
الأعراف ٧:١٣٢ .... ٤
الأعراف ٧:١٣٧ .... ٤٤
الأعراف ٧:١٣٨ .... ٢١
الأعراف ٧:١٤٢ .... ٢٠, ٢٧
الأعراف ٧:١٥٩ .... ٥٩
الأعراف ٧:١٦٥ .... ٥٠
الأعراف ٧:١٦٨ .... ٥٩
الأعراف ٧:١٦٩ .... ٣٣
الأعراف ٧:١٧٥-١٧٦ .... ٥٥
الأنفال ٨:٣٠ .... ١٤, ٢٤
الأنفال ٨:٤١ .... ١٠٠
الأنفال ٨:٤٢ .... ٨٢
التوبة ٩:٤٨ .... ٦٠
التوبة ٩:٤٩ .... ٤٧
التوبة ٩:٦٠ .... ٩٠
التوبة ٩:٦٩ .... ٣
التوبة ٩:٩٨ .... ٩٧
التوبة ٩:٩٩ .... ٩٧
التوبة ٩:١٠٣ .... ٨٦, ١٠١
التوبة ٩:١١١ .... ٧٩, ١٠٠
التوبة ٩:١١٥ .... ١

فهرس الآيات القرآنية

يونس ١٠:٨٣ .... ١٥
يونس ١٠:٨٧ .... ١٧
يونس ١٠:٨٨ .... ٢٢
يونس ١٠:٨٩ .... ٢٢
هود ١١:١٢ .... ١٠
هود ١١:٤٠ .... ٦٣
هود ١١:١٠٦-١٠٧ .... ٤٦
هود ١١:١٠٨ .... ٤٦
يوسف ١٢:٧ .... ٢٥
يوسف ١٢:١٦ .... ٢٤
يوسف ١٢:١٨ .... ٢٤
يوسف ١٢:٢٦-٢٧ .... ٢٤
يوسف ١٢:٩٣ .... ٢٤
النحل ١٦:٢٧ .... ٤٦
الكهف ١٨:٢٨ .... ١١
الكهف ١٨:٥٥ .... ٥
مريم ١٩:٥٤ .... ١٨
مريم ١٩:٥٩ .... ٣٣
طه ٢٠:٢٩-٣١ .... ٤٢
طه ٢٠:٢٩-٣٢ .... ١٨
طه ٢٠:٧١-٧٢ .... ١٢
طه ٢٠:٨٦ .... ٢٧
طه ٢٠:٨٨ .... ٢٧
طه ٢٠:٩٧ .... ٥٣
طه ٢٠:١٣٢ .... ٤٢
الأنبياء ٢١:٤١ .... ٦
الأنبياء ٢١:٩٥ .... ٦٤
الأنبياء ٢١:١٠١-١٠٢ .... ٤٧
الأنبياء ٢١:١٠٢-١٠٣ .... ٤٧
الحج ٢٢:٣٧ .... ٩٨
الحج ٢٢:٤٠ .... ٣٩
الحج ٢٢:٧٧ .... ٩٦
المؤمنون ٢٣:١٢-١٦ .... ٦٤
النور ٢٤:٣٣ .... ٨٢
النور ٢٤:٥٥ .... ٤٤, ٦١
النور ٢٤:٥٩ .... ١٠٦
النور ٢٤:٦٣ .... ٥٥
الفرقان ٢٥:٧ .... ٥
الفرقان ٢٥:٢٠ .... ٥
الفرقان ٢٥:٤١-٤٢ .... ٧
الشعراء ٢٦:١١١-١١٤ ...... ١٠
الشعراء ٢٦:١٢٠ .... ٢٨
الشعراء ٢٦:٢١٤ .... ٦, ٥٦
النمل ٢٧:١٣ .... ٥

القصص ٢٨: ٢١ .... ١٧
القصص ٢٨: ٢٢ .... ١٦
القصص ٢٨: ٢٣-٢٤ .... ١٣
القصص ٢٨: ٢٦ .... ١٣
القصص ٢٨: ٤٨ .... ١٢
القصص ٢٨: ٤٩ .... ١٢
العنكبوت ٢٩: ١-٣ .... ٣
الروم ٣٠: ٤-٥ .... ٦١
الروم ٣٠: ٦ .... ٤٤
الأحزاب ٣٣: ٥ .... ٤١
الأحزاب ٣٣: ١٢ .... ٢٣
الأحزاب ٣٣: ٣٢-٣٣ .... ٥٦
الأحزاب ٣٣: ٣٣ .. ١٥, ٤٢, ٦٢
الأحزاب ٣٣: ٤٠ .... ٤١
الأحزاب ٣٣: ٦٩ .... ٢٢
الأحزاب ٣٣: ٥٣ .... ٢٢
سبأ ٣٤: ٣١ .... ١٢
الصافات ٣٧: ٧١ .... ٦٣
الصافات ٣٧: ١٠٢ .... ١٨
ص ٣٨: ٢٥ .... ٣١
ص ٣٨: ٢١-٢٤ .... ٣٠
الزمر ٣٩: ٢٠ .... ٦١
الزمر ٣٩: ٧٣ .... ٤٩
غافر ٤٠: ٥ .... ١٤
غافر ٤٠: ١١ .... ٦٤
غافر ٤٠: ٢٥ .... ٢٨
غافر ٤٠: ٢٦ .... ٥١
غافر ٤٠: ٢٩ .... ٦١
فصلت ٤١: ٤٣ .... ٥
الشورى ٤٢: ٢٣ .... ٥٤
الزخرف ٤٣: ٣٦ .... ٦٤
الزخرف ٤٣: ٤٥ .... ٢٢
الزخرف ٤٣: ٤٧ .... ٦
الزخرف ٤٣: ٥٢-٥٤ .... ١٠
الجاثية ٤٥: ١٧ .... ١
الأحقاف ٤٦: ٧ .... ١٢
محمّد ٤٧: ٣١ .... ١٠٢
محمّد ٤٧: ٣٦ .... ٨٧
محمّد ٤٧: ٣٧ .... ٨٧, ٨٨
الفتح ٤٨: ٢٣ .... ٣
الحجرات ٤٩: ٩ .... ٥٠
الذاريات ٥١: ٢٢ .... ٤٤
الذاريات ٥١: ٥٦ .... ٣٥
القمر ٥٤: ١-٢ .... ٥

القمر ٥٤: ٤١-٤٢ .... ٧
القمر ٥٤: ٤٣ .... ٧
القمر ٥٤: ٥١ .... ٧
الحديد ٥٧: ١٦ .... ٦٣
الحديد ٥٧: ٢٧ .... ٤٨
المجادلة ٥٨: ٥ .... ٣
المجادلة ٥٨: ١٢ .... ٨٦
المجادلة ٥٨: ١٣ .... ٨٧
الممتحنة ٦٠: ١٠ .... ٨٣, ٨٤
الصف ٦١: ٢-٣ .... ٣٦
الصف ٦١: ٦ .... ٦
الجمعة ٦٢: ٥ .... ٣٢
المنافقون ٦٣: ١٠ .... ٨٨
التحريم ٦٦: ٨ .... ٤٦
نوح ٧١: ٢٥ .... ٢٩
المزمل ٧٣: ٢٠ .... ٩٩
النازعات ٧٩: ١٧-١٩ .... ١٠١
عبس ٨٠: ٥-١٢ .... ٩٠
عبس ٨٠: ١٣-١٤ .... ٩٠
عبس ٨٠: ١٥-١٦ .... ٩٠
البروج ٨٥: ٤-٨ .... ٥٩
البروج ٨٥: ٨-٩ .... ٥٩
الأعلى ٨٧: ١٤-١٥ .... ٨٩
الغاشية ٨٨: ٢-٤ .... ٤٥
البلد ٩٠: ٨-١٠ .... ٨٢
البلد ٩٠: ١١ .... ٨٢
البلد ٩٠: ١٢-١٣ .... ٨٢
الشمس ٩١: ٩-١٠ .... ٩١
الليل ٩٢: ١-٤ .... ٨٠
الليل ٩٢: ٥-٦ .... ٨٠
الليل ٩٢: ٧ .... ٨٠
الليل ٩٢: ٨-٩ .... ٨١
الليل٩٢: ١٠ .... ٨١
الليل٩٢: ١١-١٣ .... ٨١
الليل٩٢: ١٤-١٦ .... ٨١
الليل٩٢: ١٨-٢١ .... ٨٢
الزلزال ٩٩: ٧-٨ .... ١٠٤
الإخلاص ١١٢: ١ .... ١٩

فهرس المصطلحات

ابن عبّاس ٢٦
ابن ملجم ٤٥
أبو بكر ٣٠, ٦٩
أبو الحسن البغدادي ٧٦
أبو عبد الله ,..................... ١, ٧٦
أبو العادية ٤٥
إدريس بن إدريس ٥٩
آدم ٤٣, ٤٦, ٩٥, ١٠٢, ١٠٧
الأساس ٩٢
الأسس ٩٠
إسمعيل ١٧
آل فرعون ٧, ٦١
آل محمّد......... ١٤, ٣١, ٤٣, ٦٠, ٦٢
الإمام ....
٦٦, ٨٥, ٩٢, ٩٤, ٩٦, ٩٩,
١٠٤, ١٠٦
الإنجيل ٢, ٩٨
الأنصار ٢
البَشيرية ٦٦
أمّ سلمة ٤٢, ٦٩
إمام ظاهريّ ١٠٧
أمير المؤمنين ٦٤, ٦٩, ٨٦

أهل الظاهر ....
٨٤, ٨٦, ٩٠, ٩١, ٩٢, ٩٣, ٩٧,
١٠٨
أولاد رسول ٥٣
بخت نصّر ٧١
بنو إسرائيل ....
١, ٢, ٣, ٤, ٦, ٧ , ٩, ٨, ١١,
١٢, ١٤, ١٦, ٢٠, ٢١, ٢٣, ٢٤,
٢٨, ٢٩, ٣٢, ٣٣, ٣٥, ٣٧, ٣٨,
٤٠, ٤٢, ٤٧, ٤٩, ٥١, ٥٢, ٥٤,
٥٧, ٥٨ ٦٠, ٦٢, ٦٣, ٦٤, ٦٦,
٦٨, ٧١, ١٠٢
بنو أميّة ٥٧, ٥٩
بنو جَذيمة ٦٩
تأويل ٨١
التوراة.............. ٢, ٣٢, ٣٥, ٦١, ٩٨
الجبابرة ٢٥, ٦٠
جبريل................. ٢, ١٩, ٢٥, ٥٧
الحجّ ٩٨, ١٠٦, ١٠٨
الحجّاج بن يوسف ٤٥
الحجج ٩٠
الحجّة ٣٦, ٨٢, ٨٧, ٩٦, ١٠٥
الحروريّة................................ ٥٨
الحواريون ٦٢

حدود دين الله............... ١٠٦, ١٠٨
الحدود الروحانية السماوية ١٠٧
الحدود الروحانية والجسمانية ٨٠
حَذْوَ النعل بالنعل..........................
١, ٤, ٧, ١٠, ١١, ١٢, ١٣, ١٤,
٢٦, ٣١, ٣١, ٣٧, ٨, ٥٩, ٦٠,
٦٥
الحُدَيبية.......................................٥٢
حُذيفة بن اليَمان............................. ٢
خالد بن الوليد...............................٦٩
الحسن ١٦, ١٧, ٤١, ٦٨
الحسين.......................... ٤٠, ٥٨, ٦٥
خليفة رسول الله ٩٩
الداعي..
٨٢, ٨٣, ٨٥, ٨٦, ٩٦, ٩٥,
١٠٤, ١٠٦
الدعوة ٨٥, ٩٠, ١٠٤
الرافضة ٦١
رسول الله.....................................
٢, ٤, ٦, ٧, ٨, ١٠, ١٣, ١٥,
١٦, ١٨, ١٩, ٢١, ٢٢, ٢٣, ٢٤,
٢٥, ٢٦, ٢٩, ٣٠, ٣١, ٣٤, ٣٤,
٣٨, ٣٩, ٤٠, ٤٢, ٤٣, ٤٥, ٤٨,
٥٠, ٥٣ ٥٥, ٥٦, ٥٧, ٦٨, ٨٧,
٩١, ٩٣, ٩٤, ٩٦, ٩٧, ٩٨,
١٠٣
رهابن الأمّة ٤٩
رهبانية ٤٨
الزبير ٥٥
الزكاة..................................٨٧, ٩٢
زيد بن علي ٥٩
سام وحام ويافث ٢٨
السامري ٢٦, ٥٣
سُدير الصيرفي الكوفي..............١٠١
سنّة بني إسرائيل................ ٢٠, ٦٥
السنّة ....
٣, ٣٨, ٤٨, ٥٩, ٩٢, ٩٤, ١٠٤
شقيق ٤٩
الصادق ٧٧, ٩٢, ١٠٠, ١٠١
الصحابة ٤٣
صدقة ٨٦, ٨٧, ٨٨, ١٠٣
الصفا ٦, ١٠٧
صفراء بنت شعيب.......................٥٥
الصلاة ....
......٣٣, ٤٢, ٤٨, ٨٧, ٩٤, ٩٦
طلحة ٢
الظاهر...............٨٢, ٨٣ ٨٥, ٩١
الظاهري ٨٥

فهرس المصطلحات

عائشة ٤٢
عُبادة بن الصامت ٢
عبد الله بن عمر.......................... ٣
عبيد الله بن زياد....................... ٤٥
عثمان بن عفّان ٧٠
عثمان ذو النورين ٦٨
العجل ٢٦
عمّار ١٠
عمر بن سعد ٤٥
عمرو بن عوف بن طلحة المُزَني ٢
عيسى بن مريم ....
...٨, ٢٤, ٦٢, ٦٦, ٦٧, ٦٧, ٧٠
عيصا ٤
العهد................ ١٠, ٣٥, ٨٥, ٩٠
فاطمة ابنة رسول الله ٦٨
الفئة الباغية ٥٠
فراعنة أمّتنا ٦١
فراعنة بني أميّة ٥٩
فرعون ....
.....٤, ٩, ١٢, ١٤, ٢٢, ٦٠, ٦١
فُرقة واختلاف............................ ١
فطرة.................................. ١٠٣
قابيل ١٠٢
قائم القيامة ٩٥
القيامة ٧٠, ١٠٧
الكاهن ١٠٣
لاوي ٥٥
اللعين بن اللعين ٥٨
المأذونون الأوّلون ٩١
المأذونون المحدودون.................... ٩١
محمّد.................. ٥, ٦, ٨, ٤١, ٦١
المرجئة .. ٣٩, ٤٥, ٥٧, ٦٠, ٦٥, ٧٠
مريم ٦, ١٥, ١٧, ٣٤, ٦٧, ١١٤
المستجيب ٨٢, ٨٥, ٩٤, ١٠٤
المستورد بن شدّاد ٢
المصطفى ٣٣, ٦٤, ٧٥
المعتزلة الأول ٥٠
الملائكة المقرّبون ٢٥
مُعاذ بن جبل ٤٨
مكّة.................................... ٧, ١٠٨
الملكانية من النصارى ٦٦
منى...................................... ١٠٧
المهدي ٢٧, ٣٤, ٤٤, ٦٠
موسى بن عمران.........................
٧, ١٣, ١٤, ١٦, ١٨, ٢٠, ٢١,
٢٢, ٢٣, ٢٤, ٢٥, ٢٦, ٢٩, ٣٥,
٤١, ٥٢, ٥٩, ٦٠
الموقف.................................. ١٠٧

فهرس المصطلحات

المؤمن ٩٣, ٩٥ ٩٧, ٩٨, ١٠٠
الناطق ٨١, ٨٢, ٩٢, ١٠٧
النجوى ٨٧, ٨٨, ١٠٤
نخل ٢
نصارى............................. ٢, ٥٧
نوح ٢٤, ٢٨, ١١٦
هابيل ١٠٢
هارون.................................١٤
..........., ١٦, ٢٠, ٢٢, ٢٧, ٥٢
هاشم ٤, ٣٠
وصيّ رسول الله ٥٧
وليّ الله ٧٩, ٨١, ٨٦, ٨٨, ٩٤
يزيد بن معاوية ٤٥
يعقوب ٤
اليعقوبية من النصارى ٦٦
اليهود ....
٢, ٣١, ٣٢, ٣٣, ٣٥, ٣٧, ٣٨,
٣٩, ٤٤, ٥٠, ٥٧, ٥٩, ٦٢, ٦٣,
٦٤, ٦٧, ٦٨, ٧١
يوشع بن نون ٢٥, ٥٥
يوسف.......................٧, ٢٣, ١١٤